SOCIOLOGICAL PRACTICE

D1362568

Sociological Practice

Linking Theory and Social Research

Derek Layder

SAGE Publications
London • Thousand Oaks • New Delhi

First published 1998

SAGE Publications Ltd
6 Bonhill Street
London EC2A 4PU

SAGE Publications Inc.
2455 Teller Road
Thousand Oaks, California 91320

SAGE Publications India Pvt Ltd
32, M-Block Market
Greater Kailash – I
New Delhi 110 048

British Library Cataloguing in Publication data

A catalogue record for this book is available
from the British Library

ISBN 0 7619 5429 5
ISBN 0 7619 5430 9 (pbk)

Library of Congress catalog card number 98–60952

Typeset by Mayhew Typesetting, Rhayader, Powys
Printed in Great Britain by Biddles Ltd, Guildford, Surrey

CONTENTS

LIST OF TABLES

LIST OF FIGURES

PREFACE

My objectives in this book are twofold. First, to provide an introduction to approaches to the theory-research relation, and secondly, to develop an alternative which focuses on generating social theory in conjunction with ongoing empirical research. I call this alternative 'adaptive theory' because it combines the use of prior theory to lend order and pattern to research data while simultaneously adapting to the order and pattern contained in this emerging data. Although I describe it as an 'alternative', it also shares and builds upon key aspects of existing traditions in social theory and method. In this respect it is complementary to other approaches and hence may be employed alongside them. Adaptive theory is research-based but is related to and consistent with my 'theory of social domains' outlined in *Modern Social Theory* (1997). However, it also connects with, and in a certain sense grows out of, my work on research strategies (1993) and the philosophy of method (1990).

Several people have been associated with the genesis of this book. Early on Paul Secord provided much needed support for some of the embryonic ideas. More immediately Chris and Robert Rojek of Sage and an anonymous reviewer encouraged me to go forward with the book. In its draft form Alison Drewett went over the entire manuscript with a fine-tooth comb and made some telling and extremely useful 'interventions' and suggestions. I have incorporated as many of these as possible. Similarly, Bob Carter read through the draft and made several important suggestions concerning amendments and possible inclusions. I must also thank Alison and Bob for the infectious enthusiasm with which they greeted the project and which undoubtedly fed into my own readiness to complete it. It goes without saying that none of the above people are in any way implicated in the shortcomings that this book may possess.

The final revisions of the book were undertaken while I was a Visiting Fellow in the Humanities Research Centre at the Australian National University, Canberra in July–August 1997. I would like to thank the Centre, its staff and its Director, Graeme Clarke, for providing excellent facilities and support. During my stay at the ANU I greatly enjoyed the company of Alice Bullard, Jack Barbalet, Margot Lyon, and Doug Porpora. I also enjoyed and appreciated my visit to the Ashworth Centre for Social Theory, Melbourne University, at the invitation of the Director, John Rundell. Thanks are also due to Kate Spratley for her help and support.

Derek Layder, December 1997

CHAPTER 1

THE LINKS BETWEEN THEORY AND RESEARCH

This book is aimed at social researchers who wish to incorporate more theory in their research (either by using it as a guide or by attempting to generate it from data) and at social theorists who wish to give their ideas extra weight by grounding them more firmly in empirical evidence and data. To this end, I examine the most common links between social theory and social research with a view to outlining a new approach ('adaptive theory') which attempts to serve the needs of both theorists and empirical researchers. Adaptive theory endeavours to combine the use of pre-existing theory and theory generated from data analysis in the formulation and actual conduct of empirical research. I believe that this kind of approach challenges the gap that has grown up around those who specialize in social theory on the one hand, and those who are specialists in data collection and empirical research on the other.

With regard to these general aims there are two sorts of audience that I attempt to address in this book. First, within the discipline of sociology the above-mentioned gap between theory and research is particularly marked and I believe that it is an obstacle both to the development of sociology as a discipline and to the possibility of the development of a cumulative body of 'theoretically informed' knowledge. Thus my widest objective is to attempt to provide some ways in which the gap may be overcome and the connections between theory and research made stronger. I shall say more about these matters later in this chapter so I shall not expand upon them at this juncture.

However, it is important to say that, apart from clearing a path through the rather confusing maze of theory-research links, this book attempts to develop an original approach to theorizing in social research. As I have indicated, what I call adaptive theory challenges some entrenched sociological orthodoxies about research methodology as well as about the uses and nature of social theory. In this sense it offers what can only be called a new set of rules of sociological method without insisting that previous practices are somehow outmoded or worthless. Thus, adaptive theory attempts to capitalize on some of the strengths of existing approaches by expanding their range at the same time as providing a new approach and a group of alternative strategies which move beyond the established range of orthodox approaches.

However, my remarks are also addresssed to an even wider audience of social researchers who come from a variety of different disciplines and who are perhaps not aware of, or *au fait* with, the sort of general social theory that I have in mind here, and thus are not conscious of the gap between theory and research that I identify. Nonetheless I believe that this audience will be more aware of other kinds of problems which surround the relationship between theory and social research. In particular, I think that many social researchers often experience a lack of guidance as to how to deal with theory, how to use it and how to develop it from the data they unearth during their research. This is because methodology texts and others which describe how to conduct social research typically either do not address the issue of theory and theorizing directly or they take it for granted. Also, even where there is some minimal guidance provided, very often textbooks utilize a very limited range and number of exemplars and perspectives with regard to the question of using or generating theory in social research. In this respect this book aims to expand the range of possibilities for those engaged in social research who either have little training in theoretical matters or who crave for alternative approaches.

The sequence of my discussion will be as follows. Following these introductory comments, I elaborate on some of the background or contextual issues that serve as organizing themes of the book. These include some of the issues that constitute the widest parameters of the climate of opinion in which the central themes of the book are situated. Thus I attempt to contextualize the discussion in terms of contemporary ideas about the significance of theory and theorizing as well as attitudes to the whole project of social analysis in general. I develop themes around several topics, including the debate about the relevance and significance of classical social theory and its role in securing adequate, valid and cumulative knowledge about social reality. In turn, these questions are bound up with debates about the nature of social science, its claims to objectivity and truth, and the role of explanation. I also take issue with the postmodern attempt to denigrate theory and with the paucity of attempts to redress the continually growing gap between general theory and social research that I have already highlighted.

My arguments in all these areas will become apparent as the discussion unfolds but I should like to point out that as with the question of recent attempts by postmodernists to disavow or denigrate the role of theory in social analysis in general, I am opposed to any approach which simply cuts itself off from a sense of tradition and continuity in social analysis. This is because I believe that such a posture ultimately leads to a stagnation of knowledge rather than its cumulative growth and development. Connected with this claim, I also argue strongly that it is unwise and premature to abandon wholesale, claims to objectivity and the search for 'truth' in social science and analysis – even though what we regard as the truth may be significantly reconfigured in the process of reclaiming it. Implied in this is the idea that social analysis (or 'science' understood in an amended sense) must be defended as a species of *explanation*, especially in the face of recent attempts to decompose and dissolve it into mere reportage and/or descriptions of 'local narratives' – the voices of those people studied.

After tracing through some of these arguments – and here I must point out that the discussion will be brief and strictly tailored to my central concern with theory-research links – I then move to a consideration of some of the existing approaches to understanding these links as they are available in the methodological and theoretical literature of social research. I do this by presenting a number of dimensions of theorizing in social research, in terms of which I suggest we can understand the variety of styles of theorizing that are employed in actual social research projects. This background is necessary in order to understand the way in which, in later chapters, I attempt to develop new ideas and approaches to the theory-research connection. Thus the discussion of existing dimensions and varieties of theorizing in research informs the later chapters by providing a benchmark from which to judge both continuities and deviations from existing approaches.

Chapter 2 forms a bridge into the later chapters which are concerned with mapping out the contours of my own alternative views on the sort of theory-research linkages that I would endorse and would like to see playing an active role in the conduct of research. In this respect Chapter 2 concentrates on the elements or 'stages' of the research process as they are normally conceived in the methods literature. Instead of viewing these as a relatively fixed sequence of stages, I suggest that from the point of view of stimulating the generation of theory and the theoretical imagination it is often more profitable to see the different elements as loosely and flexibly positioned in relation to each other. Furthermore, in contrast to many conventional texts, I suggest that theorizing should be understood as a continuous process which accompanies the research at all 'stages' rather than as a discrete aspect that is only of relevance at the beginning or end of data-gathering. In this respect I recommend overall that theorizing should be accorded a much more important place in the research process than is normally the case.

Chapter 3 concentrates on the actual dynamics of theory-construction from the point of view of adaptive theory – although I reserve a systematic discussion of the formal and practical characteristics of adaptive theory as a distinct and coherent alternative to conventional positions until Chapter 6. Chapter 3 examines the process of theory-generation from the point of view of the analysis of research data. In this sense it advocates a form of emergent or 'grounded' theory, since I believe that this kind of approach facilitates theoretical discovery and thus helps to offset the problem of theoretical stagnation which results from the routine application of established theory or theoretical perspectives. However, it is extremely important to understand that this form of emergent theory is an integral part of the wider adaptive approach, and thus it parts company with conventional notions of grounded theory.

I argue that gounded theory is inherently limited by its dogmatic exclusion of other kinds of theory and alternative strategies designed to generate theory from data. Chapter 3, however, is not simply a formal discussion of methodological issues. By far the bulk of the chapter is concerned with outlining practical techniques which will help the researcher to transform data analysis into a form in which the theoretical imagination is stimulated. Thus I discuss and give examples relating to the coding of data and writing theoretical memos. Finally, I discuss the question of the development of theory in the context of multiple strategies of research, including the collection and analysis of quantitative and qualitative data, historical analysis, sampling, interviewing, coding, memos and the construction of typologies.

Chapter 4 focuses on the concept-indicator problem in social research. This connects the practical issues of theory-generation as they are spelled out in Chapters 3 and 5 to rather more formal questions about the status and validity of concepts. However, this is not simply a 'formal' exercise since the concept-indicator problem points us to the concrete link between theoretical concepts and the things to which they refer empirically. To this end, I identify and describe different types of concept ('behavioural', 'systemic', 'mediating' and 'theoretical') as they relate both to data and to wider aspects of society. Very often the concept-indicator problem is glossed over in methods texts, but here I centralize its importance not only for issues connected with the nitty-gritty of research practice, but for fundamental ones about the nature of social reality and the influence of general theoretical problems in empirical research.

Chapter 5 reverses the emphasis outlined in Chapter 3 and focuses on theory-building by applying existing theoretical materials to the research process as a means of stimulating novel theory. One of the features that distinguishes the approach I advocate from grounded theory is that I believe that it is not possible to approach research in a theory-neutral manner, and thus it is better to acknowledge, harness and attempt to control the inputs of prior theory and concepts as they intrude or otherwise make themselves felt in the research process. Thus, Chapter 4 tackles this question head on by suggesting strategies which facilitate the utilization and application of prior theory in the context of ongoing research. In this respect I argue that the use of 'background' and 'orienting' concepts may help both in the ongoing formulation of research problems and in the manner in which the data are explained and analysed in the long run. I also give examples of how theory may be elaborated during the course of research by drawing on both extant theory and theory and concepts as they emerge through data collection and analysis.

Chapter 6 brings the threads of the previous discussions together by laying out what I mean by adaptive theory as a distinct and unified approach. In this respect I specify what I mean by adaptive theory in terms of a number of points and then elaborate on them. In a nutshell, adaptive theory, as I conceive it, is an original amalgam of different influences and approaches that falls somewhere between what are variously referred to as deductive or theory-testing approaches on one side and inductive or theory-generating approaches on the other (although the proponents of each of these approaches would claim, wrongly in my opinion, that they contain in equal measure both deductive and inductive elements).

That it occupies something of an intermediate zone in relation to these approaches is not the only distinguishing aspect of adaptive theory. As may or may not be apparent, I feel very strongly that the gap between general social theory and 'empirical' theories (associated with the analysis and explanation of empirical data, information and findings) should be closed down in order to harness the potentially productive interplay between them. Thus, my vision of adaptive theory attempts to incorporate the insights of general theory into the practical and strategic thinking of researchers who are collecting and analysing empirical data with a view to coming up with new theories, concepts and insights.

The word 'adaptive' is meant to convey that the theory both adapts to, or is shaped by, incoming evidence while the data itself is simultaneously filtered through, and is thus adapted by, the prior theoretical materials (frameworks, concepts, ideas) that are relevant to their analysis. Again I provide practical examples and rules of thumb concerning the way in which this approach can be applied by researchers who need guidance or alternative sources of stimulation in their search for theory and the analysis, explanation and organization of their findings. Chapter 7 functions as a concluding chapter which both summarizes the main arguments of the book as a whole and also views adaptive theory in the wider context of approaches to the theory-research relation. My overall view is that adaptive theory can exist alongside those theories currently available but may also function as a radical alternative to them. However, even in this latter sense, I do not envisage that adaptive theory should be understood as entirely 'replacing' existing orthodoxies. Rather, it must be seen as a branching out in a new direction but as one among a healthy diversity and plurality of approaches. To this end I describe some of the general characteristics of adaptive theory as well as some new rules of method which are implied by this approach.

The current climate of ideas

As I intimated in my opening comments, this book may be regarded as a direct intervention into a debate about the most adequate approach(es) to social analysis in general and the uses and functions of social theory and social research in particular. One of the book's central themes – and one which underlies the more particular and practical recommendations that I make about the use of theory in the research process – is my belief that there are and should be continuities between classical and contemporary social theory. This flies in the face of much current writing, fashion and 'orthodoxy' which insists that there must be a radical break with the modernist project of theory and theorizing. This is commonly associated with other views, such that there are no longer any grounds for defending objectivism (or objectivity) and the search for truth in any guise, and the idea that social analysis is about describing (rather than attempting to explain) aspects of social life. Taken together, these views add up to a profound pessimism about the possibility of cumulative knowledge, which I would like to counter in the most direct and robust manner possible. Let me deal with these as a series of points.

First, I believe that contemporary social analysis must trade on, refashion and re-establish a continuity with classical sociology in order that we retain some hold on important and essential components of social analysis. Writers such as Marx, Durkheim, Weber and Simmel concerned themselves not only with empirical inquiry but with developing theoretical and conceptual frameworks with which they could understand society as a whole and the larger processes of social development that provide their historical context. A significant number of contemporary social analysts and commentators in relatively recent times have questioned this kind of approach. They suggest that a concern with 'meta-narratives' (or grand theories) is inappropriate and that a concern with local and subjective narratives is more apposite. This position, which is shared by poststructuralists and postmodernists (although there are others who concur over this), has the effect of dispensing with theory as an important and relatively independent component of social analysis.

As will be apparent already, I firmly believe that the project of social theory is absolutely essential to social analysis in general and social research in particular. In this sense I believe we must attempt to reproduce some of the concerns of the classical sociologists. I am not suggesting that the development of large-scale theories of society and social change is a necessary precondition of social research, nor am I suggesting that the smaller-scale concerns of much social research today are somehow less important. However, I do feel that the tie between general theory and theorizing about society and the actual formulation and conduct of social research should be reaffirmed in the present context in which a specialist and disciplinary gap has emerged between them.

This is particularly important since – as will become apparent at various junctures in this book – I believe that contemporary debates over the relation between agency and structure (or system) in social theory, as well as associated debates about the nature of social reality (ontology) and forms of representation or explanation, have profound implications for the conduct of research and the analysis of the empirical data it draws upon. Thus it is important to take seriously the manner in which general theoretical concerns directly enter into the practical calculations of research. This is a point which is as often under-appreciated by those who call themselves theorists as much as it is ignored or denied by more empirically engaged social reseachers. Both general theory and empirical research would benefit from mutual co-operation and dialogue. On the one hand, theory would be made more robust and its explanatory capacity generally enhanced by having its assumptions, axioms and presuppositions more closely and routinely measured against empirical evidence. On the other hand, empirical research would benefit from more sophisticated forms of analysis and explanation as well as enhanced generalizability and applicability.

Currently there are several forces working against this kind of *rapprochement*. It is not simply ignorance, prejudice or rivalry between theorists and researchers that stand in the way of closer links. Perhaps more important than these intellectual or practical antipathies is the fact that the disciplinary specialization which drives and underpins academic and research careers is such that the gap is routinely reinforced rather than broken down. Careers tend to be rewarded for contributions to specialized areas of competence, such as resolving particular problems in social theory, or adding to knowledge of a particular substantive area in social research, for instance medicine or education, or attempting to overcome a social problem, say drug use or prostitution. The reluctance of specialist publication outlets such as academic journals as well as book publishers to allow academics and researchers to straddle different market niches simply exacerbates this tendency to stick within disciplinary boundaries for fear of being penalized or ignored in career terms. Thus, different publication 'market areas', such as 'social theory', 'research methods', 'mental illness', 'organization studies', 'cultural studies', remain carefully segregated.

However, just as some intellectuals and theorists deride the seemingly myopic and 'pedestrian' concerns of empirical researchers – particularly those of the empiricist variety who believe that the facts speak for themselves – the force of anti-theoretical sentiments deriving from other sources cannot be underestimated. These anti-theoretical sentiments emanate from both empirical researchers as traditionally conceived (those concerned with the collection of primary data according to strict methodological canons of procedure) as well as from poststructuralists and postmodernists (and others – see later discussion). The latter insist that theory is a kind of flight from the real business of social analysis which is to give voice to particular groups and/or to depict faithfully their meaningful social worlds and their subjective experiences. This kind of response to theory is based on a very restricted view of social life which reflects a serious misunderstanding of the nature of the social world and social analysis. Such a stance is very often driven by an over-reaction to the domination of the positivist view of social science and social analysis. The approach I adopt in this book is certainly critical of naive positivist views of social analysis (as it is of naive or dogmatic humanist or interpretivist views), but I think that it is important to understand that social life has both subjective and objective components to it. By simply rejecting objectivism and/or the attempt to adopt what approximates to an objective standpoint, one is foregoing the possibility of understanding the systemic (Habermas, 1987; Layder, 1997) aspects of society and social life and how they are intertwined with the everyday lifeworld. In contra-distinction to a whole array of approaches then, the perspective of adaptive theory presupposes that we must attend to both these elements of social life in equal measure and not imagine that they are dissolved into some kind of seamless amalgam. Thus, in my view, we cannot pretend that we have somehow 'gone beyond' the problems of understanding how the partly independent realms of agency and structure and macro-micro elements are fused in different ways.

Let me conclude these comments on the wider climate of thought in which the theory-research relation is situated by addressing the question of the search for 'truth' and recent (particularly postmodernist) attempts to discredit this idea. In a sense this issue follows on from the previous discussion in so far as I believe that social research and theory should be brought together in the service of explaining how particular configurations of activity and structure (or system) combine to produce specific outcomes in any area of social life. In this and other respects, the approach to theorizing in social research which I offer in this book is wedded to the idea that the purpose of social inquiry is to produce ever more adequate knowledge. This increased adequacy and validity of knowledge is reflected in the attempt to produce enhanced and more accurate renderings of particular groups, milieux, or social problems under study, than has hitherto been the case. Secondly, it is reflected in the drive to develop ever more powerful explanations of social phenomena (particularly agency-structure interconnections).

Thus the adaptive theory approach responds to the fact of the complexity of the social world not by abandoning the search for 'truth' in the form of greater adequacy and validity (as in post-modernism), but by accelerating the effort to apprehend it and by devising increasingly sophisticated methods, strategies and explanatory devices with which to achieve it. Of course the positivist idea that there is one universal, objective truth-for-all-time for a particular phenomenon, or that there is a direct correspondence between objective truth and the 'facts of the matter', are clearly discredited notions and cannot form the centre of a viable approach to the theory-research link. Alternatively, adaptive theory proposes that greater adequacy and validity should be understood as the best approximation to truth given the present state of knowledge and understanding. It is not a once-and-for-all notion, and in this respect adaptive theory, fully formed, simply represents the 'latest stage' in the elaboration of the theory. It is always, potentially at least, revisable in terms of future research and theoretical developments. Although this kind of proviso does not in the least prevent researchers from completing their research projects with an elaborate and sophisticated theoretical end-product, it does mean that from the long-term point of view adaptive theory has to be viewed as an interim way-station which is potentially revisable and reformulable.

Dimensions of theorizing in social research

I now move on to a discussion of some of the more specific approaches to understanding the theory-research relation as they are currently on offer in the social sciences and social analysis in general. I begin by outlining some definitions and then describe some of the

Table 1.1 *Dimensions of theorizing in social research*

Theory focus	Empirical focus
Theory-testing	Theory-generating
Formal theory	Substantive theory
Epistemological	Ontological
Sensitizing concepts	Explanatory frameworks of concepts
Continuous part of research	Discrete part of research

dimensions of theorizing in research which may be found in different combinations, both in the methods literature and in particular pieces of empirical research. Thus, if social research is about the systematic gathering of evidence and data, then theorizing represents the attempt to order this information into some kind of explanatory framework. Theorizing therefore engages with questions concerning how and why particular patterns of evidence occur, and how this reflects the organization of society and social life more generally. Both 'theorizing' and 'social research' in themselves refer to a very wide and varied range of practices, while the modes in which they connect with each other are equally complex and diverse, and so any attempt to give some account of their interrelations poses rather formidable problems. I therefore propose to deal with these difficulties by identifying what I take to be the most significant dimensions of the relations between theorizing and research in terms of a series of polarities (see Table 1.1).

Let me say a few words about this procedure in order to forestall possible misunderstandings. By using a series of polarities or 'oppositions' I do not mean to imply that the two terms of each polarity represent stark alternatives, or that they are unrelated. Each of the polarities represents a continuum which indicates that most pieces of research fall somewhere between the two extremes, and this in turn helps us to understand the variety of forms and styles of theorizing in social research. One typical criticism of this analytic strategy is that it proposes 'artificial' distinctions between things which, in reality, are interlinked. Of course, there is some danger in this but if the polarities are understood as 'connected but different' (rather than as 'separate and opposed') characteristics which exist both within single pieces of research and between research projects, then this problem can be avoided. If we do not make such distinctions initially, we cannot properly appreciate the exact nature and mixture of influences that are present. Similarly, it is important to point out that each pair or coupling of characteristics is not necessarily separated from other couplings – they often overlap with each other in actual research projects and I shall point out the most common of these as the discussion proceeds.

Theory focus versus empirical focus

The polarity between research which has theorizing as a primary objective and that which is more focused on the gathering of empirical information implies that some research is closer to one side of the continuum than the other. This is true up to a point but it has to be remembered that much social research is a mixture of both tendencies. However, the distinction does point to a real difference of emphasis which is perhaps the most basic with regard to the issue of theorizing in social research, and this in itself can be subdivided into a number of others. One of these concerns whether the research explicitly 'denies' or devalues theory as compared with research which has objectives and priorities which are simply more concerned with other things (such as gathering information).

Information-seeking or policy-oriented research

Very often a lack of concern with theory and theorizing has to do with the fact that the impetus for the research derives from a social problem or policy-oriented focus. Typically, such research has very practical aims, such as to meet the requirements of a particular 'user' or 'client' group (as in, for example, community mental health or geriatric provision, or the probation service). In this sense the lack of an explicit concern with theory may be an unintended consequence of a search for basic information or evidence about the needs of client or user groups, or about the best means of policy intervention or implementation (see Richie and Spencer, 1994).

For example, studies conducted in Glasgow by McKeganey (1990) on the extent of needle-sharing between injecting drug users and the risk of HIV infection, and McKeganey, Bernard and Bloor (1990) which compared female street-working prostitutes with male rent boys in terms of the practice of safer sex and the risk of HIV infection, arose out of a 'social problems perspective'. That is, the research attempted to provide much needed information about sexual practices and drug use in a particular local area, which could feed into and inform policy formation and indicate the best means of intervention. Although the primary aim of this kind of research is to plug gaps in information about pressing social problems, there is no suggestion that the research is explicitly anti-theoretical – it is just that the priorities of the research are empirical and substantive in nature. In any case, it could be argued that such research is implicitly influenced by theoretical concerns such as the questions of why and how these phenomena are created and sustained. Furthermore, in some cases such information-gathering may, in fact, be a prelude to more systematic attempts to build and test theories – although this seems quite rare.

Although information-seeking and policy- or problem-oriented approaches to research are often well executed and perfectly viable in their own right, I do believe they could at times benefit by taking on more explictly theoretical objectives. Thus the recommendations that are forwarded in the later chapters of this book could be used to enhance the explanatory power of such research – in terms of its data analysis and conclusions. Also, by joining up the more practical concerns of policy-making with a wider body of social analytic concepts and frameworks, the goal of producing a genuinely cumulative body of general social scientific knowledge would be better served. Additionally, in this manner, the gap between theory and research would be lessened. Of course I accept that attempting to establish such linkages is not always feasible or possible in this kind of research since very often the researchers are working to strict time (and budgetary) constraints. Furthermore, typically the general agenda, objectives and purposes of such studies are determined stringently in advance of the research itself by the funding agencies. Such circumstances make it very difficult for researchers to attend to matters outside this formal remit.

Anti-theoretical approaches

The above research aims and strategies must be strictly distinguished from those which are explicitly anti-theoretical or atheoretical. This is not simply a matter of distinguishing between 'applied' and academic research, since consciously anti-theoretical views can also be found in the academic community of social scientists. For example, Becker and Rock (in Rock, 1979) and to a lesser extent Blumer (1969) have cautioned against the use of theory or the aim of theory-generation in social research. On this view theory and theorizing is understood as the product of 'armchair' theorists who are cut-off from the real world of everyday life and whose theories are irrelevant to people's lives. Such views contrast heavily with other sociologists such as Merton (1967) and Glaser and Strauss (1967) who have stressed the importance of the relationship between empirical research and the development of theory as a precondition for the cumulative growth of sociological knowledge in general (although Glaser and Strauss's views on the nature of the relation between theorizing and research are different from Merton's – see next section).

I have already alluded to the question of the denial or derogation of theory and theorizing in the introduction and I shall return to this general theme a number of times in the book. My position is more clearly in tune with the likes of Merton and Glaser and Strauss, although it also differs in various ways and sometimes in considerable measure from their respective views. Moreover, I believe that the denial or suppression of theory is based on a misunderstanding about the nature and purpose of theorizing. As a consequence, much of the thrust of this book is designed to highlight the importance of theory for empirical research and to provide practical strategies for achieving a closer union between them.

The use of single or multiple concepts

Another subdivision within the theory versus empirical focus distinction concerns the *extent* to which theoretical issues are present in the research. For example, some research which is empirical in emphasis may be concerned with clarifying or assessing the usefulness of a particular concept or concepts, as Backett (1990) has done with the concept of 'family culture' in relation to a study of family decision-making processes or as Nijsmans (1991) does with the concept of 'organizational culture' in a study of a counselling institute. Similarly, research may employ 'sensitizing concepts' to give some shape and order to the data that have been gathered. In this sense, although the primary concern is to present data or evidence in a coherent fashion, the research also has some theoretical implications, however minor, and regardless of immediate priorities. For example, Goffman's (1968) use of the concept 'total institution' in his study of a mental hospital in the USA has been highly influential in guiding subsequent studies of this and other kinds of organizations and institutions.

In this respect the issue of whether the primary focus is theoretical or empirical overlaps with other polarities – in this case that of the use of single concepts versus the employment of a more embracing network or framework of concepts. It could be argued that the use of bits and pieces of theories is not a proper use of theory in that it is not systematic and hence cannot lead to cumulative knowledge, but this would be to deny the longer-term implications of research which does not set out to develop theory in a conscious manner. Also, such a stance overlooks the fact that theory may be 'produced' in a whole host of different ways, some of which may not be the result of deliberate or systematic attempts to theorize. This overlaps with the question of whether the researcher is primarily a theorist who happens to be doing some empirical research, or someone who regards him or herself first and foremost as a researcher who is 'dabbling' in, or 'experimenting' with theory.

There are some issues here that are of direct relevance to those which I address later in this book. First, much of what I say in Chapters 2–6 is aimed at encouraging researchers who are employing single or sensitizing concepts to make more elaborate and systematic connections in their work in order to boost the explanatory power of their conclusions. Secondly, an integral part of the adaptive theory approach addresses the question of the many different ways in which theory may be produced and the different kinds of skills that are needed to do so. In this respect I try to formalize and systematize some of the more diffuse – and often unintentional – means by which theory is (or becomes) constructed. I also discuss some of the more intuitive skills required in theorizing and how to employ them with a view to developing and elaborating theory and the theoretical imagination. Finally, many of the comments I make and the strategies I suggest are aimed at encouraging researchers or potential researchers who lack confidence in their theoretical abilities to have the courage to think in theoretical terms.

The use of general theory in empirical research

Important here is the question of how we define 'research' and whether it includes the use of 'general theory' – as it is reflected in the work of theorists such as Talcott Parsons, Jürgen Habermas, Michel Foucault, Anthony Giddens and so on – as opposed to more focused empirical applications. The point about general theory is that it usually has a very broad explanatory remit and concerns itself either with whole societies and the processes involved in their development, or with very general aspects of social reality such as the relationship between agency and structure or macro and micro levels of analysis. It would be inaccurate to say that someone who dealt purely with general theory was not doing research as such, but the term research is most often associated with the idea of the collection of empirical evidence and data.

Nonetheless, someone who starts out by developing a full or general theory may wish to encourage its use in empirical investigation either to throw some light on the empirical information itself or to confirm, develop or negate various aspects of the theory. For example, in explicating and elaborating on his general theory of social interaction, Turner (1988) states that he hopes researchers will empirically test some of its propositions. Likewise Giddens (1984)

indicates some of the ways in which his general theory of structuration may be used to illuminate various aspects of empirical
research (see also Layder, 1993). Others have used empirical data to
test out some of the axioms of structuration theory (Layder et al.,
1991). It is this co-operative two-way borrowing – from general
theory to empirical research and from empirical research to general
theory – that I explicitly encourage in the later chapters. In this
manner I believe that there is a place for a union between prior
theory – acting as a model or guide to research – and theory which
has developed out of direct engagement with empirical data and its
analysis – acting as a potential modifier and shaper of the theoretical
model.

Theory-testing versus theory-generating

The distinction between theory-testing and theory-generating research
has been used by Rose (1984), and subsequently by Lewins (1992) and
Layder (1993). The distinction is useful in describing certain aspects,
emphases and priorities in research, but it should be remembered that
some elements of both theory-testing and theory-construction are
present in varing degrees in most research. However, a crucial issue
concerns what various writers and approaches mean by these terms.
Also, this distinction overlaps with other terms as well. Primarily it
parallels the distinction between 'grounded theory' (as developed by
Glaser and Strauss, 1967; Strauss, 1987; Strauss and Corbin, 1990) and
what has been variously referred to as hypothetico-deductive forms of
theorizing (Glaser and Strauss, 1971), 'analytic induction' (Bryman
and Burgess, 1994) or more simply 'middle-range' theory (Merton,
1967).

Basically, we are dealing here with two rather different approaches
to the question of how it is that, as researchers, we come up with
theory in the first place. On the one hand, the middle-range approach
(as I shall call it) emphasizes the importance of formulating theoretical
hypotheses in advance of the research in order to guide the research
and to give shape to any subsequent theorizing after the data has been
gathered. On the other hand, grounded theory emphasizes the
importance of starting the research with as little pre-formulated
theory as possible in order that it may be generated during the
research itself. In the following discussion I shall first describe
the basic characteristics of middle-range and grounded theory as they
were originally formulated and then discuss their implications for the
sort of approach that I outline in the rest of the book.

Middle-range theory

Robert Merton (1967) summarized his views on 'middle-range' research in a seminal paper entitled 'The bearing of sociological theory on research'. He argued that although we develop our initial ideas about a research problem through empirical observations of some social phenomenon (like rates of suicide in different societies), we then construct a possible theoretical explanation for the phenomenon through a logical, deductive process, which is consistent with the known facts. Research then proceeds on the basis of finding more facts and information about the topic, area or problem in question in order to 'test-out' the original hypothesis. The unearthing of evidence through empirical research either confirms the initial theoretical ideas or disconfirms them, leading to their reformulation or abandonment. The more theory is tested-out in this manner, the more likely it is that supportive evidence will be found and this can lead to a relatively stabilized body of theory which can help to illuminate other research in the area.

As the prime example of this type of research Merton refers to Durkheim's (1952) study of suicide. Durkheim began with the observation that the suicide rate in predominantly Catholic societies was lower than in Protestant societies. From this empirical generalization he constructed a possible explanation – that Catholicism represents a more strongly integrated community which provides more psychological support for its members in times of stress. In Protestant societies the bonds between individuals and the religious community are looser and people are more 'privatized'. Thus, in times of stress they are more vulnerable to psychological pressure. This leads to the conclusion that we would expect to find higher rates of suicide in Protestant (rather than Catholic) societies, thus explaining the original observation. Therefore the original generalization only becomes theoretically significant when it is related to a body of other more abstract assumptions, such as that suicide rates are related to social cohesion and the existence of supportive relationships.

For Merton, systematic theorizing is only possible in this form which is mid-way between the minor working hypotheses of everyday life and the 'grand' general theories (of writers like Talcott Parsons or Karl Marx). Middle-range theories deal with a limited number of controllable variables (suicide rates, income, status, occupation, role expectations, and so on), so that we are able to make precise empirical investigations of them and their relations with other variables. In his urge to be precise and systematic, Merton tended to favour quantitative data from social surveys and statistical techniques of analysis. In this Merton reflects an earlier concern for sociology to mimic the natural sciences, by being 'objective', impersonal and using so-called 'hard' quantitative data. Although he did advocate the use of qualitative data in certain circumstances, Merton generally regarded them as less scientific than quantitative data because they are too imprecise, flexible and open-ended, although this view of qualitative data has been challenged recently (Layder, 1993; Bryman and Burgess, 1994).

Grounded theory

Underscoring the centrality of qualitative data was, in fact, an important part of what Glaser and Strauss (1967) had in mind when they first outlined their notion of 'grounded theory' as a counterpoint to Merton's version of middle-range theory, as well as to what they called 'grand' or 'speculative' theory. Another impetus for the development of grounded theory lay in one of the limitations of middle-range theory – its tendency to view theorizing as a guide to research while research itself was regarded as a means of testing the efficacy of the theory. Although Glaser and Strauss agree that theory must always be produced in conjunction with empirical research (and that this is a problem with general theory), they do not share Merton's view of the nature of theorizing and its relation to empirical data.

In this respect Glaser and Strauss operate with an interpretivist or humanist tradition of thought which suggests that sociology (and social analysis in general) cannot model itself on the natural sciences. Social theory must reflect the experiences, meanings and understandings of people in face-to-face interaction rather than identify the empirical 'variables' that 'externally' influence behaviour which are emphasized in Merton's positivist vision of social analysis. On the other hand, the problem with grand or general theory is that it is 'preconceived' and developed prior to, and independently of, the collection of empirical data – thus it remains inherently speculative and 'ungrounded'.

But this is also a problem with middle-range theory which begins with the logical development of theoretical assumptions and propositions (even though derived from provisional observations and generalizations). According to Glaser and Strauss, when such theory is applied to the empirical world, data are typically 'forced' to fit into categories and concepts which have already been formulated. Grounded theory insists that theoretical concepts and hypotheses must *emerge* from the data as it is uncovered or gathered in the research process itself. Instead of relying on surveys and structured interviews and identifying external variables, the grounded theory approach demands much more rapport and empathy with the people it studies in order to represent their understandings and social experiences faithfully. Thus, forms of close observation (including participant observation), the use of focus groups and in-depth interviews are thought essential for this kind of research and theorizing. In short, there is far more emphasis on qualitative data than in the middle-range approach (or other theory-testing approaches).

So for Glaser and Strauss both general and middle-range theories start out (wrongly) with preconceived ideas (including assumptions about the nature of social structure and culture) and as a result they tend to be abstract and removed from the everyday lives of people. By contrast, grounded theory is directly linked with empirical data and therefore reflects the everyday realities of whichever group of people it is about. Thus one of the criteria by which we can judge the relevance and validity of a grounded theory is that it should be understandable or make sense to those whom it attempts to represent. Clearly, although grounded theory is not primarily a theory-testing approach, it does not preclude elements of testing (Strauss, 1987; Vaughan, 1992) in the sense that emergent ideas are constantly checked against (and hence 'tested' in relation to) ideas and data which have already been gathered as well as against the incoming data. In the same way, although middle-range theory is not primarily concerned with the construction of new theory from research data, it does lend itself to some kinds of 'reformulation' or development of theory (de Vaus, 1996). However, what is meant by valid theory and how it should be tested and generated mean very different things from the point of view of these two approaches.

Implications for the adaptive theory approach

In specific ways both the middle-range approach and that of grounded theory have been important sources of inspiration for the kinds of strategies and recommendations that I outline in the following chapters. At the same time, from the point of view of adaptive theory, there are many problems, limitations and drawbacks associated with these approaches. Principal among these is that as they are formulated by their originators they are 'incompatible' with each other since they both claim the centrepoint or primary focus for the use of theory and theoretical 'development' in social research. On the one hand, Merton (as is common with many predominantly quantitative approaches) only accedes a secondary role to qualitative data and the generation of new theory, while he centralizes the importance of quantitative data as means of verifying theoretical ideas which have been developed from a logical deductive system. On the other hand, Glaser and Strauss stress the primary importance of qualitative data for the process of theoretical discovery – the generation of new concepts, ideas and frameworks that apply to data drawn from a particular area or topic.

While I believe that even in their own terms both approaches have serious limitations and drawbacks, something of the spirit and the practical implications of both approaches is combined (although in a considerably modified manner) in what I term the adaptive theory approach. Specifically, adaptive theory attempts to combine an emphasis on prior theoretical ideas and models which feed into and guide research while at the same time attending to the generation of theory from the ongoing analysis of data. As I have indicated, adaptive theory is only capable of doing this by radically transforming some of the premises of both middle-range and grounded theory.

Principally, middle-range theory is limited by its exclusion of general theory (what Merton refers to as 'grand' theory) and this unnecessarily curtails its explanatory scope and power. This in turn limits its ability to add to a cumulative corpus of theoretical knowledge. In addition its overall grasp of aspects of social reality is hampered by its focus on quantifiable, so-called 'structural' variables and its relative neglect of the subjective meanings and experiences of those who are being studied. In a related manner while its claim to deal with 'structural variables' may be upheld to some extent, this does not mean that it deals adequately with social-structural or systemic phenomena as a whole. In this sense adaptive theory requires that theoretical models of forms of social organization (markets, bureaucracies, for example) and resources (power, money, and forms of ideology and signification – see Layder, 1997) are incorporated within its terms of reference. Such phenomena cannot be adequately dealt with *simply* as quantifiable variables. Finally, middle-range theory does not attend sufficiently to the problem of theory-construction as a *routine* feature of the research process and this is precisely what the adaptive approach attempts to do.

Conversely, grounded theory has certain built-in limitations. First, as I have pointed out, it too rejects the contribution of general theory and, in my view, this simply impoverishes its explanatory potential (its power and scope) in an unnecessary and inflexible manner. Such a waste of good theoretical ideas can be avoided and the overall goal of cumulative knowledge (rather than disparate and isolated fragments) can be served by accommodating general theory. Secondly, although grounded theory is good on depicting the lived experiences and subjective meanings of people, it does not have an adequate appreciation of social-structural or systemic aspects of society. This is because it is committed epistemologically (the validity of knowledge) and ontologically (its view of social reality) to denying the existence of phenomena that are not only or simply behavioural (like markets, bureaucracies and forms of domination).

By contrast, the adaptive approach deals with both behavioural (activity, meaning and lived experience) phenomena as well as systemic phenomena. In this respect it attempts to trace the reciprocal influences and interconnections between people's social activities and the wider social (systemic) environment in which they are played out. Thirdly, although grounded theory is strong in its emphasis on the discovery and generation of new theory, it is relatively weak on the theory-testing side of things – in particular in relation to preconceived hypotheses, theoretical ideas, concepts or frameworks. The adaptive theory approach has an equal emphasis on the discovery of theory and the employment of prior or extant theory which stand in a relation of reciprocal influence to each other. In this sense it takes issue with grounded theory's view that theorizing must be continuously emergent and that no conceptual schema should stand prior to initial data collection or at any point during the research process.

Formal theory versus substantive theory

I want to distinguish what I mean by formal theory from what Glaser and Strauss (1967) mean by this term. However, since they use this term in the context of a distinction between *substantive* and *formal* theory it is important to be clear about what they mean by these terms as they help us understand particular features of the relation between theorizing and research in general. In the context of grounded theory, Glaser and Strauss emphasize that the development of theories always begins with a grounding in data concerning a particular substantive area of sociological inquiry, such as patient care, racialization, geriatric lifestyles, and so on. After substantive theory about this area has been developed as a result of the researcher immersing her or himself in empirical data culled from interviews, observations (and documentary resources), it is then possible to elaborate and extend this theory so that it may cover more general and formal areas of inquiry, such as authority and power, organizations, organizational careers, status passage, and so forth.

Of necessity, grounded theory always begins with a substantive anchoring and then moves to formal theory. Formal theory that has already gone through this process may then be used as an initial guideline to further research but it should never become hardened and inflexible, turning into a search for data that fits (confirms) the theory rather than generating theory that fits the data. It is always important to stress discovery and openness in relation to theorizing. In any case, Glaser and Strauss point to the need for a multiplicity of theories (both substantive and formal) and this is in direct contrast to those who 'talk as if there is only one theory for a formal area or perhaps only one formal theory for all areas' (Glaser and Strauss, 1971: 182).

If we view the distinction between substantive and formal theory away from the context of grounded theory, it does pinpoint a divergence in social research. This is between those who understand theory to be irrevocably tied to a discrete set of empirical concerns or issues, such as suicide, stratification, sexual behaviour, mental illness, drug addiction, nursing or education, and so on, and those who are interested in the implications of research for more general theoretical issues. What we mean by formal theory here is crucial. For example, although many researchers would agree that the wider implications of theory are important, they would baulk at the idea of using elements of more general theory (such as the work of Foucault, Habermas, Giddens, Parsons, and so on) as an integral feature of research.

In terms of the approach that I outline in the rest of this book, it is crucial to disentangle this notion of formal theory from the strictures imposed by Glaser and Strauss's definition, which excludes the influence of general social theory. An exclusion of more general theoretical themes has the effect of narrowing down the possible sources of theorizing in research, both as an initial guide (part of the research design) and as an adjunct to grounded theories. In this respect it would seem more helpful to the accumulation of theoretical and empirical knowledge to accept that there are different types and levels of theorizing. As a consequence, they have their own forms of validity and thus there are a number of ways in which theory may be legitimately described as 'grounded' in data and a number of possible ways in which such theory may be generated. Although there are many problems that need to be worked out in this area, a more co-operative stance between entrenched views about what theory should be, or what it should look like, is surely a more constructive response (Layder, 1993).

Epistemological and ontological aspects of theory

At issue in developing a more inclusive approach to theorizing in research is understanding some of the assumptions which underpin particular approaches. In this respect research is connected to basic philosophical issues and in a literal sense can never be theory-neutral. Even a researcher who claims that his or her theory is unaffected by theoretical assumptions would, unavoidably, be making a theoretical claim in this regard. Thus the claims of positivism to provide 'objectively neutral' findings, unsullied by prior epistemological or theoretical assumptions, has been shown to be false (Keat and Urry, 1975; Bhaskar, 1979). However, the humanist (or interpretivist) claim to be providing a more adequate account of social reality simply by attending to subjective meanings and understandings has also been successfully challenged by the 'new realist' approach to social science (Pawson, 1989; Layder, 1990).

This is a complex issue but at this juncture I do not want to enter into a formal discussion detached from the more practical considerations I offer in the following chapters. Nonetheless, the issue of examining the underlying epistemological assumptions of particular research strategies has three major implications for theorizing in social research. First, identifying the premises upon which visions of social analysis and research strategies rest allows one to examine hidden assumptions which may affect potential theoretical developments as a result of social research. For example, if one believes that the only valid form of knowledge is empirical in nature and derived from the evidence of our senses (empiricism), then we are unlikely to be sympathetic to claims that the internal connections between concepts (rationalism) have any useful role to play in providing secure and valid knowledge.

In the context of adaptive theory I suggest (in Chapter 6) that the tension between empiricist and rationalist approaches to knowledge must be overcome and in this respect the adaptive approach presents one solution to this dilemma. Secondly, if a researcher is wedded strongly to the idea that social research must adhere to methodological criteria associated with the natural sciences, then he or she may reject the claim that social research can be based on more humanistic assumptions and involve more interpretative and empathetic responses. Again, this is an issue which surfaces in Chapter 6 where I suggest that adaptive theory draws on both kinds of approach to social analysis and social science.

Clearly, the analysis of underlying epistemological and ontological commitments allows one to deal with different levels of theorizing and the sorts of validity claims that are associated with them. Thirdly, and related to these, the question of the relation between epistemology and ontology is extremely important for social theory and research. Both Giddens (1984) and Bhaskar (1979) have argued that ontological questions (about the nature of social reality) are prior to epistemological ones about validity. However, in my view both kinds of question – the nature of reality and how we come to know it – are inextricably bound together and this has important implications for the manner in which we go about research, the sorts of research problems we pose and the questions we ask. This is especially the case in relation to the issue of how we view the interconnections between, and mutual influences of, social activities and aspects of social structure (system).

Sensitizing concepts versus explanatory frameworks

This issue relates to the one above but also refers back to the question of the degree to which particular research projects focus on empirical or theoretical questions. In so far as it relates to epistemological questions, it concerns the extent to which the use of single concepts or segments of larger theories in social research can be legitimately regarded as theory proper or merely a preparatory step towards theorizing. The wider issue here is whether single concepts have only a limited 'decorative' function in research or whether they really do add explanatory power to the analysis of the research findings. It is difficult for single concepts to provide dense and rounded theoretical explanations of the kind we perhaps expect from larger and more general theories, but there is no real reason to suppose that they are less illuminating either descriptively or theoretically.

Certainly, there are excellent examples of research which have drawn on wider bodies of theory to help illuminate and structure their findings, as in the case of Bloor and McIntosh's (1990) use of Foucault's notions of power, resistance and surveillance in their study of therapeutic communities and health visiting in the UK. There are perhaps two dangers with the use of general theory. First, where its use is selective there is the possibility of wrenching concepts out of their wider theoretical context and thus inadvertently disfiguring their meaning (which could lead either to forcing the data to conform to 'inappropriate' concepts, or simply using the concepts as decoration). Secondly, the obverse of these problems may occur when a whole conceptual network or general theory is used as an explanatory framework for research findings. In these cases it is often tempting to employ the whole package of concepts and underlying assumptions to provide a ready-made 'explanation' of the findings without due regard for the findings themselves. As a result, this may turn into an exercise in self-confirmation and/or self-justification.

Notwithstanding these potential pitfalls, my more general view in this book is that the best use of individual concepts drawn from a wider body of theory or knowledge is as a means of cranking up the process of theorizing – either by elaborating on extant theory or by generating theory in relation to research evidence. By using such concepts as orienting devices the researcher is provided with a preliminary means of ordering and giving shape to a mass of data. Such concepts may be discarded at any point during the analysis of data, for instance if it becomes apparent that they have out-lived their usefulness as orienting devices. On the other hand, further data analysis may underline the explanatory importance of the initial concepts and hence they will eventually form an important aspect of the developing theory.

However, with regard to the adaptive approach as a whole, single concepts are employed with a longer-term view to developing more elaborate theories, models and conceptual frameworks. Moreover, while I acknowledge that using one (or several) concepts drawn from existing theory to illuminate research findings is perfectly valid and acceptable as a strategy in its own right, the approach that I offer in this book combines the use of extant theory with the development of theory from research findings. This allows for both the elaboration of the extant theory in relation to research findings as well as the emergence of theory from the conjunction between prior theory (and theoretical models) and data analysis tied to an ongoing research project. This wider-ranging stance allows for a more flexible, open-ended and inclusive use of resources in the development of theory and cumulative knowledge of the social world.

Theorizing as continuous versus discrete part of research

This final opposition has to do with the extent to which theorizing is thought to be a separate and distinct activity which enters the research process only at certain junctures or whether it is regarded as a continuous and integral feature of all phases of research. Again, this overlaps with several of the other dimensions already discussed. The more it is thought that research should be led by theory in the sense of having a theory-testing orientation, then it is viewed as a discrete activity which enters into the research process at distinct junctures. With theory-testing approaches the development of a context of theoretical assumptions precedes the research proper and then re-enters the equation after the research has been conducted – as a concluding stage in the analysis of the empirical data.

When research is formulated and guided by a general framework of concepts like Marxism, developmentalism or feminism, then theorizing is a constant accompaniment of research in the sense that the framework provides a continuous backdrop. Typically, though, the findings are used simply to confirm the importance of the theory in the first place – they are rarely used as a means by which the theories can be tested. Much qualitative research (influenced particularly by the notion of grounded theory) provides a distinct counterpoint to this in the sense that it views theorizing as a continuous aspect of the research process but insists that it must be an emergent feature of data collection and analysis which continually feeds back into these activities (Bryman and Burgess, 1994). Not all qualitative research follows this path. For example, Bloor and McIntosh (1990) gathered their fieldwork data on health visiting and therapeutic communities before they realized that it was pertinent to Foucault's theoretical work on power, surveillance and resistance. Thus, this provides an example in which theorizing occurs 'after the event' of research as a way of organizing and analysing the data.

The adaptive theory approach emphasizes that theorizing should be a continuous aspect of the research process (see Chapter 2) rather than be reserved for special junctures and/or occasions. Theorizing may therefore take place at any phase of the research process, including well before and well after the data has been collected – although I believe that it must be undertaken in close association with data analysis. This reinforces the efficient use of resources by maximizing the time and space devoted to theoretical matters. Of course I do not mean that the whole research process should be monopolized by theoretical issues. Quite clearly practical, methodo- logical and technical matters are necessary ingredients of the research process – and will continue to be encountered at every step of the way. However, I believe that increasing the resources, time and energy directed towards theory development enhances the explana- tory scope and power of research conclusions as well as tying it more firmly to the empirical evidence which forms its basis.

Implications for adaptive theory

I have tried to show that theorizing and social research are related in complex and multi-dimensional ways. Although I have identified some of the main dimensions in this regard, I have also tried to convey the fact that much research proceeds on the basis of 'muddy' combinations of different elements and emphases. The general point of this discussion has been to lay bare some of the most important features of the theory-research relationship as they are present in current research practices. However, the discussion also serves as a background to the presentation of my own adaptive theory approach which forms the substance of the rest of the book. As such the different dimensions and strands that I have identified all bear some relation to adaptive theory, although it should be clear that they do so in rather different ways and with different emphases. Let me summarize the main points of divergence and overlap.

First, in terms of the extent of theoretical versus empirical focus I have suggested that in principle adaptive theory concentrates in equal measure on theorizing and data-gathering in relation to a specific research project. However, the whole thrust of the adaptive approach is to ensure that possibilities and opportunities for theorizing are never overlooked, and thus I emphasize the importance of constant attunement and sensitivity to the possibilities of theorizing. The researcher should not 'switch off' her or his theoretical sensibility when engaged in the more technical or methodological aspects of research. This takes us into the second dimension concerning the issue of whether theorizing should be regarded as a discrete stage (or limited to particular stages) or elements of analysis. In this respect the adaptive approach views theorizing as an ever-present accompaniment to empirical research and data-gathering (see Chapter 2).

As far as the theory-testing and theory-generating dimensions are concerned, elements of both are involved. However, it is important to construe this mutual involvement in the context of a re-fashioning of the premises upon which the middle-range and grounded theory approaches are based, since as they stand they are somewhat antithetical to each other. This re-fashioning draws into the discussion the importance of underlying notions of validity and the sorts of social phenomena that constitute the legitimate topics or subject matter of social inquiry and empirical research. With regard to the question of the selective or wholesale use of general theory, the adaptive approach is tolerant of both as long as they are understood simply as resources which are, in principle, revisable and reformulable. Only if general theory is used as a 'master device' which orders empirical data 'in advance', are the intentions of adaptive theory thwarted.

The adaptive approach emphasizes the *development* of theory which draws on different combinations of different kinds of theoretical and substantive resources and trades on the synergy that is created between them. Similarly, elements of the use of both sensitizing concepts and explanatory networks are incorporated and absorbed into the adaptive theory framework. Thus, while in general adaptive theory embraces the search for an explanatory framework, one way in which it does so is by encouraging the use of orienting or background concepts that serve to stimulate the theoretical imagination and further theoretical elaboration.

The above comments serve as a rather indirect depiction of adaptive theory so by way of conclusion let me outline more directly some of its distinctive features (I provide a full and detailed discussion in Chapters 6 and 7). First, adaptive theory focuses on the construction of novel theory in the context of ongoing research by utilizing elements of prior theory (both general and substantive) in conjunction with theory that emerges from data collection and analysis. It is the interchange and dialogue between prior theory (models, concepts, conceptual clusterings) and emergent theory that forms the dynamic of adaptive theory. In this sense the approach is sharply distinguishable from grounded theory, middle-range theory and the use of general theories as 'all-embracing' interpretative frameworks.

The adaptive theory which results from such an interchange and dialogue always represents an attempt to depict the linkages between lifeworld and system elements of society. That is it centralizes the interconnections between, on the one hand, actors' meanings, activities and intentions (lifeworld) and, on the other, culture, institutions, power, reproduced practices and social relations (system elements). In this respect adaptive theory focuses on the ties between agency and structure in social life and the connections between macro and micro levels of analysis. Thus adaptive theory represents a methodological approach which takes into account the layered and textured nature of social reality (its ontological 'depth'). It also acknowledges the need for an epistemological basis which reflects the interweaving of objective and subjective elements of social life. This multi-dimensional approach distinguishes adaptive theory from others which tend to focus exclusively on one dimension or domain of social life.

Adaptive theory is accretive, it is an organic entity that constantly reformulates itself both in relation to the dictates of theoretical reasoning and the 'factual' character of the empirical world. Prior theoretical concepts and models suggest patterns and 'order' in emerging data while being continuously responsive to the 'order' suggested or unearthed by the data themselves. Thus, although adaptive theory centralizes 'emergent' theory, this is very different from grounded theory in that it makes use of elaborated conceptual models which stand prior to data collection at certain points in the research. By contrast, the grounded theory approach rejects the importance of prior theory (especially general theory) and insists that theory should emerge directly and exclusively from data collection and analysis. In this respect a distinguishing feature of adaptive theory is that it simultaneously privileges (prior) theory and research data in the emergence of new theory whereas grounded theory privileges empirical data over and against prior theory of any kind.

CHAPTER 2

ELEMENTS OF THE RESEARCH PROCESS

Having outlined the main contours of, and variations in, the relationship between theorizing and research I want now to turn to the dynamics of the research process itself. My strategy will be to distinguish different elements of the research process which are common to research of all kinds. The elements I shall be concerned with are: the choice of topic and problem; the (theoretical) framework – or more accurately 'theoretical deliberations'; methods and techniques of data-gathering; sampling, coding and memo-writing. Although I do not deal with data analysis in a separate section, my assumption is that it enters the research process at every step of the way and thus I deal with it in the other sections. Even though I treat theoretical issues separately, I also want to suggest that theorizing and data analysis go hand in hand and thus theorizing should also be regarded as a continuous feature of research. Some authors have usefully attempted to present elements such as these (but not necessarily identical ones) as stages in the research process. While this has its uses and while some of the elements may be regarded as sequential stages in the unfolding of various research projects, for a number of reasons I want to leave to one side the idea that there is some necessary or relatively fixed temporal sequence.

Of course in some instances there is clearly some point in thinking about certain stages or phases of research as temporally fixed in terms of whether they come before or after others. For example, obviously one cannot talk about data analysis or results and conclusions before one has decided on a technique of gathering the data. However, this fixity is not true of most of the other elements that I have identified. Sometimes this is because research is often a 'messy' practical activity which does not follow a predictable sequence or adhere to clean conventional guidelines. The stages or phases therefore become rather jumbled. In reality, the phases are not always distinct and neatly separated from each other and thus they tend to meld into one another, making it impossible to say when one event or phase ends and another begins.

Finally, and most importantly, if one takes into account the fairly wide variety of styles that are possible in social research, then it becomes more apparent that where particular stages occur will vary depending on a number of factors. For example, the choice of

Figure 2.1   *Elements of the research process*

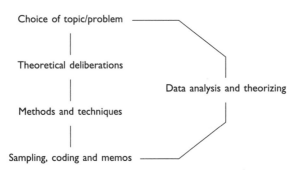

sample and sampling techniques are not necessarily limited to an early stage of the research process. If the researcher believes that sampling should be a flexible accompaniment to the unfolding character of the research, then it may be more in the nature of a continuous feature of the whole process rather than limited to a small phase. For example, this is the case with 'snowballing' techniques which are used in research where there is no reliable information on the nature of the universe being sampled (the numbers of people involved and their location). Thus, relatively invisible groups such as 'Asian carers' or 'married homosexuals' or 'active criminals' must be sampled in this fashion. (See also later comments on theoretical sampling.)

Also, depending upon the predilections of the researcher, theorizing itself may occur at any or all phases of the research and thus it is difficult to assign a 'normal' or 'proper' position for it in some sequence of research practices. In fact it is exactly this kind of undogmatic, flexible or 'anarchistic' approach to theorizing that I wish to advocate in this chapter since I believe that this is most conducive to imaginative theorizing. This conception feeds into subsequent chapters in which I suggest ways of generating theory in the context of ongoing research and develop an approach (adaptive theory) which attempts to profit from a co-operative dialogue with general social theory. Notwithstanding these aims and objectives, I shall deal with the various elements of research mentioned above in what could be regarded as a 'conventional' sequence, simply for purposes of exposition – since some order of discussion has to be observed (see Figure 2.1). But in a sense this sequence should be regarded as arbitrary (for the reasons mentioned above) and capable of being moved around or shuffled according to varying styles of research and practical circumstances.

Choice of research topic and problem

As soon as we consider the problem of the initial formulation of a research project we can understand the point about the lack of clearly segregated and compartmentalized stages. First, there may be no definite end-point to the formulation of the research problem. In fact it may resemble a rather haphazard, 'evolution' characterized by a series of oscillating phases of relative confusion and clarity rather than an immaculate conception. Secondly, there is no reason to suppose that decisions about what the research topic is and the central problems to be addressed can be disentangled from more general questions about the theoretical framework or the methods of data collection. These are issues which will, of necessity, be of continuing importance both in dealing with the initial phase of 'problem formulation' and with the other elements of the research process. However, it is worth considering the decisions and choices that are made at the beginning of a piece of research since they may have considerable impact on its later development. In a more prescriptive sense I want to argue that very often much more could be made of this phase in terms of conceptual development and theory-generation.

Very often methods texts and other books on the mechanics of research begin with the assumption that the topic or problem that drives the research, and which it seeks to address (and ultimately solve), has been chosen in advance, and therefore plunge straight into the technicalities of particular methods and data-gathering techniques, forms of sampling and the coding of data, and so on. Less often questions about the role of theory in the formulation of research problems are left out of the equation, but even where they are broached they tend either to be marginalized (as just another technical phase of research) or they are construed in a particular manner. In this sense theoretical questions are frequently covered in either of two ways (or possibly some combination of both).

First, theory and theoretical issues are thought to revolve around tightly formulated hypotheses (or sets of assumptions) which are to be tested-out in varying ways during the research. Conversely, theory is treated as the end-product of the research process which is generated from the findings or data uncovered by the research. By defining the theoretical issues associated with research in such a limited manner, textbooks often minimize the possibilities and opportunites that are open to the would-be researcher-theorist. Coupled with the tendency to go straight to the technical issues of methodology, these narrow definitions of theory have the effect of short-cutting any prolonged contemplation of questions concerning the choice of topic and the manner in which the research problem is conceptualized in the first place.

By adopting a more catholic notion of theory and conceptual issues and by refusing to assume that questions about the choice of topic and the research problem have all been sorted out in advance, one can usefully ask questions about this initial phase of the research which may lead to clues and hunches which are pertinent to the development of concepts and theory later on in the research. In this respect I am advocating an approach which is pluralistic, flexible and open, instead of sticking to a traditional or conventional approach, method or procedure which may well be 'tried and tested' but is also inherently limiting, rigid and closed to other approaches, rules of procedure or methodological protocols. In this instance the pluralism I am advocating is related to both methodological and theoretical matters as they are applied to the initial formulation of the research topic and problem. By not tying oneself to any particular set of rules of procedure or conception of what constitutes theory, a theoretical framework or a theoretical problem, one may begin to ask fairly simple questions about the nature of the research topic and problem which may eventually feed into the process of theory-generation and elaboration.

For instance, one can ask questions concerning the key words, phrases and concepts that spring to mind in thinking about the area under consideration before any data collection or even a literature search has begun. By making lists of such words, phrases and concepts and then shuffling and playing around with them, the researcher may stimulate the creative processes entailed in theory-construction. Haphazard juxtapositions of the ideas and concepts involved may yield fruitful lines of attack or inquiry, or even possible explanations or explanatory leads quite independently of previous research findings, fresh data or established theories allied to the area or topic in question. Engaging in this practice of 'imaginative rehearsal', involving the patterning and rearrangement of ideas and concepts, prevents the researcher from becoming too bogged-down by the existing or current 'wisdom' in the area or topic in question. This is certainly not an injunction simply to ignore the current literature and the accumulated findings, evidence and theoretical ideas of previous research and theory-building endeavours. Far from it. Rather, it is a precaution against being too committed to, and hence 'caught-up' in, the accepted and established views about a particular area or topic that one ceases to think anew about them.

If theory-generation is to be a primary goal of the research, then constant fresh injections of perspective and overview are a necessary prerequisite. Thus, my suggestions about the initial playing around with new ideas are not made with a view to excluding or ignoring an accumulated body of knowledge in a particular area – if such a body of knowledge does exist. Rather, if this is the case, the initial imaginative experiments must take place against the background of an existing body of evidence and theory. In such a situation it is important to incorporate the influence of the extant findings and conventional wisdom of the area while at the same time retaining the capacity to distance oneself from this body of knowledge. (This includes being willing to entertain ideas contrary to those which currently hold sway – see next section.) This is necessary in order to create the conceptual breathing-space required to generate novel ideas, hunches and insights which may, later on, lead to more elaborate theoretical schemas. Such a strategy has the advantage of creating a dynamic synergy between new thinking and accumulated knowledge.

For example, say a researcher had decided that her or his topic of interest centred on the relationships between prostitutes and their clients. General questions such as what is the nature of the relationship (the quality of the communications and interactions between them) and the reason why this is the case (what causes or determines these characteristics) may be the ones which are giving immediate impetus to the research. However, let us also imagine that the researcher is interested in the emotional dimension of the relationships (the 'emotional' tone – positive or negative). In this respect the concept of 'emotional labour' is of pivotal importance and in this example we have to assume that a preliminary reading of the literature on the sociology of emotion has led the researcher to Hochschild's (1983) work on this topic. Hochschild discusses the concept of emotional labour in general terms but her main research sample (and the main example she uses generally) is of airline flight attendants. She concentrates on the way they deal with and manage the emotional demands of the flying public as they are mediated by the airline companies for whom they work.

Already the concept of emotional labour will be of central importance to theoretical thinking about the topic and the problem-focus of the research because it raises the question of how it is that human emotion is variably expressed (sincerely, affectedly, falsely, and so on) and managed by those working (or otherwise operating) in different kinds of work environment. Therefore, simply by concentrating on this concept and thinking about (imagining) the variety of forms of emotional labour that are required in different contexts will enable the researcher to generate provisional ideas about the range of applicability of the concept and the way or ways in which it could be extended or modified in order to cope with circumstances different from those of flight attendants. This will also allow the researcher to begin to think of the sorts of categories, codes and empirical indicators of concepts that will play a role in the later stages of data collection and analysis.

For example, an interesting dimension of emotional labour concerns the degree of 'emotional distance' that people maintain from roles that they are playing, or from the (emotional) demands of other people. Initial theoretical ideas may be generated by comparing different kinds of work setting and the different kinds of demands that emanate from the positional roles that people play in them. For instance, to what extent do prostitutes maintain an emotional distance between themselves and their clients in order to preserve the integrity of their 'real selves' in the face of the emotional demands made upon them by clients? Is this distance carefully 'managed' by prostitutes so as not to allow the relationship to become too impersonal (and thus alienating for the client), hence endangering its monetary basis – that is, the willingness of the client to pay for services and to keep returning for the same services? Is this ability to maintain emotional distance (and the associated aspects of emotional composure, the ability to play-act, and so on) the same as that required by flight attendants, or school teachers, or nurses?

Such issues and questions raise a multitude of others such as to what extent are there differences in emotional labour in the different work contexts. Does this require that we extend (or decompose) the concept of emotional labour into subsidiary ones such as 'styles of emotion management' or types of emotional distance (personal, professional, economic)? What are the main dimensions of difference and what produces or causes them? What influence does the nature of the interpersonal contacts required by the job have on these questions (for example, catering for the neuroses or phantasies of clients in prostitution, as compared with inculcating appropriate responses and interpersonal emotional skills in school children). In these examples is there more pressure for sincerity of expressed emotion associated with school teachers or nurses than there is with prostitutes or even flight attendants? Questions about the economic basis of the work and the employment status of the practitioners raise themselves in connection with these issues.

These questions begin to multiply and may or may not produce interesting ideas which may or may not prove to be of lasting value in attempting to explain data on prostitute–client relationships. The *comparative* dimension of the questions naturally draws the research on to other related areas which again may feed into the primary research focus itself, but importantly, such questions may also precipitate a move outwards to incorporate other similar areas thus increasing the cumulative scope and range of thinking and theorizing. The idea of introducing in an imaginative sense a whole range of questions and accumulated observations and facts and then playing around with the resulting ideas, evidence and concepts facilitates preliminary theoretical thinking about a research topic prior to the collection of data.

This kind of preliminary work may go on independently of extant knowledge (particularly in cases where there is very little or no previous work done on the area or topic in question) or it may provide a means of thinking afresh about an area in which there has been some work or in which there are pivotal ideas or concepts (such as the case of emotional labour). In either case, the preliminary work goes on in the context of incorporating (where appropriate) bits and pieces of extant knowledge which all feed into the initial deliberations and decisions about the formulation of the research objectives as well as shaping the problem-focus of the research.

Frameworks and theoretical deliberations

In one sense the notion of a sequestered phase of research in which theoretical matters are attended to has already been queried but here I want to reinforce this by suggesting that 'theorizing' in the widest sense possible should be a continuous feature of the research process. However, it is often the case that when research is conducted or discussed in textbooks there are three typical approaches to the question of theory. The first emphasizes the primary importance of the collection of empirical information. As I pointed out in Chapter 1, this is sometimes coupled with an avowedly anti-theoretical stance which denies or rejects the importance of theory and consequently undervalues and understates the importance of theory and theorizing. However, some research which emphasizes empirical findings is not consciously anti-theoretical but simply more concerned with finding information either to plug gaps in knowledge and/or because of some greater priority such as a social policy or social problem orientation.

The second approach to the question of theory assumes that it is a matter of deciding upon and applying a body of concepts and ideas which will constitute the 'theoretical framework' of the research. There are three main variants of this. One involves either the use of a general theory (or fragments of it) such as Marxism, structuration theory, postmodernism, and so on, as a wide-angled background resource with which to contextualize the 'theoretical discussion' of the empirical data collected during the research. The second variant involves the application or 'testing-out' of single concepts such as 'total institution' or 'family culture' in the context of a particular research design. The single or focal concept may be taken from a more inclusive network (such as a general theory) or it may be taken from some other more widespread source or discourse. The third variant concerns the application of a tightly formulated hypothesis, set of premises or assumptions at the outset of the research and for which the subsequent data collection is meant as a form of testing against the evidence.

All of these variants have in common a tendency to be verificationist in orientation, although it is also true that some forms of general theory and the use of particular concepts are not always applied in quite such a strict manner. I shall deal with these exceptions in a moment, but what potentially groups these variants together is the very fact that they are 'preconceived' orderings of data. As such they are applied to the incoming data collected during a research project and thus they often have a tendency to be concerned with confirming or refuting the existing theory, concept or hypothesis rather than generating new theory. This is simply a tendency and not a hard-and-fast rule since it could be argued that even the stricter forms of theory-testing which result in non-confirmation then naturally lead to some new theoretical formulation.

This sometimes happens but the more common response is reformulation of the older or existing theory rather than discovery or construction of genuinely new theories. There is undoubtedly an important role for such theory-testing and verificationist approaches in general – particularly in cases where there is a large body of extant theory and empirical findings already established by previous research. In this respect the verificationist tendency of these theoretical approaches reaffirms the importance of continuity and dialogue between current research and past endeavours. It also establishes an important link with the idea of the cumulative nature of the development of both theory and empirical research.

As I have intimated, some general theories and the use of particular concepts are not always or inevitably employed in a strict verificationist manner although without doubt the use of some general theories to explain empirical data by 'forcing them' into preconceived categories, without much attention to their fit, certainly conforms to this verificationist model. Sometimes general theories (or concepts taken from them) are used rather more loosely as a general theoretical 'orientation' to an empirical area or set of data rather than as a rigid interpretative scheme which filters and sorts the data into the appropriate categories provided by the theory. In this sense the general theory functions more as a 'guideline' which suggests possibilities rather than as an ordering and interpretative device that imposes itself firmly on the data.

Alternatively, aspects of general theory (and concepts taken from other discourses) may be employed as 'sensitizing concepts' which have a much more provisional relationship to empirical data. For instance, referring back to the example of prostitution research, Hochschild's general concept of 'emotional labour' may initially provide a useful means of identifying and categorizing relevant data until the researcher finds that she or he needs to refine or develop further subdivisions or distinctions in order to provide more adequate explanations and accounts of research findings. Thus, in the previous example, it was suggested that a comparative analysis of other occupations that require emotional labour combined with ongoing interviews with prostitutes and their clients may yield more elaborate and refined concepts depicting, for instance, different 'styles of emotion management'. In this sense the concept of emotional labour functions more as an orienting device which is suggestive of 'possible lines of inquiry' than as a strict indicator of what the data means (see Chapter 3). Of course, it is also true that particular concepts may be used strictly for 'testing' purposes, as when a particular concept is employed to gauge its usefulness for understanding empirical data.

Overall though, in spite of the fact that general theory and particular concepts may not be used in the very strict sense of testing out the viability of theories and concepts, their more 'provisional' nature does not prevent them from retaining an indirect connection with a verificationist tendency. Their preconceived form and the fact that they suggest (but do not necessarily dictate) patterns of explanation, concepts and ideas means that they are naturally inclined towards (oriented to) the confirmation or otherwise of the home theory of which they form an integral part. That is, they are not naturally or routinely geared to the detection of concepts and ideas which have little or no connection with the theories and concepts in which they are embedded. In my view, both the direct (hypothesis-testing) and indirect tendencies towards verification can only lead to an inertial drag on, and ultimately a stultification of, theory development – as Glaser and Strauss (1967) have suggested. Thus I would argue that such approaches should and can be more closely and securely harnessed to the task of theory-generation and discovery (and I shall deal with this presently).

However, this point about the inertial drag on theory development (and the accumulation of knowledge in general) brings us to a consideration of the third approach to the question of theory in the context of research. Like those already discussed, the grounded theory approach generally appreciates the value of theory but flatly rejects the three variants discussed above on the basis that they are unremittingly verificationist in orientation. As I have said, there is a certain amount of truth in this assertion and undoubtedly Glaser and Strauss's emphasis on the discovery or generation of new theory by ensuring that it is grounded in data is to be applauded (even though I would question the method of grounding the theory advocated by Glaser and Strauss). However, the grounded theorists' rejection of the other forms of theorizing in research is both wasteful and based on some erroneous assumptions about the nature of theory and theorizing in social inquiry and about the nature of social life and social organization.

It is wasteful in the sense that, by rejecting other forms of theorizing, grounded theory simply becomes a dogmatic and ultimately unsustainable ideological claim to the truth which precludes other legitimate attempts to grasp the relation between theorizing and research. In this sense grounded theorists simply miss out on some valuable resources which can be drawn into a more comprehensive and far-reaching set of strategies for the generation of theory. Even more serious though are the grounded theorists' assumptions that these other approaches are only capable of yielding speculative, ungrounded 'armchair' theories which bear little or no relation to the empirical world.

This is a profound misunderstanding of the verificationist position on the relation between theory and empirical data. In this respect the grounded theorists fail to understand that there is a plurality of forms in which the theory-research relation is to be understood and that verificationist forms of theory bear a different kind of relation to the empirical world (Layder, 1990, 1993). Similarly, the grounded theorists' rejection of other forms of theorizing is based on a misunderstanding of the manner in which the social world is organized and the fact that these other approaches focus on different aspects of social organization (Layder, 1993, 1994, 1997). In essence, because the grounded theorists' position precludes any consideration of social-structural or social-systemic phenomena (on the basis that such phenomena do not exist and hence can play no role in people's everyday lives), they are unable to deal with these pivotal phenomena. I deal in more detail with these and related issues at various junctures of the book.

The adaptive theory approach

In Chapters 6 and 7 of this book I develop what I call an 'adaptive theory approach'. At this point I want to describe some of the ingredients of this approach with reference to the present discussion of the more conventional or established approaches. My position is that all the approaches I have just described have something valuable to offer but that it is important to develop a more comprehensive and integrated approach. Although grounded theorists are wrong about the nature of social organization and about the assumptions behind the verificationist approaches (bearing in mind my qualification that they are not all equally concerned with verification), their emphasis on the generation of new theory is extremely important. This is also a feature of the adaptive theory approach – but without the attendant limitations inherent in grounded theory.

That is, the adaptive theory approach includes attention to theory which emerges in conjunction with specific research projects, as well as to theory which exists prior to specific research projects such as general theories, hypotheses in need of testing, or some other body of accredited assumptions and axioms about a particular facet of social life or substantive area. In this sense adaptive theory draws upon the whole range of approaches to theorizing in research (as well as a range of methodological traditions and techniques) as resources which may be brought into some kind of dialogue with each other. The 'adaptive' part of the term is meant to suggest that the theory both adapts to, or is shaped by, incoming evidence at the same time as the data themselves are filtered through (and adapted to) the extant theoretical materials that are relevant and at hand. The exact nature of this approach will be the subject of the chapters to follow, but here I simply want to suggest some of the preconditions that are necessary in order for the adaptive approach to draw upon this diversity of theoretical elements.

I shall have more extended comments to make about general theories presently because one of the most well-defined themes of the adaptive approach is an attempt to fashion a stronger and closer alignment between the resources of general theory and the endeav-ours and methodological considerations of empirical social research. Hitherto there has been something of a gulf between those who regard themselves as general theorists and those who engage in the nitty-gritty of primary data-gathering empirical research. Although it is rare to find any sociologist – theorist or empirical researcher of any type or persuasion – who would deny the importance of establishing or reaffirming the closeness of the ties between theory and research, there are in fact few, if any, attempts to overcome the specialist divisions between these areas and the multiplicity of 'competing' epistemological positions which hinder this kind of dialogue. From the point of view of adaptive theory, it is therefore necessary to specify some of the prerequisites that would allow for a greater dialogue between the approaches to theorizing in social research that I have identified and discussed.

From the standpoint of using adaptive theory as an organizing device which may process the dialogue between the other general approaches to theorizing, it is important to establish the basic conditions that determine the inclusion or exclusion, the manner of use, and so on, of elements of the other approaches. The most important of these and the one that applies to all four general approaches to theorizing (the use of general theories, particular concepts, hypothesis-testing and grounded theory) insists that they must be 'epistemologically open' as discourses. That is their tendency to erect boundaries which exclude other approaches must be thwarted in order that they may be opened up to a plurality of other influences. My point is that frequently discourses on the nature of the theory-research relation operate as closed universes which, although necessarily self-consistent, also tend to be self-referential. As a consequence, they are inclined to exclude other approaches which are viewed as necessarily competing for the same territory of knowledge (in this case a particular construal of the theory–research relation).

To become open implies that such discourses must not be regarded as always or necessarily competing, but rather as complementary approaches to the same area. This is not to say that there are no points at which serious inconsistencies may arise and at which incompatibilities of an epistemological nature may prove insurmountable. This may necessitate modifications in the epistemological and ontological commitments of various discourses/approaches. The basic precondition here is that discourses cease to be regarded as sacrosanct, monolithic and self-referentially true. Instead, each becomes regarded as a working resource – just one of several in the context of an overarching framework. In this sense the adaptive theory approach operates as a means of distributing and co-ordinating the diverse influences of the other approaches. This implies a certain level of self-consistency, especially in terms of its epistemological commitments. But since these commitments are extremely wide and comprehensive (for example, embracing moderate versions of both objectivism and subjectivism – see Layder, 1997), it cannot become absolutely fixed, rigid or dogmatic and hence it remains open to the influence of innovations and developments beyond its current terms of reference.

If this precondition applies to all the approaches to the theory-research relation that I have described, then the necessity of openness is no less important when we consider some of the internal distinctions in these discourses. In particular, I want to concentrate here on the contribution that general theories may make to the adaptive theory approach. By general theory I am referring to those schools of thought, and networks of ideas, that are associated with particular authors and which are defined within the disciplines of social science in general and sociology in particular. There are many such schools of theory, for example functionalism (and neo-functionalism), Marxism (and its different varieties), symbolic interactionism, ethnomethodology, (phenomenology, humanism, existentialism), structuralism, poststructuralism and postmodernism to name but a few. Likewise, there are numerous general theories associated with particular authors, for example Foucault's discourse–power analysis, Habermas's 'theory of communicative action', Giddens's 'theory of structuration', Archer's 'morphogenetic theory', Parsons's 'theory of the social system', again, to name but a few. These general theories tend to be quite abstract and deal with very general features of social life, such as the nature of the ties between power and social practices or the links between social action and social structures (or systems). However, my contention is that such theories can play a valuable role in the formulation of new (adaptive) theory by providing background stimuli in the form of concepts and chains of reasoning associated with wider conceptual clusters. For example, Giddens's theory of structuration is composed of an integrated cluster of concepts such as the 'duality of structure', the 'dialectic of control', 'discursive consciousness', and so on. Such resources can be brought into a dialogical relation with others, such as freshly gathered empirical data, more substantively grounded theories, various methodological techniques (such as memo-writing, forms of coding, and so on), in a manner that is productive of new theory about an area which is currently the subject of research activity. In order for them to be able to function as resources in this way it is of paramount importance that each school of theory or author-specific theory is epistemologically open to the influence of these other resources and the theoretical developments and modifications that are entailed in producing new (adaptive) theory.

This requires the relinquishing of implicit assumptions that such theories are perfected end-products in their own right and hence are thought to capture and monopolize 'the truth' in particular areas. This means that these theories should not be used in a dogmatic manner as a blanket background framework which precludes other forms of explanation (as is often the case with dogmatic applications of rigidly held, all-embracing frameworks of thought such as forms of Marxism, feminism, poststructuralism or postmodernism). This may be a convenient way of ordering data through a form of pre-interpretation, and it may also be a very efficient way of asserting and affirming (rather than demonstrating) the explanatory powers of the theory in question, but it does not and cannot lead to novel theorizing which is the point of the adaptive approach. Of course, one must also be aware of the potential pitfalls of too much openness in the form of unthinking borrowing from, and unreflective co-operation between, radically discrepant discourses. The inconsistencies and incompatibilities between discourses must be taken seriously and attended to accordingly.

Apart from the spirit of epistemological openness, general theories must also be attuned to the question of theoretical discovery and this implies a turn away from their natural inclination towards a verificationist orientation (of course this also applies to the hypothesis-testing approach). This involves a further step on from openness to the influence of other theories and discourses to an active readiness to be transformed or absorbed into new theoretical forms in the service of theory-generation. General theories must become equally and naturally predisposed to theory-generation as well as the testing or verification of existing theory. In other words, they need to exhibit a simultaneous orientation to, and emphasis on, verification and theoretical discovery. Conversely, grounded theory must be radically transformed to accommodate the verificationist orientations possessed by general theories and theory-testing approaches. Thus, instead of presenting a uni-dimensional approach fixed rigidly upon the constant generation of new theory from data, grounded theory must aquire a dual orientation which allows a role for the influence of 'preconceived', 'prior', or 'extant' theory.

Such an approach demands the relinquishment of the misconceived idea that general theory is simply detached and disconnected from the real world. This view must be replaced by the recognition that general theories are often connected to the empirical world in fundamentally different ways from so-called 'grounded' theory. I say 'so-called' because I would claim that general theories are as anchored to the real empirical world as are grounded theories. What typically differs is their mode of connection with the empirical world. General theories are expressed in a more *abstract* manner and thus they refer more *indirectly* to aspects of social life and empirical data. Allowing a role for prior theory also means abandoning the claim that theory should only be about representing people's everyday lives (the intersubjective understandings, meanings and reality negotiations of interpersonal conduct). This must be replaced by an acceptance that theory should equally be about representing and/or depicting the social settings and contexts (system elements) that provide the social environment of people's lives (or lifeworlds). An adjunct of this is the notion that both lifeworld and system elements are mutually and inseparably interwined at the same time as they are partly autonomous from each other.

Given the qualifications and necessary modifications mentioned above, all approaches to theorizing in research may be harnessed to a programme of theoretical discovery and theory-construction in the context of ongoing research – as envisaged within the parameters of the adaptive theory approach. As I have already indicated in the first section, theorizing in this sense is not limited to any particular phase or stage of the research process. It is a continuous, ongoing practice since adaptive theory evolves in terms of theoretical elaboration (its internal connection with extant theory and the conceptual clusters and chains of reasoning that this entails) as well as in its dialogical relation with incoming data. Thus, adaptive theory shapes emergent data at the very same time as it is itself shaped by this data. Theorizing can therefore never be regarded as a completed process in the sense of giving rise to a perfected product in the form of a theoretical formulation. It can only ever be regarded as a best approximation to such a theory in the light of its potential revisability at any stage of the research process (including before it starts and after it has been completed).

Methods and techniques of data-gathering

The range of methods and techniques of data-gathering open to the researcher include the use of qualitative or quantitative data, or some combination of the two, the use of surveys and fixed-choice question-naires, case studies, observation techniques, including video record-ing, forms of participant observation, in-depth interviewing, focus groups and documentary research of all kinds. There is no reason to suppose that all the considerations discussed in the previous section, as they apply to purely theoretical matters, do not apply both to the choice and subsequent employment of methods and techniques used to gather data during research. That is, the adaptive theory approach also encourages a multi-pronged strategy (Layder, 1993) in terms of the employment of methods and techniques in order to maximize the potential for theory-generation. Again, the principle of openness is important from this point of view since the practicalities of data-gathering are often influenced by the rules of procedure, epistemo-logical assumptions and theoretical allegiances associated with par-ticular methods and techniques. Thus before any real commitment to a dialogue between different methods and techniques can take place, it is worth considering some of the underlying assumptions and commitments which may prevent or work against the accomplish-ment of this objective.

The notion of a multi-pronged or multi-strategy approach requires that any existing 'artificial' barriers are broken down and this is why the adaptive theory approach sides with those authors (Bryman, 1988; Silverman, 1985, 1993) who have argued for the dissolution of those barriers which have frequently separated the use of quan-titative data from qualitative data in social research. Clearly, both types of data may utilize and/or yield theoretical ideas (Layder, 1993), but I believe that the conditions under which theory-generation is maximized are only fully met if they are accompanied by the use of the sorts of strategies and resources that I have indicated in relation to adaptive theory. Namely, there has to be some dialogue with all the kinds of resources available: general and substantive theory, theory-testing types, sensitizing concepts, and empirically emergent theory. If these resources are not fully mobilized *in toto*, then there is the distinct possibility that theory-generation may not be maximized.

A possible problem with quantitative data in this respect derives from its close (although not exclusive) association with surveys, fixed-choice questionnaires and theory-testing approaches in general. This 'close association' does not mean that this type of data or the techniques for collecting them mentioned above are inherently incapable of generating theory. However, it does mean that if the context of the research is dominated by a concern for quantitative data and the application of techniques for their collection, then there is a possibility for a bias towards the verificationist tendency, and its predilection to work with pre-established hypotheses, to creep into the entire operation. Furthermore, this reaffirms a predisposition to view the research process as one in which any new angles or theoretical ideas will emanate primarily from the working hypothesis or some set of assumptions derivable from the body of ideas associated with it.

Clearly, under such circumstances the amount of attention given over to the quest for theory will be minimized. Another associated problem here concerns the fact that the exclusive use of techniques which generate quantitative data, such as surveys and fixed-choice questionnaires, means that the researcher has to establish in advance and in some considerable detail the conceptual parameters of the research. This frames the sorts of question asked, the kind of data collected and the nature of the sample used (the number and types of people interviewed), and makes it difficult to jettison these ideas quickly in response to changing theoretical ideas and emerging data which may lead to a questioning of the original framework. Also, the traditional association between quantitative data (and collection techniques) and theory-testing approaches has the effect of deflecting attention from more complex and abstract general theories upon which adaptive theory depends to help it respond flexibly to changing research circumstances.

That such large samples are used in conjunction with these techniques means that it is an expensive business. These factors make it difficult for such an approach to respond quickly and flexibly – in terms of changing the conceptual framework in relation to unanticipated data and changing ideas. The ability to adapt to the routinely changing circumstances of the research is the keynote of the adaptive approach and represents the conditions under which it thrives and bears fruit. The difficulties posed by the general lack of flexibility are compounded if the dominance or priority of quantitative data is not at some point balanced by qualitative concerns. In this respect the adaptive approach requires some attempt to register in theoretical terms the dynamic social processes involved in the unfolding intersubjective 'lifeworlds' of those people under study, and this, of necessity, requires a good deal of qualitative involvement by the researcher with those who are the subjects of the research. Coupled with the fact that the meanings and intersubjective understandings of people are not easily registered through quantitative data, this means that an exclusively quantitative approach will be doubly disadvantaged in this area.

Conversely, there are several possible problems associated with research which involves the exclusive use of qualitative methods and techniques of data-gathering. First, problems revolve around the tendency of such research to become too entangled with descriptive rather than theoretical objectives and concerns. This is patently not a problem for research that sets out consciously with such aims in mind (although one might want to question the exclusive pursuance of such aims). However, as I have pointed out in Chapter 1, such research may have a legitimate objective in its own terms, such as plugging gaps in knowledge or providing information on a social policy or problem-related issue, and may eventually be used as a background resource for future theoretical endeavours. The exclusive use of qualitative data may give rise to atheoretical research simply because it has no theoretical commitments. Such research will produce descriptive rather than explanatory conclusions, perhaps even inadvertently. This descriptive orientation, though, is often linked with an anti-theoretical stance – a conscious disavowal of the project of theory.

This sort of attitude is common to many schools of thought which favour or prioritize the use of qualitative methods. Many symbolic interactionists (Blumer, 1969; Becker in Rock, 1979), ethnomethodologists, phenomenologists, poststructuralists and postmodernists (Blumer, 1969; Becker in Rock, 1979; Denzin, 1990; Rosenau, 1992) are of this persuasion and actively suggest that the creation of theory is not a fit and proper objective of social analysis. These writers confuse a number of things. First, they confuse the idea of theory-creation with the notion of a move away from a supposedly more 'authentic' descriptive account of the meanings that play a direct role in people's lives (symbolic interaction and phenomenology). Postmodernists focus more on the idea that theory allegedly marks a distancing from a concern with what people want – the local voices and narratives particularly of oppressed groups. Of course, a cursory glance at the work of Glaser and Strauss (1967, 1971), Strauss (1987), and Strauss and Corbin (1990) on grounded theory would immediately dispel this confusion and point to the fact that a concern with theorizing is perfectly compatible with a preoccupation with lifeworld phenomena.

Conversely, when research which prioritizes qualitative data is geared towards theory-construction – particularly grounded theory – it is often too conceptually innovative in that it tends to produce an endless supply of newly minted concepts. In such cases it is not clear how the conceptual innovation must at some point be limited and related to the way in which data collection and analysis is dialogically linked to the independent role of theory. Of course, this does not necessarily help in the construction of theory that is linked to other forms of theorizing and which is therefore systematically cumulative in nature. Moreover, such a position wholeheartedly endorses an empiricist position in which the data constantly shapes the manner in which it is theoretically represented. Thus, it has nothing to say about (and actively rejects) prior theory (general and substantive) and the way in which this may be employed to shape the analysis and interpretation of data.

Included in the grounded theorists' rejection of prior theorizing is a blanket rejection of theory-testing approaches in general. While this may in the past have served to re-focus the spotlight on previously neglected issues of theory-generation, a continuing rejection of verificationist approaches, including both deductive (theory-testing) and general theoretical approaches, is dysfunctional. It marks a failure to capitalize on opportunities to build more comprehensive approaches to research methodology and the cumulative development of theoretical knowledge as well as a more general understanding of social organization. Clearly, what is needed from an adaptive theory point of view is a wide-ranging and inclusive attempt to utilize diverse methods and techniques of data-gathering in a concerted and systematic manner. Such an approach must also give due attention to the problems that stem from different epistemological and ontological commitments which may unwittingly prevent the maximum utilization of resources.

Data-sampling, coding and memo-writing

Choosing a sample of people to interview or events to observe is a key feature of any research project. In this section I do not intend to discuss sampling in a systematic manner (see O'Connell Davidson and Layder, 1994 for a detailed discussion). I merely wish to indicate some broad outlines and then home-in on some specific features which follow from the previous discussion and feed into the concerns outlined later in the book. In this respect social research relies on two broad forms of data-sampling. Probability or random sampling draws a statistically representative sample from a wider population and allows the researcher to generalize confidently from the sample to the wider population on the basis that every unit in the population (or universe) has an equal chance of being selected in the sample. This kind of sample is most often required in survey research and/or the use of fixed-choice interview questionnaires, along with quantitative techniques for analysing the data. Such research is most pertinent when there is a great deal of existing knowledge available about the nature of the population under study so that a truly random sample may be drawn.

The other type of sampling technique is the non-probability sample in which there is no means of estimating the probability of all units of the population being studied – in fact no guarantee that every element has a chance of being studied. This is often referred to as 'purposive' sampling and its logic and power lies in selecting information-rich cases for in-depth study. As Patton (1990) observes, information-rich cases are those from which one can learn a great deal about issues of central importance to the purpose of the research. Such samples are most frequently associated with qualitative data culled from in-depth interviews or various kinds of involved (participant) observation. There is nothing predetermined about the size of these samples and flexibility is the keynote.

Generally, the researcher gathers information or data up to the point where she or he either has enough to supply answers to the questions that originally prompted the research, or has enough to test-out or produce a theory or explanation to account for the data. The researcher stops gathering information (expanding the sample size) at the point when no new information or theoretical ideas are appearing in the data (the interviews or observations or documentary analyses). The validity, meaningfulness and insights gained from qualitative inquiry using purposive samples have more to do with the information-richness of the cases selected (time periods, people or events) and the observational and analytical capabilities of the researcher than with the sample size as such.

There are a number of sub-types of purposive sampling (as there are of probability or random sampling) but the one that concerns us for immediate purposes is 'theoretical sampling'. This is a sampling technique originally developed and advocated by Glaser and Strauss (1967), and although in principle it may be used independently of their grounded theory approach, it was specifically designed to deal with the issues and preoccupations of that approach. The basis of theoretical sampling is the selection of events, people settings and time periods in relation to the emergent nature of theory and research. In this respect the researcher is enjoined to collect and analyse the data simultaneously so that there is an immediate feedback from the data collection which in turn suggests various implications for theory-generation. On the basis of the emerging nature of the theory the researcher decides what data to collect next (which people to inter-view, what events and settings to observe over what periods of time) in order to develop the theory or theoretical ideas in the most fruitful manner possible.

The adaptive theory approach to theoretical sampling requires that Glaser and Strauss's ideas are both amended and supplemented in order to fit in with its more comprehensive and dialogical outlook. In principle, the idea of being able to adjust the sample (both in terms of size and quality) in relation to the emerging nature of theoretical ideas is a good one and overcomes the obvious problem of the lack of flexibility associated with the use of probability samples. This is an absolute necessity if one is to generate theory on a flexible (adaptive) basis. However, Glaser and Strauss's formulation neglects the role of prior theory (general, substantive, hypothesis-testing, and so on) in the research process and it is this which the adaptive approach wants to draw in and include within its terms of reference.

In this respect Glaser and Strauss's approach is driven by the unremittingly empiricist and (inductivist) premise that the data give rise to the theory and that more data should be collected and thus the sample adjusted in terms of how previous data have shaped the theory. The adaptive approach considers that this greatly under-estimates the significance of prior theory in research in terms of both its productive and constructive roles in shaping data in relation to preconceived explanatory models (or schemas, or even single con-cepts), as well as the manner in which it can respond and 'adapt' to incoming data. More generally, in so far as it neglects the role of extant theory, the grounded theory approach represents a waste of good theory!

The adaptive approach insists that so called theoretical sampling must be true 'theoretical' sampling on a wide-ranging basis and not limited exclusively to the sampling of people, events, settings, and so on, in relation to theory that has emerged from the data. Thus, new people or groups or events are included in the sample not simply on the basis of some purely empiricist directive informed and thus determined by the incoming data, but rather, people and events must be progressively included in the sample through the combined force of prior theoretical ideas or models and the collection and analysis of data in relation to them. Thus it is the dialogical relation between prior theory, data collection and analysis, and the adaptive theory that emerges as a result, that is the decisive factor. The most important factor prompting a move away from such an empiricist position is that it then allows for theoretical registering of the system elements of social life (settings and contexts of activity) rather than simply those to do with the lifeworld (personal identity and situated activity).

This is necessary because the empirical focus of the adaptive approach centres on the lifeworld–system linkages that characterize the structure of social reality in general, and which are also principal defining features of that area of social life which is currently the research focus. Theoretical sampling must therefore be performed in relation to the primary theoretical focus of adpative theory – the ties and interconnections between social agency and system elements that are at the heart of social life. The acceptance of both lifeworld and system features as part of a comprehensive, interconnected and stratified social ontology also enables a proper treatment of issues of power, control and domination, and the resources that underpin them (including the analysis of ideology and other cultural discourses). This is because it is impossible to understand fully the nature of social interaction in the absence of a concern with system factors and the manner in which these two essential features of social life intertwine with each other. The pervasive influence of power (and control) and the manner in which it manifests itself in different domains of social life cannot be understood properly if its systemic (or structural) aspects are not recognized or registered in the first place (Layder, 1985, 1997).

What goes for the question of theoretical sampling also applies to the issues of coding and theoretical memo-writing. In the following chapters I shall be dealing with these issues in some detail, and in the context of empirical examples from research. Here I merely wish to flag their significance for research in general and to indicate provisionally how they fit into the wider framework of the adaptive theory approach. Coding is of primary significance for the analysis of data (either quantitative or qualitative) and has to do with the choice of symbols (codes) which summarize the meaning or implications of units of data. What I have to say about coding in the later chapters primarily concerns the analysis of qualitative data since (as with the use of theoretical sampling) it may be used in a much more flexible manner than that associated with quantitative data and random samples. With the latter, the relative rigidity of the samples is also linked to a relative fixity of coding systems or 'frames'. Qualitative data and purposive sampling allow for the possibility of readjustments to coding frames *in situ*, and thus may become a potent resource for the generation of theoretical ideas. As such, it may form a continuous feature of the research which dovetails neatly with the organic and unfolding nature of theorizing in the context of the adaptive approach.

Memo-writing is another technique which Glaser and Strauss (1967) have employed as part of their grounded theory approach, and again, like theoretical sampling, it has the great virtue of concentrating on the important process of theoretical creativity. However, in the light of what I have already said about the crucial shortcomings of grounded theory, it is no surprise that the notion of theoretical memo-writing has to be suitably emended for use in the context of the adaptive theory approach. Principally, memo-writing entails writing detailed commentaries on the significance of data and their theoretical implications. Memos often have the effect of stimulating the theoretical imagination and as such they play a crucial role in any research enterprise which has theory-construction as a principal aim.

However, it must be borne in mind that the adaptive approach centralizes the importance of the inclusion of elements of general and substantive theory as the source of prior models or modes of explanation for the ongoing collection and analysis of data. Thus the notion of memo-writing in this context must be extended to include such theoretical elements. Also, memo-writing must attend to the internal characteristics of theoretical perspectives or frameworks, such as their degree of coherence or their embeddedness in chains of reasoning and models of explanation. In this context, memo-writing becomes much more directly concerned with what I call theoretical elaboration (of which I distinguish several forms) and the potential that this has for theoretical development and the co-ordinated and integrated accumulation of social scientific knowledge in general.

Conclusion

I have organized this chapter to facilitate the discussion in the chapters that follow. My central point has been a fairly straightforward one: that in the context of the sort of approach to theorizing in social research that I wish to advocate it is necessary to envisage 'elements' of the research process as fairly fluid and flexible both in terms of their sequence and in terms of their employment in the general process of theorizing. As I have tried to make clear, the notion of theorizing itself has to be understood as an integral part of the overall research process as well as organically connected to the wider literature and findings of previous research and scholarship. Although the adaptive theory approach is inherently synthetic and eclectic, it is so in a systematic and disciplined manner and in this sense does not underwrite an 'anything goes' approach. Nevertheless, it is much more tolerant of a diversity of standpoints and potential resources than is to be found within the conventional approaches to theorizing in research. In this sense the adaptive approach represents a plea for a more inclusive conception of methodological and procedural 'rules' (and their employment) as they apply to theory-generation in social research.

CHAPTER 3

ANALYSING DATA WITH THEORY IN MIND

This chapter examines some of the practical problems of theory development from the point of view of ongoing data analysis during research. (Chapter 5 reverses this emphasis and concentrates on applying theoretical materials to the process of social research as a means of elaborating and developing new theory.) I must underline the fact that this is a matter of emphasis since, as I hope to show, all social research and theorizing contain elements of both deduction (theory guiding data) and induction (theory emerging from data). Likewise, the associated questions of theory-testing (verification) and theory-generation (discovery, theory-building) are equally closely linked in research although the relative emphasis varies from case to case. So although in this chapter I concentrate on the problem of generating theory from data, it will become apparent that I believe that all observations and forms of data-collection are influenced by theory and prior 'theoretical' assumptions in some way (Layder, 1990).

The chapter falls into three sections which concentrate on related issues of data analysis: coding, theoretical memos, and multi-strategy research. In the first two sections I draw on illustrative material mainly from my own research on actors' careers in the UK. This allows me to tease out in detail some of the practical problems and issues that stem from attempting to generate theory from data. In this case I deal with transcripts of in-depth interviews with various members of the acting profession. Although the immediate focus is on interview transcripts, it will become apparent that other kinds of data, such as documents, surveys and quantitative data, enter into the process of theory-generation as I describe it. This is a feature of my own approach and is not necessarily followed by all researchers, although I would argue that a multi-strategy frame-work is preferable in order to tease out the multi-layered nature of social life. A general theme of this chapter is that we never enter research with a mind clear of theoretical ideas and assumptions. Indeed, part of my argument will be that systematic recognition of one's theoretical assumptions (including prejudices) and the attempt to harness them to research purposes actually facilitates the production of more powerful and adequate explanations of empirical data.

Coding and analysing interview data

The interview materials I refer to here were conducted with various members of the acting profession (Layder, 1984). Although my primary focus was on actors and their careers, as the research unfolded it became clear that other people involved in the profession (show-business, entertainment) were of pivotal importance to this concern. Thus, agents, casting directors and producers were also interviewed at various stages. (This is an example of 'theoretical sampling' which I discuss later in the chapter. In this case it involves interviewing people on the basis of their importance for the emergent theoretical ideas as they develop during the course of the research.) The interviews were all of the in-depth variety, and although I had a number of questions, issues and topics that I wanted people to talk about (these, of course varied with the different jobs they held), they were not administered in a rigid way. If particular people were forthcoming on a specific issue or question, then I would allow them to talk at length (as long as it remained pertinent to the research). Nor did I stick to a rigid sequence or wording of questions. Such matters were largely dependent on the atmosphere and degree of rapport that I felt I had with the person being interviewed, even though the whole point of in-depth interviewing is to elicit a person's subjective view of the world – to tap into their lived experience and the meanings with which they construct their everyday worlds. A semi-structured interview schedule and in-depth probing to some extent restrain the researcher from 'imposing' his or her own prior assumptions about what is relevant.

The basic problem I want to concentrate on in this section is how to deal with the mass of data that accumulates as one transcribes interviews. Five or six interviews, which are about an hour or so long, translate into quite a bulk of information once they have been transcribed. After about 20 to 25, we are seriously confronting the problem of sustaining the 'manageability' of the data. How, therefore, does one begin to select out and highlight the relevant portions of information instead of ploughing backwards and forwards through the whole lot? Traditionally, this problem is solved by the process of coding the data – that is, by applying labels to particular extracts from the interviews in order to be able to identify them as belonging to various descriptive or analytic categories. A problem here is what system or coding frame to use? I want to draw attention to the fact that the issue of coding is directly relevant to the question of the analysis and interpretation of the data, as well as the development of theory and concepts from the data. Similarly, what is known as the concept-indicator problem (Rose, 1984; de Vaus, 1996)

– that is, the extent to which particular concepts can be said to 'point to' or 'indicate' particular aspects of empirical data, or vice versa – is integral to the issue of coding and the question of theory-generation from empirical research.

The following is an account of how I dealt with these problems in relation to my transcriptions of interviews with members of the acting profession. It is important to note that I transcribed quite a number of the earlier interviews (with different categories of personnel) in full. (There were several interviewees who would not allow me to tape the interviews so in these cases the data were simply my recollections of the conversations noted down as soon after the interviews as possible.) This is significant in that during the later stages I began selectively to choose extracts from tape-recordings, eventually leaving the bulk of each interview untranscribed but preserved on tape just in case it was needed later. This 'selectivity' is only possible when one has arrived at a system of coding (classification or labelling) the interview data. Such a coding system is built-up in the early phases of the collection and analysis of the data. After the researcher has decided what the main coding categories and labels are, then he or she can begin to look for indicators of the concepts that the codes imply in the data itself. That is, one can selectively seek out, or home-in on, data that is relevant to the codes as they have emerged from the earlier phases of the analysis.

Pre-coding and provisional coding

How does one arrive at a suitable coding system? I shall describe the particular way in which I derived the labels I used for coding my interview transcripts, although I should say that my purpose is not to suggest that this is the best, or the only way of proceeding. Rather, my intention is to lay bare the exact nature of the procedures I used in order to generate theoretical ideas and concepts relating to actors' careers. On many of the transcripts I have used primitive pre-coding devices, such as underlining parts of the text or putting an asterisk by certain sections of text in order to highlight their importance or relevance. However, the fact that no particular label (or formal code) has been used in these cases suggests that they were simply notations of 'interesting' answers or quotations. Thus they indicate the existence of pre-coding – that is, the targeting of segments of data because they seemed significant, but with no explicit awareness of why they were so. In other cases I would use 'provisional' code labels or names to indicate parts of the transcript which triggered some association with a particular concept, category or idea. In essence, the provisional code indicated a tentative attempt to order and classify the data in some way which could be revised or confirmed at a later date.

'Pre-coding' or provisional coding suggests a partial parallel to what is known as 'open-coding' in the methods literature. However, my position is very different from those (including grounded theorists) who stress the use of open-coding as a preliminary way of analysing data. The parallel between the two consists simply in the fact that in my version there is an openness to the discovery of new and provisional codes, particularly at this early stage of the proceedings. But there are marked differences. For example, the notion of open-coding advocated by the likes of Glaser and Strauss (1967) presupposes two things which are not part of my own practice. First, the grounded theory method insists that open-coding is about generating as many codes as is warranted by the data in order to be then able to reduce them in number as some of them are reinforced by the further extension of data collection and analysis. In this sense the openness is one in which the researcher has no presuppositions about what might be the appropriate codes prior to the data collection and analysis. The idea of operating with a 'clean slate' is an essential precondition for the grounding (in data) of emergent theory.

The other essential element in the grounded theory approach is the idea that the initial open-coding should give way to a much more closed or restricted type as the research proceeds. This movement to what Strauss (1987) calls 'axial coding' occurs because as the initial codes, indicators and concepts are exposed to more and more data one is able to identify which are to be the core codes and categories central to the specific piece of research in question. Again, as these are subject to the 'test' of data, one can be more certain of the validity and efficacy of the concepts and codes because the data 'guarantees' them to be 'properly' grounded. In this sense the researcher moves from a situation of total openness in coding to a form of closure dictated largely by the empirical data themselves.

My own views of precoding and provisional coding are quite at variance with the one described above. First, although there is an openness to the discovery of new codes (and concepts and ideas), the point is neither to generate a maximum number at this early stage nor to produce them *ex nihilo*. It has been generally acknowledged that all observations and interpretations are theory-laden to some degree or other. Thus it is impossible to start literally with a 'clean slate' so to speak. Related to, yet distinct from, this (and as I shall go on to show), the objective of theory-generation is enhanced if one starts with some (more or less systematic) prior theoretical ideas since they help to both organize the data and stimulate the process of theoretical thinking. This is both more realistic in a practical sense and more justifiable epistemologically in so far as it refuses to endorse a naive empiricism in which the data are thought to speak for themselves and 'suggest' codes and categories (as they are in grounded theory). Thus the search for new codes and concepts goes on in tandem with the use of extant theoretical assumptions and relevancies. That is, theoretical 'openness' is dialogically combined with assumptions about the relevance of extant material (concepts, frameworks categories) in the service of further theoretical generation.

Secondly, unlike in grounded theory, my version of provisional and pre-coding does not give way entirely to a more restricted type as a result of the development of core categories and concepts. Pre-coding (in the form of highlighting and marking text), in fact, may give rise to provisional codes which are subsequently firmed-up and 'validated' by ongoing data collection and analysis and may eventually be adopted as core codes and categories. However, this does not mean that open-coding is abandoned altogether in favour of these core materials. In this sense what I have termed pre-coding or provisional coding should be retained throughout the analysis in parallel, and dialogically engaged with, both emergent core concepts and the extant theoretical materials.

Such a standpoint has two advantages over the procedural sequence advised by grounded theorists. First, the idea of the continual receptiveness of the research to new codes (and hence novel theoretical ideas) means that there is no wastage produced by closure of the emergent theory within and around the core categories that emerge *in situ*. Such closure functions automatically as an exclusionary device once the core and axial concepts and theoretical ideas have been established. Rigid closure of this kind is always premature because it means that the whole analytic endeavour is no longer open to revision in the light of new ideas and theoretical insights. Thus, with primitive coding as a continual (and forever incomplete) accompaniment to the whole research trajectory, serendipitous discovery in the realm of theoretical ideas is never pre-empted.

Secondly, the idea that pre-coding and provisional coding always take place in the context of a dialogue with emergent theory and extant theory (including general theory) ensures that the emergent theory is not cut-off or isolated from the ongoing established body of theoretical concepts and ideas (both classical and contemporary). That is to say, pre-coding and provisional coding are potential conduits to extant theoretical ideas which can be brought to bear upon the emerging theory and in this sense complement the extant materials. However, provisional coding is inherently open-ended, unlike the extant 'informative' theory, and hence it is a continuous and sensitive barometer of changes in theoretical direction brought about either by unanticipated findings or fresh theoretical insights, or some combination of the two. The three-way interchanges between these sources of theoretical ideas ensures that a truly comprehensive accumulation of theoretical knowledge occurs or is at least a possible outcome of this kind of strategy. With the grounded theory approach only a very limited accumulation is permitted because it is entrapped entirely within the parameters of emergent theory and other so called 'formal' theories which have been grounded in the same manner.

Core and satellite codes

The above considerations relate to pre-coding or provisional coding whose open-ended character is reflected in the fact that they simply refer to marking or highlighting the text of interview transcripts either with an asterisk or with some provisional name or label. Such notations indicate possibilities and potentialities rather than worked-through ideas or fully formulated concepts supported by data. However, I regularly used another method of indicating significances in the data and this relates to coding in the traditional sense of applying particular labels and names to 'classify' sections of text. Coding in this sense helps to develop a more specific focus on the emerging data and gives direction to the analysis by highlighting relevant questions that one might want to ask about the data. Giving names to the 'main points' also helps the researcher to become more familiar with what the findings include or contain and hence begins to define what is still missing and what, if possible, needs to be gathered or to become the object of search. Overall, coding in this sense helps to answer questions such as what themes and patterns give shape to this data. I was using core and satellite code names like the following: appraisal; casting; work routines; appraisal criteria; actors' perceptions; status mobility; agents; referral; contact networks; billing disputes.

I agree with Glesne and Peshkin (1992) that such codes are, or can be, quite personal in that they are meant to fulfil a specific researcher's immediate requirements and need not necessarily be useful or clear to anyone else. This is particularly the case with a single researcher. However, as soon as there is a research team to be taken into account and findings and analysis have to be co-ordinated, clarity and under-standability are essential requirements. The important thing is to be able to identify a segment of interview data as belonging to a certain category. However, I would not go too far along this path since codes need also to be in a form which will ultimately yield theoretical ideas. Thus they need to be readily convertible into a precise and general conceptual form which means that one cannot afford to be too idiosyncratic in the first place. In my view, therefore, codes may be personalized in the sense that they may be condensed and not necessarily identifiable by an outsider, but this condensed form must be capable of easy and ready elaboration into an alternative form which relates well to established conceptual ideas and practices.

This point connects with the issue of the role of prior theoretical ideas in establishing code names (and ultimately deciding on core categories). This in turn links back to the previous discussion of open-coding (pre-coding and provisional coding in my terms). In the use of the codes illustrated above I was clearly departing from the advice of Glaser and Strauss in two ways. First, as I have said, where I was not sure of concept-indicator links and the codes that reflect them I used provisional or pre-coding instead of generating as many new codes as possible in the initial stages. Indeed, Strauss's (1987) advice is to code the initial interviews in great detail, line by line, to maximize the number of codes that may be generated. Such a procedure can only create an enormous number of codes which prove to be quite irrelevant in the end. Surely the point is to be able to target the theoretical pertinence of data as soon as possible and this requires caution, clarity and parsimony in one's urge to produce results. This kind of detailed, minute coding can prove to be far too cumbersome and wasteful of energies that could be directed elsewhere.

Secondly, there was a clear departure from the grounded theory approach in that my use of codes was not predicated on the notion of beginning research with a 'clean slate'. Although some of the core and satellite codes I was using emerged directly as a result of scrutiny of the interview transcripts (such as 'billing disputes', actors' perceptions', 'fee-bargaining' and so on), many of the others were already formulated and derived from the theoretical baggage I had acquired through prior reading and parallel theoretical labour. Thus I knew early on some of the code categories like 'appraisal system', 'appraisal criteria', 'status system', 'status mobility', 'occupational organization', and I started looking for links between them and the interview data (concept-indicator links). These code categories derived from theoretical ideas which were 'independent' of the specific project and its 'internally' emergent characteristics. These comprised a number of elements and I shall describe them in more detail later in the discussion. Here I merely indicate them in broad outline as below:

- *General and formal theories* – Status passage; organization theory; social integration; power, control and authority; labour markets.

- *Substantive ideas* – Occupational careers; nature of acting – organization of career; actors as personality types.
- *Typology building* – Main types of occupational career; bureaucratic, collegiate and market types; situating acting in a comparative context.

The first two of the above clearly constitute prior theoretical and substantive ideas and assumptions about the area (or adjacent areas) in question and were derived from literature searches and exposure to various aspects of general theory. In this sense their existence as resources was somewhat prior to and independent of the actual research project itself. The third source of theoretical material – referred to as typology-building – is rather different from the other two in that it existed partly prior to the investigation of actors' careers but also constituted an ongoing feature of the project itself. That is, the typology of occupational careers was constructed in some measure through theoretical work on documentary sources (literature surveys and analyses) but was also in large part an organically emergent feature of the research project itself.

As I say, I shall deal with these elements in more detail later in the discussion because here I want to concentrate on the specifics of coding and interview data analysis. However, in order to understand the latter fully, the wider context of theoretical assumptions that influenced proceedings needs to be borne in mind. The main implication of the existence of prior assumptions and ongoing (partly independent) theoretical work is that I did not approach the interviews (and could not) in a totally 'open' mode, unaffected by prior reading and the important analytic ideas and concepts that flow from it – as advised by grounded theorists. I went with an armoury of concepts, theoretical ideas and categories. On the other hand, I did not initially regard these as sacrosanct – early on they were regarded as provisional in the sense that they could be modified, abandoned, confirmed or retained as required by the unfolding of new data or changing theoretical priorities and relevances.

Coding and theoretical memos

A crucial question is how does coding or labelling data 'add-up' to something more? How does it become theory? The short answer is that devising codes and applying them does not, in and of itself, add up to theory. This is where the importance of memo-writing enters the equation. Memo-writing is about making notes, primarily for oneself, which ask questions, pose problems, suggest connections, and so on about how the properties of concepts or categories are revealed, exemplified or contradicted in some way by the incoming data and the process of coding. Memo-writing therefore is meant to generate discussion and self-dialogue which fashions a conjunction between theoretical reflection and the practical issues surrounding data collection and analysis. The issue of concept-indicator links is centrally involved here. Memos provide a means of exploring and teasing out whether or in what sense particular codes, concepts and categories really are illustrated (indicated) by data – in this case extracts from interviews. It is in the area of concept-indicator linkages that the dynamic of theory-generation is situated.

The nature of memo-writing

An essential feature of theoretical memos is their cumulative nature in that they trace the evolution of one's thinking about particular issues over the time period covered by one's research involvement. Thus, the whole sequence of memo-writing functions rather like a journal as a record of how and what the analyst was thinking at different points in the research. However, the actual form and structure that memos may take is variable. Let me deal with a few of the most useful and common of these.

Theoretical memos – or notes to oneself – may take the form of one-off entries in a note-book or storage system which are filed and organized in terms of labels, categories and concepts – perhaps arranged in alphabetical order. Thus each time that one makes a note about a particular concept or category it is systematically filed away under the appropriate heading. In such a filing system new codes and categories can be added (or subtracted) at any time. A variant of this is the notion of a sequential log-book in which the researcher keeps regular notes on the progress of the research and which is ordered in a strict temporal sequence following the exact contours of the research.

Theoretical memos may also take the form of *marginal notes* on the actual transcripts of documents (qualitative or quantitative) that are being analysed. The disadvantage of this (if it is done by hand) is that the notes tend to remain scattered and thus difficult to find unless one is constantly referring to a particular document. If the transcripts are stored on a computer, then this problem can be obviated by using the retrieval systems provided by software packages which allow one easy access to relevant sections of a transcript. Thus memo-writing may be conducted in conjunction with various software packages which deal with the analysis of qualitative data.

My adopted practice was to use a *combination of methods*. In the earlier phases of data collection and analysis I used the marginal notes method, but this became less and less satisfactory because as the research progressed there was a tendency for theoretical memos to become more elaborate, analytic and discursive. This created the need for more space to develop points and arguments in a systematic manner. My solution to this problem was to write memos as separate documents or commentaries, concentrating on one particular transcript at a time. I would go through a transcript, which had already been either formally coded or pre-coded (simply marked or higlighted in some way), and attempt to reduce it to its essentials. That is, I would spotlight the important extracts which contained core codes, concepts or pivotal information and make detailed notes regarding why these were the core extracts. I shall give a concrete example of this in a moment, but let me first comment on the way in which this form of memo-writing (in conjunction with coding) helps in the management and organization of data.

As I indicated earlier in the discussion on coding, one of the main problems of field research concerns the amassing of too much data. The problem is how to reduce this data to make it more manageable and in this respect much of the data one gathers will need to be discarded (or at least stored away) for immediate purposes. The combination of coding and memo-writing, as focused on whole transcripts, provides a means of reducing the data to manageable proportions by identifying and isolating the relevant segments. This is perhaps easier to do in the later stages of the research when the bulk of interviewing (observing, reading and analysing documents) has been completed – although this does not preclude coding and memo-writing as ongoing continuous aspects of the research process. Writing extended, focused memos gives one an overview of the data and one's analytic thinking on it. As a consequence, this kind of procedure allows one to identify gaps (if any) in the data. It indicates where one needs to fill-out information both to illustrate relatively well-honed theoretical ideas as well as to help fine-tune or structure ones that remain vague, ill-defined or inadequate in some way.

Memos and theory-generation

From these extended memos I developed discussions of many important concepts and ideas, for example, 'shared control', 'types of appraisal systems', 'stratified (internal) labour market', 'work routines of casting personnel' and so on. I did this by constructing a running discussion or commentary on the data contained in the interview transcripts and this involved two main elements. First, it required a continual reshuffling or rethinking of what the data meant (how, what and why questions) in order to produce new angles, ideas and explanations. Secondly, it involved a sustained teasing out (elaboration, extension, modification) of the concepts and ideas that were already playing a significant role in the analysis and interpretation of the data.

In order to indicate what this means in terms of memo-writing, let me give an example of the way in which I developed the concept of 'typification' and its relation to a cluster of associated concepts such as 'type-casting', 'appraisal criteria' and 'work routines of casting personnel'. Typification refers to the way in which casting directors (or anyone who casts, such as directors and producers) 'think of' actors as being relevant to a range of (types of) theatrical roles when they are making routine decisions about which actors are going to play particular parts in specific productions. These considerations are worked through in the context of an extended theoretical memo written as a commentary on one of the interview transcriptions – in this case with a theatrical producer. Incidentally, the memo turned out to be 4,000 words long, so my account will obviously be abridged and selective.

The following is a schematic outline of the progression of the memo through a number of topics (and the transitions between them) culminating in an elaborate discussion and definition of typification and its implications for actors' careers as well as the organization of the occupation as a whole. The memo starts off quite 'quietly' by making incidental notes about the first five pages of the transcript. However, on page five my comments on what the producer was saying about the difficulties of predicting which productions will be theatrical 'hits' subsequently begin to 'take-off' on an elaborate trajectory of their own. Here is the sequence of topics and transitions:

1 Memo starts with a discussion of the problem of the 'predictability' of hits – the success-potential of theatrical productions.
2 Memo moves on to a discussion of the market conditions of theatrical production.
3 This leads to a comparison of management systems in industries with different product market conditions (Burns and Stalker's (1961) distinction between organic and mechanistic systems).
4 Following from this, the memo turns to a comparison of the different forms of innovation and creativity required in industrial versus artistic production (like the theatre).
5 The above leads off on a tangent and ultimate cul-de-sac in pursuit of the question of how to define innovation. This portion

of the memo ends in confusion and the discussion is left off at this point.

6 The commentary begins again by taking up the question of the importance of 'newness' in ensuring the success of plays, shows and films as well as for actors' careers.

7 This leads to a discussion of casting directors' problems of producing 'new ideas' when casting. This eventuates in a conceptual distinction between two kinds of 'type-casting'.

8 I abandon the idea of two variants of type-casting and instead develop the notion of 'typification' of actors by casting directors as an aspect of the work routines and as the antithesis of 'type-casting'.

9 This then leads into questions about status mobility in the career and how typification helps to reinforce and reproduce the segmentation of the internal labour market for actors.

Before commenting on the 'logic' and sequencing of the theoretical memo as a whole, let me unpack some of the ideas contained in the list above since the exact meaning and significance of some of them may be rather obscure. There is pressure on casting directors to come up with new ideas when casting productions because their own careers depend not only upon getting the right actors for the right parts, but also making unexpected, perceptive matches in this respect (often prompting the comment 'what a wonderful piece of casting!'). Casting directors tend to resolve the problem of newness not by finding new actors but by linking actors with whom they have already worked (or are in some way acquainted) with unfamiliar roles. My first attempt to conceptualize this was to think in terms of two kinds of type-casting because the term was commonly in use and the phenomenon to which it referred undoubtedly existed.

Type-casting occurs when an actor is constantly cast in one type of role (dumb blonde, romantic lead, heavy criminal/ thug) because of prior success and public association of the actor with that role. This leads to a reluctance by those who cast to use the actor for any other kind of role. As a result, the career of the actor suffers both in terms of the number of roles available and the development of acting skills and being stretched artistically – all of which are highly valued by actors, critics and public audiences alike. For casting personnel, however, the problem of dreaming-up new ideas for plays and productions is tackled by engaging in a practice which is the exact opposite of the tendency to stereotype actors.

Thus, by routinely thinking of actors who are already known to them as being relevant to a range of roles, they are able to make original casting decisions and to expand the range of the actor. This, of necessity, not only expands the potential employment opportunities (in a profession in which there is chronic unemployment) but also aids the upward movement of careers in terms of the artistic and technical development of skills. This contrasts markedly with the consequences of type-casting that often lead to a career dead-end (sometimes successful, sometimes on a definite downward curve). Thus I originally conceptualized these two as 'inhibitory' type-casting versus 'facilitational' type-casting.

I eventually settled on the term 'typification' not only for the sake of elegance but because it was confusing to think of it as a form of type-casting. (I therefore made the decision to abandon a conceptual formulation which was dependent upon an *in vivo* (originated by the people who use it in everyday life) category – 'type-casting' – in favour of one which was sociologically defined – 'typification' (used by sociologists with a technical meaning). However, although this final conceptualization was a formal 'sociological' one, it was also clearly related to my discussions with actors, agents, casting directors and producers. So, in this sense, the concept of typification was generated as a direct consequence of talking to people in the field.

In particular some respondents mentioned the issue of 'casting against type'. Although this was normal colloquial usage and thus did not immediately prompt any conceptual or theoretical reflection, I eventually realized that casting 'against type' (using actors in types of role which are the complete opposite of those they normally play) could only occur prior to a situation in which type-casting had set in (when the actor is viewed as only applicable to one type of role). Therefore, what I was calling 'facilitational' type-casting in fact had nothing to do with type-casting since casting against type could only occur within a process which envisaged the actor as applicable to more than one type of role. The idea of typification suggested itself to me as expressing the manner in which casting directors routinely think of actors they know in terms of a range or span of potential roles.

Finally, the notion of typification linked with the general issue of actors' career status mobility in the occupation as a whole. In turn this threw further light on another strand of the analysis which was concerned with the organization of the internal labour market for actors. From other interviews and two surveys of employment and earnings in the profession (see Layder, 1985), I knew that the labour market was segmented. There was an elite group of star actors who comprised around 5 per cent of the population of actors and beneath them there was a segment comprising about 15 per cent of actors who were 'in the swim' of employment opportunities. These were actors who, although not necessarily star names, in a public sense are 'known' in the profession – that is crucially, they are 'known' to, and regularly used by casting personnel. Underneath them was the great mass of actors (80 per cent) many of whom spent most of their time unemployed or engaged in work other than acting.

The question that this raised was how was this segmentation of the labour market produced, stabilized and maintained over time as the surveys suggested? There are a number of factors involved here which do not concern us for present purposes. However, the notion of typification provides part of the answer in so far as the casting directors' constant use of actors they already know (those 20 per cent already in the swim of employment opportunities) ensures that the same actors will be employed time and time again. This has the effect of blocking the mobility chances of the mass of actors in the lower echelons of the status structure – the base of the labour market. Therefore an unintended effect of typification as a regularized means of the co-ordination and allocation of acting labour is the stabilization and reproduction of the segmental structure of the labour market. I must emphasize that this is but one of the elements involved here. A more detailed analysis of the occupational organization of acting (including the interrelations between agents/personal managers and casting directors among other things) is needed to give a compre-hensive answer to this question.

The inner logic of theory-generation

If we scrutinize the sequence in which the concept of typification (including its properties, characteristics and social-organizational consequences) is arrived at, we can see that it results from a combi-nation of elements of serendipity, contingency, blind searching and false leads, as well as systematic and logical connectedness and the reasoned elaboration of concepts and ideas. In short, overall the memo seems to constitute a very messy amalgam of all these. While this is quite true, it also represents the kind of dynamic upon which theoretical creativity rests. Let us examine this more closely. The whole sequence moves from one set of ideas through to a seemingly unrelated end-product (the notion of typification) with an obvious break in continuity between points 5 and 6 in the list on pages 61–62. It might be tempting to conclude that the fact that the ground covered in points 1 to 5 leads to a cul-de-sac in analytic thinking, renders it irrelevant to the final outcome. This, however, would be a misinterpretation of the significance of the earlier sections of the memo and their relation to the emergence of the concept of typification and its properties.

The basic flaw in proposing the irrelevance of the earlier part of the memo to its eventual outcome is that such a view misunderstands the importance of finding a direction and theme for theoretical reflection. The whole process starts from a rumination on the significance of the problem of the commercial predictability of shows and theatrical productions in general and then goes straight into a consideration of market conditions in different kinds of industry and artistic production. Although the discussion becomes somewhat sidetracked by an attempt to define innovation in these varying conditions, by this time definite theoretical and conceptual themes and foci have already emerged. The themes are centred around the question of how newness, innovation and creativity play a role in a milieu highly influenced by the market, such as commercial theatre (television and film). This subsequently leads to the question of casting productions and the problems of type-casting and typification as aspects of the work routines of casting personnel.

So although there is an apparent discontinuity in the memo in terms of a dead-end and confusion at point 5, there are also underlying thematic continuities which carry forward the theoretical logic and the overall impetus of theoretical elaboration and generation. Admittedly, the logic is carried forward apparently in a rather shaky (haphazard) manner – more a kind of word association than a logical and sequential form of reasoning – but it is this mode and train of thought, set off by a comment on a interviewee's response and then perpetuated by the immediately preceding ideas, that gives focus and momentum to the earlier parts of the memo. Furthermore, it subsequently provides the overarching thematic thrust required to bridge the hiatus that occurs between points 5 and 6. Now although there is undoubtedly an internal logic or connectedness in the memo, this is not the only process that is operating to produce the sequence and the specific form of theoretical elaboration. That is, although it is true in one sense that the ideas seem to 'grow out of' and 'follow-on' from each other, in another sense there are many 'external' influences that are also being brought to bear in the reasoning process and help to make it happen in the first place.

There are two main sources of influence here. First, there are the prior assumptions, theoretical and substantive knowledge, and so on, that the reseacher brings with him or her to the research. Secondly, if other kinds of research strategies and methodological techniques are being employed concurrently with the focal one (in this case interviewing), then the theoretical generation and analysis has to be understood in important measure as an outcome of this wider context. I shall argue further on that research which aims to generate theory benefits from a multi-strategy approach, but first I shall examine some of the prior theoretical assumptions that influenced the theoretical elaboration as it is traced in the memo analysed above.

Theory and data analysis

I mentioned earlier that although theorizing and data analysis are distinguishable aspects of social analysis and should not simply be equated, it is nonetheless important to understand them as operating in conjunction with one another. Also, in Chapter 2 I mentioned several of the more general theoretical assumptions with which one begins research and the way in which they may seep into the research process considered as a series of stages. At this juncture I want to carry this analysis further by examining more specific theoretical orientations that influence the progress of research and theory construction. My more general purpose here (as it is with the above example of the theoretical memo) is to recommend certain practices as important ingredients of the process of analysing data with theory-generation in mind. Thus, my position is very different from a number of existing approaches. First, it differs from the approach of those who insist on an empiricist and supposedly atheoretical approach to social research. However, it also differs from those who believe that theory-construction should be an entirely deductive, rationalist enterprise or who imply by their own practices that theory-construction should be largely separate from 'applied' empirical research (rather than used to illustrate theoretical ideas).

Crucially, my position differs from that proposed by grounded theorists who insist that theory should be generated only in the context of ongoing research and in an exclusively internalist manner. That is, the researcher should have no theoretical (a priori) assumptions with which to influence ('infect' might better convey the attitude of those who dogmatically believe in the superiority of grounded theory) the purity of the theory which should emerge directly and solely from the collection and analysis of data. Such an approach is inevitably attached to an empiricist epistemology and thus constricts the range, flexibility and explanatory power of the theory that results from it (Layder, 1990, 1993). My recommendations, therefore, are first that it must be acknowledged that all research is to some extent influenced by theoretical assumptions and that it is better to deal with them openly and systematically in order that they do not unwittingly distort the data analysis or the 'findings' of the research. Secondly, and more importantly, as empirical researchers we should positively value prior theoretical ideas as a means of giving focus to data collection and analysis.

With regard to the example of typification as expressing a feature of the behavioural routines of casting directors and other aspects of sociological analysis, there are several sources of prior assumptions and theoretical ideas that influenced its evolution from the data analysis. The first is the phenomenological sociology of Alfred Schutz (1972) who uses the concept of typification to refer to a general process whereby, through language use, people 'typify' objects and features of their environment and absorb them into their routine spheres of relevance. The effect of this is to reduce the complexity of the environment and the potential confusion produced by it, and in the process to render it more manageable, understandable and to some extent predictable. According to Schutz, this process of typification also facilitates social interaction by enabling a 'reciprocity of perspectives' to occur between people.

Clearly, although there are some overlaps in my own and Schutz's versions of typification, there are also considerable differences, one of which is that attention to the reciprocity of perspectives is not as important for my version of typification. Thus, by using the concept I was not generally concerned with understanding how it is that people are able to tap into each other's perspectives and thus facilitate shared understanding. Rather, I was concerned with how casting personnel deal with a routine work problem and the way in which the process of typification as a cognitive process helps them in this regard. The overlap with Schutz's usage occurs in respect of the common focus on the manner in which typifying aspects of the social environment allows a person to simplify that environment and impose some pattern on it.

Secondly, the sociology of work and organizations provided several influences. In this respect the process of typification directly links with the notion of productive processes and work flow, as well as problems relating to the co-ordination and allocation of personnel. Although the acting profession is very different from bureaucratic organizations, the nature of power and authority and the way it is deployed in the routine functioning of such organizations provides a pertinent analogy to the work tasks and problems of casting directors. Typification (of actors) refers to a process by which casting directors (as occupational practitioners) have developed a system to facilitate the organization and flow of their work to co-ordinate and allocate actors to available parts and roles. Thus work on formal organization and labour markets directly influenced my thinking and made me look for pertinent aspects of the data. (I deal with the question of perceiving data through a theoretical lens in detail in Chapter 4.)

Similarly, Durkheim's work on the nature of social integration and patterns of social bonding was influential in my thinking about aspects of occupational organization. I was also interested in notions of power and control generally, and here the work of Marx and Weber was an important background influence. In this sense the concept of typification did not just arise 'out of the blue'; there were definite conceptual precursors and theoretical perspectives that directed my attention to various features of the data and suggested particular forms of conceptual appropriation.

Theory-building in the context of multi-strategy research

The following discussion will attempt to show that within the terms of a multi-strategy approach to research there are often no clear dividing lines between theory-generation as the outcome of data analysis pure and simple (that is, theory derived from data) and theory as the outcome of the constant influence of prior and ongoing theoretical reflection (or reasoning processes) which actively influence the direction of the research. The main point about a multi-strategy approach is that the idea of using as many sources of data and/or methodological and analytic strategies as is possible and feasible for the research project in question greatly facilitates the process of theory-generation.

I want to show that using a multi-strategy approach increases the strength, density and validity of theoretical ideas and concepts that emerge from data collection and analysis. This is so for two reasons. First, using as many sources and strategies as possible and feasible ensures that one is approaching the research from as many angles as possible and that one is making as many 'cuts' into the empirical area and data as possible. The natural advantage of such an approach is that it automatically contributes to 'triangulation' which ensures cross-checks on the validity of findings and, of course, the concepts that may emerge from data analysis. The more one relies on one particular source, strategy or method, the more the researcher's attention will be trained on specific dimensions of the empirical area or problem at the expense of equally important areas or problems. A multi-strategy approach produces a multi-perspectival 'overview' which increases the potential for more and more robust theoretical ideas.

Finally, the coalescence of a number of approaches to the empirical area or problem produces a synergy which is conducive to re-orderings and re-interpretations of the findings which may lead to theoretical breakthroughs. As such, this synergy amounts to a force which encourages or stimulates serendipity! In what follows I shall outline five dimensions in which multi-strategy research may move.

Multiple data sources and collection techniques

A basic contention of the multi-strategy approach is that the use of as many different sources and techniques of data collection as possible and appropriate for the research problem in question will have a greater potential yield as far as the production of theoretical ideas and concepts is concerned. One implication of this is that any predilection or prejudice about the use and efficacy of either quantitative or qualitative data must be broken down. Although theory-generation is perfectly possible using only one form of data, I want to suggest that it is using both (especially in tandem with each other) that creates fertile conditions in which novel theorizing may occur (see Layder, 1993). Also important in this regard is the willingness of the researcher to employ both ethnographic techniques of data-gathering (such as participant observation, in-depth interviewing, documentary interpretation, and so on), in conjunction with survey data, official statistics, pre-structured interviews, and so forth. In particular, the use of various combinations of types of data and collection techniques allows one to gain a stronger and more sophisticated analytic purchase on the interconnections between macro and micro features of the social world.

Of course, this injunction to use as many sources and techniques as possible must be tempered by the important qualification that such an approach must also conform to criteria of feasibility, practicality and relevance. Clearly it is sometimes not appropriate or feasible to use certain data sources or collection techniques, but the main point is that they should not be ruled out a priori because of some personal preference or prejudice of the researcher. It is equally essential when employing multiple sources and techniques not to adopt an arbitrary or 'unprincipled' eclectic approach. The crucial point is contained in the phrases 'in conjunction with', or 'in tandem with each other'. Theory and concepts emerge most often and most frequently in a robust form where there is a genuine interchange and dialogue between methods and strategies, sources and techniques (see Layder, 1993).

Historical analysis

Although it is not always necessary or practical to adopt an historical perspective on a particular problem, it certainly may add both empirical and analytic depth to a research project. Questions about the manner in which particular aspects of social life have evolved over variable periods of time are intrinsically 'causal' in nature since the past always impresses itself on the present in some way, even though this may not always be apparent. Investigating such questions involves reading history in a sociological way – that is, it means using historical materials in order to draw out the relevant sociological factors and concepts. Historical materials include primary (original) sources such as documents – both public, as in state papers, autobiographies and so on, and private, as in diaries and journals – as well as secondary sources such as biographies and historical reconstructions or interpretations of particular eras. All these may provide important sources for the generation of new theoretical ideas on a topic or problem by concentrating on the antecedent social conditions which prevailed and which, therefore, in some way influenced present circumstances. Historical analysis may be used as part of a general multi-strategy approach to serve as a validity check on both the substantive and formal theoretical elements that emerge during the research on the contemporary situation.

Theoretical sampling and key interviews

According to Glaser and Strauss (1967), theoretical sampling is most often used with qualitative data (although I would argue that it is equally applicable to quantitative research). The basic underlying principle of theoretical sampling is that the researcher should not rigidly pre-determine the sample (its size or composition) in advance of the research. In this respect questions about which people or which events or activities should be included, or how many people or events should be examined, cannot be answered prior to the research, especially if one wants to generate theory. These questions will be dealt with in an ongoing manner according to the emergent nature of the theory.

Thus the number of people interviewed and how they are chosen is an ongoing, flexible response to the unfolding nature of theoretical and analytic ideas about what the data 'adds up to' or 'means' in terms of an overall explanatory account. A basic objective of theoretical sampling, according to Glaser and Strauss, is to preserve the pristine and 'grounded' nature of the theory that is generated by helping to ensure that the theory is constructed in a truly emergent way and is not imposed on the data. While there is a point to this, I do not think that we should abandon the idea that prior theoretical ideas, concepts, models or propositions may also be helpful in relation to the notion of theoretical sampling and theory-generation.

A good example that highlights some of these issues again comes from my research into actors' careers. After conducting several interviews with actors, it became apparent to me that they were not perhaps the best informants when it came to understanding the underlying social organization of the profession and the functioning of the labour market for actors. I therefore drew into my sample some agents and personal managers. The more I learned from them, the more I realized it was necessary to interview casting directors as well. This of course led to the emergence of the concept of typification which I have already documented.

At the same time as my theoretical sampling was adding to my list of potential interviewees, I was also utilizing a number of other data sources, including two surveys of employment and earnings conducted by the actors' trade union, Equity, and documentary information on patterns of ownership and control in the entertainment industry in general. Thus the theoretical sampling was proceeding in conjunction with a broadly multi-strategy approach (which also included a comparative analysis of careers and the development of a typology of career structures – see comments below on the uses of typology-building for theory-generation). So the data analysis and theory construction overall has to be understood as occurring in the context of a combination and coalescence of all these different data sources, techniques of collection and analytic strategies (including theoretical sampling).

This illustrates the point I made earlier. It is the synergy of these processes which produces 'breakthroughs' in thinking about the meaning of the data (including its theoretical implications) and which leads to re-interpretations or re-orderings of the analysis. The emergence of concepts and theoretical ideas in such an overall context ensures that they will be firmly grounded not only in data but also in robust chains of reasoning and analytic depictions. As I suggested earlier, the multiplicity of lines of attack produce a density of coverage of the area and of perspectives on it. Such circumstances produce favourable conditions under which breakthroughs, insights or the 'eureka' principle may flourish.

Although this sounds rather contradictory, in a sense the multi-strategy approach encourages 'serendipity' to happen. An instance of this from my research concerns the emergence of key informants and what, in the light of the overall context, turn out to be 'key interviews'. The key interview in this sense is one in which a number of ideas suddenly come together through the surfacing of important information. Such key interviews also highlight the importance of small extracts or phrases culled from other interviews which may trigger the perception of connections between different aspects of data.

In my case, one of my interviewees, an executive from the central casting agency, came up with the phrase 'in the swim of employment opportunities' when talking about a particular group of actors. When considered in relation to the other materials I was analysing at the time, particularly the surveys of employment and earnings and other interviews with casting personnel and producers, this phrase (and the interview as a whole) became a 'key' feature which brought together a number of themes, hunches, insights, and so on. It was instrumental in crystalizing my ideas on the segmentation (or stratification) of the acting labour market and how the interrelations between casting directors, personal managers and producers and their routine working practices served to reproduce and reinforce the labour market hierarchy. It was not that this interview, or the phrase itself, stood out on its own and 'suggested' these insights and interconnections in a true 'serendipity' fashion, as if it were pure chance or accident. The insights or the 'eureka' effect of the phrase 'in the swim of employment opportunities' only became significant as a result of all the other aspects of the puzzle simultaneously fitting into place. In this quirky sense the serendipity is induced by the simultaneous interaction and interlinking of many different influences and bits of information which had been 'evolving' relatively independently for some time.

Overall then, the notion of theoretical sampling that I have advocated here is in many crucial respects very different from that suggested by Glaser and Strauss (1967). In a nutshell, my version of theoretical sampling actively encourages the use of extant theoretical resources (including the use of general theory) as a means of facilitating the development of theory from ongoing research. In this sense I do not envisage a stark contrast between the 'emergence' of theory (from data) and the alleged 'forcing' of data into preconceived concepts and categories. My vision of the place of extant theory allows for an intermediate alternative whereby preconceived theory guides data-gathering in conjunction with the unfolding nature of information and analytic thinking. Thus, theoretical sampling does not simply and blindly follow or 'chase' the data, but it is always open to the possibility of being informed by established concepts and rational forms of reasoning that derive from more developed theoretical frameworks or approaches.

Coding, memos and concept-indicator links

I have already covered the main issues that I want to raise about coding and theoretical memos earlier in this chapter, however I do want to emphasize their importance in this context. That is to say, these issues in themselves constitute an integral aspect of the multi-strategy approach which feeds into the overall conjunction of effects and the resultant synergy. The coding of data, and the theoretical memos that result from, and feed into, the ongoing analysis of data, do not exist as independent aspects of research, neatly separated from other influences. Quite the contrary, the whole point of the multi-strategy approach is to induce a cumulative and developmental effect in theoretical thinking and the production of ideas.

Typologies, theory-generation and the research process

Developing typologies (or building typological models) alongside data analysis is a very useful means by which the theoretical imagination is fired during the research process itself. Typologies are systematic classifications of types of social phenomenon as they fall within a particular category. Thus one could have a typology of political parties, of authority or control relations, of types of organization, of religious movements, of types of prison inmate, sex tourist, or of types of staff–client interaction (Clegg et al., 1996), or of techniques of client resistance (Bloor and McIntosh, 1990). Having the objective of building a typology (of whatever is the primary focus of the research) at the start of the research gives direction and impetus to theoretical thinking for a number of reasons.

One primary reason is that it forces the researcher to begin to ask questions about the data and the social phenomena to which the data refer. Essentially the questions are to do with comparative analysis concerning why some phenomenon (a group, a relationship, a 'type' of participant) is the same or different from others. Choosing comparisons which highlight large differences has the effect of stimulating ideas, concepts and categories which are formed in terms of the questions why and how are they different. On the other hand, comparing an aspect of social life with one which is very similar encourages questions about why and how they are the same or similar, and thus stimulates the generation of ideas concepts and categories around these questions. Asking comparative questions with a view to developing a typology has the advantage of ordering one's observations and analyses in a systematic fashion rather than simply making one-off comparisons via thought experiments.

Secondly, typology-building allows the researcher to engage in theoretical elaboration and thus to think in terms of chains of reasoning rather than simply in terms of one-to-one correspondences between concepts and data (concept-indicator linkages). It does this first by suggesting connections between emergent concepts and ideas which may not have otherwise been apparent while at the same time confirming more 'obvious' or apparent connections. Secondly, by tuning into a comparative perspective the researcher is led to countenance extant theory around the focal area itself – or in adjacent areas – and thus is presented with the possibility of other theoretical inputs and connections. In this sense the researcher's interests become attuned to a wider array of theoretical materials which may eventually add to or complement the organic growth of theoretical thinking about the current research project. (I discuss theoretical elaboration in more detail in Chapter 5.)

Overall, the development of typologies can clarify thinking, suggest lines of explanation and give direction to the theoretical imagination. In so far as theoretical elaboration is an important feature of the research, then typology construction can also be a stepping-stone to and from more general theory (approaches and schools of thought). The pursuit of an organic connection with theory elaboration and the establishment of interconnections with general theory are not, of course, necessary features of all typology-building. The development of a typology may be undertaken as a rather discrete activity and regarded as a complete and self-sufficient analytic strategy in its own right. However, in the context of the multi-strategy approach that I am advocating, the goal of theory development is paramount.

Very often these theoretical advantages of typology-building are missed by those who view it as a self-sufficient strategy devoid of potential connection with formal or general theory. For example, typology-building is sometimes advocated in methods texts but is restricted to typologies based around emergent empirical material relating to various dimensions of behaviour or activity. Examples of this are Glaser and Strauss's (1965) 'awareness contexts' surrounding dying patients, Lofland's (1966) typology of 'entrance styles' in public establishments, or Richie and Spencer's (1994) typoplogy of sexual attitudes and behaviours. The restriction of typologies to 'categorizing different types of attitudes, behaviours, motivations' (Richie and Spencer, 1994: 176) is almost always coupled with a lack of concern with distinguishing between what I term (Layder, 1993) action or behavioural typologies and structural or system typologies.

As I have indicated, action or behavioural typologies restrict themselves largely to the depiction of lifeworld elements of society concerning subjective meaning, lived experience, motivations, attitudes, and so on. The importance of system or structural typologies is that they concern themselves with depicting the settings and contexts of behaviour and thus provide the necessary requirements for more inclusive and powerful explanations of social life. Any comprehensive depiction of the social world will automatically utilize concepts relating to both behavioural and systemic aspects since social practices are an amalgam of the mutual influences of lived experience and systemic aspects of social life. (See Chapter 4 for a detailed discussion of these types of concept-indicator link.) However, it is important to make the distinction in the first place since otherwise the relative impact of the different but connected influences of these aspects of social life will be neglected or obscured.

Those approaches to research which emphasize action or behavioural typologies do so at the expense and consequent neglect of structural or system typologies. Therefore it is important to acknowledge that forms of behaviour, attitudes, motivations or 'types' of people *always* exist in some kind of setting or context (or linked series of them) and thus to achieve depth and power of analysis it is crucial that the influence of these settings and contexts is registered and understood. It is also crucial to emphasize the important role that structural or system typologies may play in research; otherwise their influence on the behaviour or people in question will be vague and partial, or treated as an implicit, inchoate backdrop to the analysis. The use of system typologies has the effect of broadening the scope of analysis by attending to wider aspects of social organization and social relations. This effectively makes the analysis more complex in the sense of being more dense, rounded and comprehensive.

Developing system or structural typologies is especially useful in helping to map the interconnections between system elements and the behaviours and activities which take place within this wider (systemic) environment. This in turn has the effect of stimulating theoretical thinking since there is a greater number of 'variables', 'factors' or 'elements' to be taken into account and these raise theoretical questions about the manner in which they interrelate. The effects of the development of a system or structural typology are not simply one-way in the direction of theory. They also feed into the research process in a very practical manner by identifying gaps in information which may lead to readjustments in sampling. In consequence, such re-thinking or re-calculation may bestow greater direction to the investigation as a whole. Thus, the great virtue of developing such typologies in the context of ongoing research is that it highlights the intrinsic interconnections of theory, research and data analysis, and actively encourages the mutual impact and influence of them all in the research process itself.

Let me briefly illustrate this with the example of my own research on the acting profession. Initially, my primary focus was on actors themselves and on their careers in particular. However, as I have pointed out, it became apparent that interviewing actors could not furnish me with information about the labour market in acting and for this I needed to interview others in the business (casting personnel, personal managers) and to use other sources of data (such as surveys on employment and earnings and studies of ownership and control in the media). This gave me some indication of the systemic aspects of the occupation – the settings and contexts in which actors' careers are worked out in a larger sense. However, to give a much fuller picture of the nature of the wider career context it was necessary to situate the acting profession in relation to other kinds of occupation and career. Thus, by asking questions about how and why a career in acting was similar to, or different from, other kinds of occupational careers (such as the civil service, the armed forces, medicine, sport, music, and so on), I began to develop a typology of occupational career structures.

By examining and analysing the existing literature and research on occupational careers I found that there was quite a lot of material on bureaucratic and professional careers (like managers in industry or civil servants) but there was relatively little on craft-like occupations like acting, in which naked market forces play a large role, and virtually nothing at all on acting itself. However, by analysing the published material I was able to begin to develop a 'provisional' typology of career structures. This yielded three main types – bureaucratic, collegiate and market careers. My initial analysis suggested that the concepts of power and control and the issues that flow from them, such as which groups in the occupation are able to control career status movements (successfully or otherwise in the career), were important in distinguishing between types of career structure. However, until I began researching careers in acting, I had no real way of understanding the form of control in this career. By interviewing casting directors, personal managers and using survey data I came up with the concept of 'shared control'. This points to the fact that career mobility is 'shared' by a multiplicity of group influences (employers, casting directors, agents, critics and audience reactions).

This illustrates the zig-zagging pattern of the research process and the mutual influences of typology-building and the unfolding nature of data collection and analysis. The provisional typology initially raised the issues of power and control over career mobility and thus alerted me to its importance. At the same time the absence of information on market-type careers highlighted a gap in knowledge and helped to re-focus the substantive analysis of acting on issues of mobility control in the career. This, as I say, yielded the category of 'shared control' although this, in itself, did not simply derive from the data collection on acting – it only became relevant and important in relation to the forms of control in the other two types of career structure. In the bureaucratic type, control over the career (decisions about promotions, career development and patterns of progress through companies) was vested in the hands of employers – and high status members of the organization acting in the interests of employers – thus the concept of 'employer control' was relevant here. In the collegiate careers of professionals like medics, lawyers, and so on, the category of 'collegiate control' was relevant and indicated the manner in which professional colleagues may exert some control over status mobility, depending also on the type of work context involved (private practice, organizational employees, and so on).

In short, the development of a typology alongside a substantive analysis facilitates a process of mutual influence between theoretical ideas and concepts and the collection and analysis of data in an ongoing manner. Thus typology-building is yet another strand of a multi-strategy approach which can feed into theory elaboration and development in a cumulative sense. It actively encourages a dialectical interplay between 'emergent' theorizing based on the discovery (collection) of data and information and the use of extant theoretical materials derived from different sources. Each influence tempers and conditions the other. Such an approach to research underlines the fact that it is not a unilinear process of steady development whereby the researcher gradually uncovers material and develops ideas in a highly ordered fashion. Rather, it suggests a zig-zagging back and forth between theoretical ideas, data collection and analysis – with each pointing to gaps and insufficiencies in each other and thereby prompting creative and investigative responses which produce a cumulative and organic theoretical end-product.

Conclusion: theory from data?

Although I have dealt with the question of theorizing distinctly from the point of view of someone who is directly engaged in research, this has been a matter of emphasis since I have also tried to make plain that to view theory-development or construction simply as a matter of 'emergence from the data', as the proponents of grounded theory suggest, is both debilitating and inaccurate. It is debilitating in the sense that it attempts to limit 'legitimate' theorizing to concepts and ideas which are directly suggested by the data themselves. This conveniently leaves out of the account the fact that there are always 'imported' assumptions in theory-building since the researcher always brings with him or her a whole host of diffuse (and sometimes specific) assumptions about data and about appropriate and legitimate forms of explanation and analysis. It also nullifies the possible influence and role of extant theoretical materials (including general theory) in the process of theory-generation. Such an arbitrary severance only impoverishes social analysis at the very moment when there should be an attempt to establish connections between different strands of theorizing in pursuit of the goal of cumulative knowledge.

In the context of these more encompassing considerations I have specified some practical procedures and strategies designed to serve the objectives mentioned above. I began with the problem of how to sort, select and otherwise order empirical data via the use of various types of coding. The main example I dealt with was transcripts from in-depth interviews but in principle the same procedures and techniques can be applied to other empirical materials such as documentary sources or even survey research. I suggested that it is useful to distinguish between pre-coding, provisional coding and coding around core and satellite concepts. The usefulness of these coding procedures hinges upon their ability to incorporate and engage with aspects of general, formal and extant theory at the same time as being sensitive to the emergence of codes and concepts as they are influenced by the new data that is unearthed by ongoing research.

I then moved on to the question of how theory may be constructed in conjunction with the analysis and general scrutiny of data. Again in relation to in-depth interview transcripts, I showed how the practice of memo-writing could be harnessed to the goal of theory-generation. In this respect writing theoretical memos draws upon a diversity of sources and skills in an effort to construct new theory. I traced through the evolution of the concept of typification during the course of an extended theoretical memo. This illustrated the manner in which concepts and theoretical ideas may be developed from the conjunction between direct engagement with empirical data and the application of the theoretical imagination as it has been fashioned through prior reading and exposure to theoretical materials.

Finally, I suggested the viability and efficacy of employing a multi-strategy approach in order to facilitate theory-generation. I argued that using multiple sources, methods, strategies and types of data creates a dynamic synergy which maximizes the efficient use of resources and encourages strongly anchored theory. At the same time it increases the possibility of serendipity and the emergence of novel theory. I concentrated on the advantages of incorporating multiple data sources and collection techniques, historical analysis, theoretical sampling, as well as the importance of key interviews, coding, memos and concept-indicator links. I ended by suggesting that there has been a one-sided emphasis in the methods literature on action or behavioural typologies and that this needs to be balanced by an emphasis on structural or system typologies.

SOCIAL RESEARCH AND CONCEPT-INDICATOR LINKS

This chapter serves as a transition in terms of the themes treated in Chapters 3 and 5. In simple terms, Chapter 3 emphasizes the move from data to theory, while Chapter 5 takes the opposite tack and focuses on the theory to data connection. In this respect Chapter 4 takes an interim position in that it concentrates on concept-indicator links (and hence theory-data links) from the point of view of their formal intersection. However, this is not simply a formal problem – it has very practical implications for the formulation of research problems, and the gathering and analysis of data. Understanding the nature of concept-indicator links means that one has a firmer grasp of the connections between theoretical ideas (concepts, frameworks, typologies) and the empirical materials (the data, information) that they represent. Moreover, being clear about the implications of these connections is essential for an overall grasp of the research process itself as well as the more specific links between theorizing and research.

In order to understand the importance of this question it is first necessary to appreciate that concept-indicator links operate at two levels – as both 'underlying' and 'surface' aspects of research activity. Both levels are intimately related and neither exists in isolation from the other. Often the 'surface' aspects are given more attention in methods books and discussions about methodology generally. Thus, for example, establishing linkages between the concept of 'emotional labour' and specific empirical indicators of this phenomenon – such as smiling behaviour in flight attendants – is important in ensuring the success of a research project centred on this topic. After all, knowing that this is a valid, accurate and reliable empirical indicator of the concept is essential for the production of well-executed research. However, it is equally important to understand the more underlying aspects of the concept-indicator problem.

The concept-indicator problem

The 'deeper' aspects of the concept-indicator problem raise more general issues about the nature of society and social reality, and these in turn prompt questions concerning the validity or adequacy of the concepts that are employed to represent or depict different aspects of social reality. Asking these deeper questions also connects us to the more general theoretical issues that are the subject of contemporary debate – such as the agency-structure problem or the relation between macro and micro levels of analysis of social life. Understanding and engaging with these issues facilitates the production of more powerful and inclusive research conclusions and explanations. Furthermore, it helps to overcome the 'false' gap between general theory and research.

In this sense the discussion in this chapter follows on from one of the issues raised at the end of Chapter 3 concerning the distinction between behavioural (action) and system (structural) typologies. There I suggested that there had been an unfortunate skewing of attention towards behavioural or action typologies and a consequent neglect or ignoring of the system types. Here I want to raise such issues in the context of a wider discussion of the nature of social reality and the sorts of concepts which we use to describe or represent it. I argue that it is of pivotal importance to understand social reality as 'layered' or 'multi-dimensional' and that, as a consequence, the validity or adequacy of our concepts should be judged in relation to its variegated nature. Specifically, I identify four types of concept-indicator link that are directly involved in routine aspects of social research but which are rarely discussed in methods texts or by researchers.

I begin by focusing on the concept of typification which I initially discussed in Chapter 3. By examining the meaning of this concept in relation to its empirical indicators in social life, I am then able to suggest that it represents a specific type of concept-indicator linkage. In this case typification is an example of what I term a 'bridging' or 'mediating' concept and can be distinguished from the other main types which I term 'behavioural' or 'system' concepts. By way of conclusion I focus on the final type of concept-indicator link by discussing 'theoretician's concepts' – concepts drawn from a body of general theory or theoretical framework – and suggest that their role in social analysis is under-appreciated and that they have direct implications for the conduct of social research. The chapter ends with some practical advice concerning the manner in which awareness of, and sensitivity to, these issues adds to the quality, explanatory power and potential of both theorizing and social research.

Concepts, data and epistemological questions

It is important to be aware of and to value positively the prior theoretical baggage we bring with us to data analysis, in so far as we can use it in a systematic manner to guide theory-construction. However, it is of equal importance to be aware of the epistemological status of the concepts we use (their validity and adequacy) and how they relate to the data or the slice of social reality that is being analysed (their ontological status). In this respect I want to concentrate on matters relating to two of the most important problems in sociological analysis – the interrelations between agency and structure and macro and micro levels of analysis. What I have already said about the concept of typification and the manner in which it was generated provides a useful introduction to these problems as well as to the question of how data analysis is deeply connected with them. I shall begin, therefore, with a discussion of the epistemological and ontological status of typification and use it as a means of introducing a distinction between three types of analytic concept. From this point on, the discussion will become more general, drawing on a range of material and examples from empirical research.

Given that the concept of typification, as I have outlined the process of its emergence, is derived from a consideration of two other member-defined concepts, namely 'type-casting' and 'casting against type', we can appreciate that it is a product of an epistemological transmutation. That is to say that once in the form of the concept of typification it had become an analytic (formal, sociological) concept quite removed from everyday employment by (social) actors 'on the social scene', to use Schutz's (1972) phrase. My sociological definition and usage of typification both added to and omitted some of the meanings and references contained in the *in vivo* concepts of 'type' and 'against type' casting. The addition of a reference to the work routines of casting personnel and the facilitation of allocation and co-ordination of actors in the labour market had the effect of distinguishing it in large part (although not totally) from 'common-sense', 'everyday', 'subjective' definitions and meanings of members of the profession. It also separated it out (though again, not wholly) from the stream of 'local narratives' that characterize the lived experiences of those in the profession.

Thus, typification could no longer be defined entirely in terms of the raw, on-the-ground practices of members (unlike 'type' and 'against-type' casting). In short, the concept of typification itself would not be recognizable to actors or casting directors unless its formal sociological meaning was first explained to them. As I have implied above, this sets apart the approach I am advocating from those of symbolic interactionists, phenomenologists, ethnomethodologists, postmodernists, poststructuralists, as well as grounded theorists and others who dogmatically limit their concerns to intersubjective meaning and understanding, local artful practices (Hilbert, 1991) or local narratives (Denzin, 1990). Such authors eschew the importance of objectivist, social-structural (or systemic) features of the social world and reject concepts which represent these aspects in some way and which, as a result, are not necessarily understandable or meaningful to the 'subjects' of the research. Although the concept of typification (and others like it) does not necessarily accord with members' definitions, meanings and narratives, it is nonetheless descriptive and analytic of the everyday behavioural worlds of the people to whom it relates (in this case primarily casting directors, but also actors).

I am arguing two main things here. First, that typification is a synthetic concept which merges the subjectively experienced world of research subjects with the analytic and conceptual predilections and directives of the researcher. Secondly, by undergoing such a transformation it is no longer simply a behavioural concept sub-jectively defined (from the point of view of the behaviour of those to whom it applies). Rather, it remains essentially a behavioural concept which is subjectively relevant, but that now also possesses analytic, rational and formal properties which both transcend and include the lived experiences of those to whom it applies. I am not implying that the vernacular concepts of 'type' and 'against-type' casting are thereby made redundant by the invention of this new concept. Quite the contrary, since they refer to quite different things. But, I am arguing that typification fills up a conceptual space concerned with behavioural implications which are not represented or captured in common-sense or everyday understandings. Therefore such concepts should be regarded as existing alongside member-defined concepts since they are not in competition for the same 'factual' ground or semantic territory. Importantly, however, such concepts do add to the corpus of knowledge about everyday practices since they are grounded in the (pristine) data of everyday life as much as are the so-called *in vivo* concepts. The difference is that synthetic concepts are not simply grounded in the data of lived experiences or local narratives, but are also anchored to a chain of reasoning and an analytic vantage point which gives their conceptual representation of the behaviour in focus a rather different basis (Layder, 1990). In this sense such concepts are a unique amalgam of member-defined and formally defined elements which make them epistemologically (and ontologically) distinct.

The distinctiveness of these sorts of concept is further extended in so far as they also represent a blending of elements of different aspects of social reality. Specifically, they are centrally concerned with combining aspects of individual social agency – including the intersubjective world of social interaction – with the non-acting aspects of reproduced social relations and practices which constitute the settings and contexts in which social activities are played out

(Layder, 1997). For the sake of brevity I shall refer, following Habermas (1984, 1987), to the latter as social system (or structural) elements. So the kind of concept of which typification is an example blends agency and systems in that aspects of each are connected in equal measure. In this sense I would suggest that they are 'bridging' or 'mediating' concepts which represent the connections or linkages between these fundamental aspects of social reality.

This is reflected in the concept of typification in so far as it is an amalgam of both the actual behavioural predispositions, decisions and actions of casting personnel as well as part of a system of power, control and allocation which serves to underpin a hierarchically organized labour market. The power and control of casting personnel does not derive from their personal capacities (although they undoubtedly have personal powers as well – see Layder, 1997). It derives from the workings of a labour market and the organized (reproduced) practices which flow from the system of allocation of labour in the market for acting work. As such, this power is in large part (though not wholly) systemically embedded and historically emergent from the practices of previous generations or cohorts of people involved in casting and theatrical production in general.

Thus, the behaviour (or practices) of casting personnel has to be understood not simply as the outcome of their interpretative capacities and the interpersonal processes in which they are engaged. A good deal is the result of the power, authority and control which they exert as a result of their position in a nexus of reproduced social relations set within an organized labour market. It is the social position of casting personnel as *mediators* between the influence of market forces and the consequences these have for actor's careers in general (and individual actor's career fortunes in particular) that marks out their distinctive role in the occupational organization. It also underlines the duality of reference indicated by the concept of typification.

Types of concept-indicator link

In the above section I have endeavoured to describe a kind of concept, exemplified by 'typification', which could be said to occupy a unique place 'in between' members' (or 'lay') definitions and those of social analysts, as well as representing crucial linkages between aspects of both systemic and interpersonal features of social life. On the basis of this I want now to show that such bridging or mediating concepts in fact represent a middle-ground between two other types of concept and their empirical indicators which I shall term 'behavioural' and 'systemic' (or 'structural') concepts. In so doing I hope to demonstrate that although the distinctions between them are crucially a matter of emphasis – and that they do not indicate absolute or clean separations – they are nonetheless very real in that they highlight important differences in social reality. As such they also indicate important differences in the epistemological basis of certain concepts as they relate to the empirical world (concept-indicator links) and thus they have important implications for the manner in which theory may be derived from social research.

The question of emphasis is important because I do not want to create the impression that it is only bridging concepts that blend systemic and interpersonal aspects of social life. This may indeed have been the apparent 'drift' of my previous statement about the distinctiveness of concepts like typification. However, my argument is not that bridging concepts are the only ones that link systemic and interpersonal aspects. In fact, all concepts about the social world include some reference to both these elements. Nonetheless, the distinctiveness of the three types of concept that I am here drawing attention to is that they are involved with these elements of social life to varying degrees and in fundamentally different ways. I say that all concepts about the social world involve some reference to both agency and systems (structures) because these two aspects of social life are inextricably bound up with each other – they are 'deeply implicated' in each other as Giddens (1984) says. That is, the effects of each cannot be completely separated out from each other since they are interconnected and thus they continually influence each other. However, a crucial difference between Giddens's position and my own is that I believe that the effects of agency and systems on social activities and practice is variable and depends upon the relative influence of different aspects of social life ('domains' as I call them (Layder, 1997)) at different points in time and social space. These variable factors are reflected in the four types of concept depicted in Table 4.1.

Behavioural concepts

What I have termed behavioural concepts have a fairly broad range of application and are perhaps the most commonly used in social research. They include distinctions between 'types' of participants in particular kinds of social activities, for example types of sex tourist (O'Connell Davidson, 1995), or social settings (as in Giallombardo's (1966) classification of women prisoners). However, they may also refer to the nature and/or quality of interpersonal relationships in

Table 4.1   Concept-indicator links

Type of concept	Aspect of social reality
Behavioural	Types of participant (sex tourist, inmate, careerist), interpersonal events, behaviour and communications, self-identity, face-to-face conduct.
Systemic or structural	Reproduced social relations, practices, positions – the settings and contexts of behaviour: bureaucracy, markets, types of organization. Underpinning power relations.
Bridging or mediating	(a) Objective–subjective duality of reference; 'career', 'emotional labour'. (b) Behaviour of social agents who control and mediate: 'typification'. (c) Social relations strongly influenced by system: 'alienative', 'calculative'.
General or theoretician's	Any of the above

particular settings and the meanings and intepretations that people attach to them. An example of this is Clegg, Standen and Jones's (1996) account of staff–client interactions with adults with profound learning disabilities (producing the classifications 'provider', 'meaning-maker', 'mutual' and 'companion') which focuses on the emotional and cognitive fulfilment provided by different kinds of relationship and involvement. Brewer's (1990) study of typical communication styles among members of the Royal Ulster Constabulary (yielding the 'skills', 'fatalism' and 'routinization' vocabularies), which help them deal with stressful and dangerous situations by normalizing them, provides yet another form of behavioural concept. In this instance the vocabularies represent typical, occupationally-induced forms of response to a threatening environment.

The point about behavioural concepts is that they directly describe some aspect of a participant's behaviour, predisposition or attitude and include some reference to his or her identity or the quality and meaning of the relationships in which he or she is involved. Although these concepts may in fact be either member-defined or observer-defined, in all cases they must conform in some measure to criteria of 'subjective adequacy' (Bruyn, 1966). Some of the criteria that Bruyn notes deal with methodological issues such as the length of time spent studying the group, the degree of intimacy achieved, and the number of different vantage points from which they were studied. These all bear some relation to helping to ensure the adequacy or validity of the concepts that the researcher produces as a result. Other criteria of subjective adequacy concern the extent of the researcher's familiarity with the language of the group and his or her ability to communicate with the members of the group. Such factors affect the researcher's ability to render accurately and adequately the lived experiences of those studied – as reflected in the central concepts used to describe them and their behaviour.

These criteria are also close to those emphasized by Glaser and Strauss (1967) who insist that concepts and theory must 'fit' the data and be relevant to the people involved. Moreover, concepts must be recognizable, make sense and be understandable to those who are the subjects of the study (even if not routinely employed by them). For example, Glaser and Strauss's (1965) classification of 'awareness contexts' around dying patients ('closed', 'open', 'mutual pretence' and 'suspicion awareness') are not the sorts of label and descriptor that patients' families or medical staff themselves would use. However, as Glaser and Strauss emphasize, the validity of such concepts is crucially dependent upon these same people agreeing that they are relevant to, and representative of their own experiences, meanings and behaviour. Now Glaser and Strauss's idea that formal concepts (such as those that describe the awareness contexts) do not have to be defined or used by those to whom they refer is an important advance by those who argue or strongly imply (such as Bruyn, 1966; Becker in Rock, 1979) that concepts must not seriously depart from the vernacular vocabulary of participants. However, they do still restrict their prescriptions in that grounded concepts have to be understandable, recognizable and make sense to the people studied.

While all these criteria of subjective adequacy obviously do play a significant part in determining the validity or adequacy of behavioural concepts, it is important to distinguish the position I am outlining here from the overall position of Glaser and Strauss and others of similar persuasion. The crucial distinction is that the latter restrict *all* research concepts to those which conform to criteria of subjective adequacy while I am suggesting that subjective adequacy is largely restricted in applicability to behavioural concepts. Furthermore, I am arguing that researchers can and should utilize other kinds of concepts (systemic and bridging types) as well as, or in conjunction with, behavioural ones in order not only to maximize theoretical potential, but also to ensure that all facets of social life are taken into account. I am arguing that the range of legitimate research concerns should be much more inclusive than that proposed by Glaser and Strauss (1965), Bruyn (1966) and Becker (in Rock, 1979), who are committed to an exclusively interpretivist (humanist or phenomenological) conception of the nature of social analysis and research.

The position I am advocating here is broadly realist (Layder, 1990, 1993) in that it suggests that social reality is not simply composed of actors' meanings and subjective understandings, but that there exist systemic (or structural) factors which exert considerable influence on the nature of people's lived experiences. The influence of behavioural and system aspects of social life on each other is mutual and their mechanisms and effects are deeply intertwined. On the one hand, systemic factors depend upon the reproductive activities of human beings to ensure their continuity in time and space, while inter-subjective experience and social activity is heavily influenced, shaped and formed by the same systemic factors that they help to reproduce continually through interaction and the social routines in which they are embedded. Social research should therefore attempt to trace the modes in which both subjective and objective factors combine to mutually influence each other.

It is in this sense that all theoretical concepts pertinent to research 'contain' references to both agency and systems aspects but differ in the extent to which they connect with these distinct but interrelated aspects of social life. Thus it is that behavioural concepts are, in relative terms, more concerned with the agency side of the equation in that they concentrate on depicting the behavioural worlds and the intersubjective 'lived' experiences of those who are the subjects of the research. The importance of subjective understanding and subjective adequacy, therefore, automatically play a large part in adjudicating the validity of such concepts. However, as I have said, from the realist position that I defend here, social research and the concepts that emanate from it are also necessarily implicated in concepts which register the influences of systemic factors. This is because social activity and subjective or lived experience are never 'free' of the social settings and contextual resources which are constitutive of social system elements. Thus, especially in regard to these other concepts, criteria of subjective adequacy cannot be the decisive ones or the only ones to be taken into account.

Even with behavioural concepts validity cannot simply and solely be subject to criteria of subjective adequacy even if they are largely so. There must always be some sort of 'convergence' with more formal analytic criteria relating to the validity of systemic and bridging concepts. That is a concept which may seem faithfully to depict the research subject's worlds (local narratives and the voices of oppressed groups), but this does not necessarily guarantee the truth or efficacy of these concepts – especially if they are flatly contradicted by an examination of wider aspects of the social setting and context. Perhaps the important point to bear in mind for the researcher who wants to generate theory from data is that the empirical indicators of behavioural concepts are primarily to do with illuminating the sub-jective worlds of people from a broadly 'insider' point of view. Of necessity, this requires some attempt to depict the social experiences of those studied from a subjective point of view and that the concepts themselves should register the inner texture of this lived experience in a way that is recognizable to those to whom they apply. However, these concepts must also be concordant with knowledge of the wider social conditions in terms of which social experience is played out.

Systemic or structural concepts

In order to provide clarity (in a rather over-drawn manner, it must be admitted) systemic concepts may be thought of as a species of 'non-behavioural' concept. That is, such concepts refer primarily to the reproduced social relations which represent the historically emergent standing conditions of an ongoing society. To say that they are standing conditions does not mean that they are static and unchanging or that they are somehow beyond the reach and influence of human agents. Such things as institutions, language, culture and various forms of knowledge are all susceptible to the transformative powers of individuals and social groups, but they nonetheless confront particular individuals and groups as the products of previous generations (Marx and Engels, 1968). In this sense they confront people in their day-to-day lives as 'already formed' social circumstances. In Popper's (1972) terms, they have an objective (or Third World) existence independent of 'knowing (or participating) subjects'. In my terms, they have a relatively independent existence from the routine social practices in which people are regularly engaged (Layder, 1997).

Although they have these ontological properties (of 'depth'), such standing conditions are not static. They are integrally involved in social processes. First, such standing conditions are inherently 'in process' as a result of long-term historical processes of social change at both macro and intermediate levels of social reality. Importantly, different aspects of the settings and contexts (the 'standing conditions') of social activity are differentially resistant and susceptible to change through the transformative activities of individuals and groups. This is because they vary in terms of their sedimentation in time (the hold of history and tradition), their pervasiveness in particular societies and the extent of their entanglement with established forms of power and domination.

Secondly, at the level of situated activity there are always a number of productive processes in which people are creating localized meanings and understandings and which are deeply implicated in the reproduction of the wider social forms (the settings and contexts) which comprise the standing conditions. It is important to note, however, that the vast majority of these creative aspects of behaviour remain localized in terms of their transformative effects, while the creativity involved in system reproduction is minimal in terms of making a difference to these 'established' elements of social life (see Layder, 1997, Chapter 5).

As these latter comments indicate, there are a number of senses in which systemic aspects of social life are related to social activity and subjective experience. First, they provide resources and facilities which people draw into their behaviour as they make it happen in the particular face-to-face situations in which they are recurrently involved. Conversely, routine social activities provide the 'life-blood' of system elements in so far as they contribute to (and hence help to ensure) their continuity in time and space, while they simultaneously reproduce these systemic forms. All in all, although system factors (and hence the concepts which stand for, or indicate, them) stand slightly apart from social activities, individuals and groups in society, their autonomy from them is only relative since, as we have seen, system aspects are indissolubly intertwined with social activities and subjective experience. However, this relative autonomy is of crucial significance and makes a world of difference in terms of the status of the concepts we use to analyse these features of society.

Thus it is that system factors predominantly denote the reproduced aspects of social relations as they have been stretched through time and space and away from face-to-face activities (which ultimately feed into their continuity and reproduction). In this sense they cannot be understood in terms of the motives, reasons or the intersubjective 'lived' experiences of people, and instead they must be viewed as part of the (contextual) conditions which constitute the wider social environment of social life and activity. This view departs from approaches like phenomenology, interactionism and grounded theory which do not envisage any role for, and in fact radically deny the existence of, these aspects of social life and therefore reject the efficacy of concepts which endeavour to take such features of social life into account. In this respect such theories and approaches over-react to system concepts, fearing that they involve some kind of reification of social life – that it is beyond the reach and trans-formative capacities of people. However, as I have pointed out, the inherent tie with social activity and subjective experience rules this possibility out of the present account.

An important feature of systemic aspects of social life is their inherent involvement with relations of power, control and domination. All sets of reproduced social relations, as reflected in the settings and contexts of social activity, are very closely interwoven with the powers and practices which underpin them in various ways and are therefore associated with different modes of power and power relationship. Examples of systemic concepts themselves display considerable variation. Some refer to society-wide (macro) phenomena such as 'capitalist', 'feudal' or even 'postmodern' 'types' of society. Others refer to intermediate modes of social organization such as 'organic' or 'mechanical' solidarity by which Durkheim (1964) referred to the different ways in which society or sub-sectors of it are 'held together'. Under organic solidarity people are held together (integrated) through dissimilarity (individuality) and the complementarity of the roles and functions they fulfil, while under mechanical solidarity likeness or similarity helps to produce lasting (integrative) bonds.

This distinction has been subsequently used by various authors to help describe and explain various aspects of society. Bernstein (1973), for instance, employs it in developing his account of differences between speech codes that predominate in different social classes and families. On the other hand, Burns and Stalker (1961) talk about mechanistic and organic management systems to describe variations in the flexibility of the organization of firms in different kinds of industry and market conditions (for example, electronics versus manufacturing). All these usages refer to different kinds of reproduced social relations and the way in which they provide the settings and contexts in which various kinds of social behaviour and activities are enabled and constrained.

As Habermas (1984, 1987) has emphasized repeatedly, the areas of bureaucracy, markets and power are perhaps some of the principal 'systemic' foci – and this is reflected in the examples of the concepts just cited. Other classic examples of such concepts, as they relate to bureaucratic organization, are to be found in the work of Etzioni (1961), who distinguishes between coercive, remunerative and normative types of power in organizations, while Gouldner (1954) refers to what he terms 'mock', 'representative' and 'punishment-centred' bureaucracies. An example is provided by Edwards (1979), who, in tracing the historical emergence of modern forms of 'structural control' (which he terms 'technical' and 'bureaucratic') in organizations in the manufacturing industry, also identifies preceding types ('personal' and 'hierarchical' control). Foucault's (1977, 1980) characterizations of modern forms of power as 'disciplinary' and 'biopower' are also examples of what I consider to be systemic concepts (although it has to be said that there is some doubt about whether Foucault himself would agree with the label 'systemic').

The detailed empirical meanings and indicators of these concepts do not concern us at this juncture. Rather, it is the epistemological basis of the concepts and the nature of the social reality to which they refer that is of crucial significance. Now while, as I have said, there is always some link between system phenomena and the behaviours of people who are subject to their influence (that is, the concepts are not simply self-referring), the primary reference point of these concepts is not social behaviour in and of itself. It is rather the reproduced social relations (and the powers and practices which underpin them) that form the settings and contexts in which social behaviours are enacted. Therefore criteria of 'subjective adequacy' cannot play a large part in the construction of these concepts and the meanings they convey. Thus the understandability of such concepts to participants or their usage by participants cannot determine their validity.

Other important criteria concern the logical or rational connections between these and other related concepts or the ability to derive or deduce empirical propositions from them – say about the behaviour of people or the functioning of various kinds of social organization like labour markets or bureaucracies. That is, not only do such concepts refer to aspects of the empirical world, but they are also locked into a chain of reasoning related to a wider body of theory or theoretical propositions (see Chapter 1 for a discussion of Merton's ideas on this). The crucial point about this chain of reasoning is that it is primarily to do with the analyst's (researcher's) efforts to locate the empirical phenomenon in a wider, more generalized and abstract context of ideas. So for example, although lay people refer to 'bureaucracy', what a sociologist means by this is much more specific and in this sense quite different from colloquial usage. Therefore the colloquial usage cannot be relied upon to give a precise and technical definition. These concepts are predominantly observer-defined rather than participant-defined.

Also, the question of relevance or connection with people or participants is different from behavioural concepts. The validity of systemic or structural concepts is not, and cannot be dependent on criteria associated with whether they make sense subjectively to participants or even whether participants believe these concepts to refer to real entities in the social world. For example, some phenomenologically inspired authors have suggested that concepts have no validity unless they enter into the daily lives of people or they are grounded in people's concrete local practices (Hilbert, 1990). But such views simply restrict the range of empirical phenomena to which researchers may legitimately attend while also limiting the range of social phenomena that can be analysed or explained.

Whether people actually believe in the reality referred to by the analyst's (or observer's) concepts cannot adjudicate their validity. For example, whether people working within bureaucratic organizations believe themselves to be participating in 'coercive' or 'disciplinary' regimes of power is neither here nor there as far as the meaning of these terms is concerned, or with regard to their usefulness in analysing or explaining the sectors of social life to which they refer. In this respect the validity of such concepts is defined precisely in these terms – their capacity to explain and analyse social reality not with regard to their employment in everyday life or their capacity to evoke understanding based on common-sense usage.

Bridging or mediating concepts

In the light of the definitions of behavioural and systemic concepts we can now more clearly understand the role of bridging or mediating concepts. The former two are distinguishable in terms of the relative importance of criteria of 'subjective adequacy' as opposed to 'objective' or 'analytic adequacy' and the predominance of their reference to behavioural as opposed to systemic aspects of social life. By contrast, bridging or mediating concepts represent a fairly balanced, synthetic combination of the two. That is, such concepts (like 'typification') represent a focus on the combined effects of behavioural and systemic (or structural) elements of social life in equal measure. These concepts then reflect a dual emphasis on the effects of objective and subjective aspects of social life. There are three broad kinds of phenomena which such concepts indicate, or upon which they focus attention.

First, a typical focus of attention is on specific linkages between objective and subjective phenomena. Concepts such as 'career' (Hughes, 1937; Stebbins, 1970) or 'emotional labour' (Hochschild, 1983) are of this nature in that they have a duality of reference both to subjective behaviour and to the objective social conditions under which they are worked out.

Secondly, there are concepts which denote the fact that certain kinds of social actor or personnel occupy strategic positions of control in social life such that they mediate the effects of systemic aspects of social life. Those holding positions of authority or influence in various organizations and settings are typically involved in these kinds of situations – for example, managers of firms, 'intermediaries' like critics, agents, personal managers, employers, and professionals of all kinds. The concept of 'typification' which expresses the mediating role of casting personnel in the careers of actors is exactly of this nature – as is Foucault's notion of 'surveillance' as it applies to relations of control and resistance between professional social workers and their clients (see Bloor and McIntosh, 1990).

Finally, there are concepts which characterize the nature of social relations that are significantly influenced by systemic features but which also express the nature of people's involvements and their motivations. Etzioni's (1961) distinctions between 'alienative', 'calculative' and 'moral' forms of involvement of participants in organizations are good examples of these kinds of bridging concept.

In general it can be appreciated that in slightly differing ways such concepts represent both the social systemic circumstances – the settings and contexts – which embed people's lives and activities at the same time as they reach into and depict some specific aspects of their behaviour, such as involvements, attitudes, motivations and relationships, which significantly reflect these circumstances. In this respect it is important that both criteria of subjective and analytic (or objective) adequacy play a role in determining their validity and usefulness as analytic devices. In this sense validity has to be judged in terms of the duality of reference of the concept – the genuinely combined effects of subjective and objective adequacy.

General or theoretician's concepts

To complete the overall picture let me touch on a fourth type of concept-indicator link which is often neglected by applied researchers because it is thought to be the sole province of specialists in general social theory. Another reason for its neglect is that it often goes unrecognized as part of the prior assumptions that researchers bring with them to their research. Thus some researchers claim to be 'uncommitted' theoretically or only interested in people's 'concrete', 'actual' behaviour and yet at the same time they draw upon general theoretical ideas to underpin their assumptions about the behaviour in question. Concepts used in this latter sense are perhaps the least interesting for present purposes, concerned as I am primarily with the intended theoretical possibilities that arise from data analysis, although they remain important in a more general sense. The main types of theoretician's concept are ones which derive from the armoury of particular theorists, approaches or schools of thought.

For example, Giddens's (1984) theory of 'structuration' is replete with concepts like 'the duality of structure', 'discursive conscious-ness', the 'dialectic of control', and so on. Habermas's (1984, 1987) theory of 'communicative action' includes concepts such as 'colon-ization of the lifeworld', 'system steering media' and 'strategic action'. Foucault's (1977, 1980) work depends heavily on the concepts of 'discourse', 'practice', 'power/knowledge', among others. My own 'theory of social domains' (Layder, 1997) includes concepts such as the 'duality of social relations', the 'dialectic of separateness and relatedness', 'primary consciousness', and so forth. In Chapter 5 I shall argue that social researchers should more readily draw such concepts into their research calculations in so far as they may enhance the possibilities for theoretical advance and generation. Here I want to stress the status of these concepts as depictions of social reality and indicate in a provisional manner the way in which they may be utilized in developing concepts and theoretical ideas from the analysis of data.

The first point to make about theoretician's concepts is that they are often disregarded because they are thought to be unconnected to the empirical world of 'real' facts and data. In this (erroneous) view the fact that such theory is expressed in a rather abstract form is confused with the idea that it is somehow disembodied or disengaged from the real world and floating in some ethereal world of pure intellect. This is not only a view that can be attributed to those who regard themselves as applied researchers and have no time for such 'ungrounded', 'fictional' narratives that (allegedly) bear no actual relation to the concrete social world, but unfortunately it is also a view that is perpetuated by some theorists who, although committed to the value of general theory, unwittingly underscore the faulty image of the nature and functions of abstract theoretical reasoning by choosing to describe it as 'meta-theory'. I feel that this is an unhelpful and misleading term and only gives ammunition to those who are ignorant about the nature of general theory and wish to devalue it. The term gives the false impression that abstract theory is somehow, and exclusively, theory about theory, and thus disengaged from the empirical 'core' or substance of the world. Nothing could be further from the truth and this is an impression which must be countered at every opportunity. In my view there is no such thing as meta-theory: there can never be just theory about theory since all theory is connected with the empirical world (although variably in terms of level of abstraction), otherwise it would not qualify as 'social theory' in the first place. The error here, as I have implied, is based on confusing a high level of abstraction with the idea of a lack of empirical content or reference. In this respect it must be recognized that there are different kinds of theory and levels of theorizing which connect with the empirical world of data, 'facts', and so on, in varying ways. The point about general theory (and discussions about its nature) is not that it is disengaged from the 'real' empirical world, but rather that it is couched at a fairly high level of abstraction and thus its relation to the world of empirical data is often oblique and/or indirect.

This is compounded by the idea that although one might want to discuss the nature of theorizing – which suggests that one is simply engaged in discourse about theorizing – this neglects the fact that such talk would be meaningless if it contained no reference to those aspects of the empirical world which are indicated by theoretical concepts. Of course this does not involve the claim that such theory or theoretical discourse is directly related to, or based on, fieldwork. Nonetheless, this in itself does not mean that it has no direct bearing on such empirical work, as is illustrated by many of the themes of this book. I contend that this issue is entirely separate from another (which is, in fact, part of the overall confusion) – that involved in the distinction between good and bad theorizing. Indeed, the central criterion by which we may judge the value of abstract general theory is the extent to which it throws light on the empirical world. Any theory (or, for that matter, talk about theory) which fails to do this would indeed qualify as 'defective', 'bad', or irrelevant theory.

Of course, this is the whole point of my inclusion of these kinds of concepts in this discussion about data analysis and the possibilities of theoretical construction or development that flow from it. In my view, all general theory is connected with the empirical world in some way. However, and this is the crucial point, general theories differ in terms of their degree of abstraction (and thus their apparent 'distance' from empirical matters) as well as in relation to the question of how they may be tested or adjudicated. Very often general theories cannot be tested in any simple or straightforward manner because they deal with matters that cannot be empirically 'measured' as easily as variables such as income, occupation, social standing, and so on. For example, Giddens's 'structuration theory', Habermas's 'theory of communicative action' and my own 'theory of social domains' are concerned with characterizing the nature of social activity and social institutions in a general sense, as well as teasing out some of the interrelations between different elements of social life. As such, it is not a straightforward matter to 'test-out' the respective adequacy or validity of the various axioms and propositions of these theories simply because such phenomena are not always empirically discrete, measurable or conducive to the yielding of unambigous evidence. This is not to say that there can be no reliable ways of going about checking the adequacy or validity of such concepts and theories, but rather it is to point to some of the complexities and subtleties involved.

Another issue that concerns theoretician's concepts is that of the criteria of adequacy or validity which we may bring to bear on them and this makes for some rather interesting comparisons with the other types of concept-indicator link I have identified. Clearly, many aspects of the notion of subjective adequacy are of little relevance here. For example, the issue of whether lay people or participants actually use or understand such concepts is of little or no pertinence because they are not actually participants' concepts (nor were they meant to be). By definition, they are analysts' (researchers', observers') concepts first and foremost, and as such the two most important criteria by which we may assess their validity concern first, the broader context of reasoning in which they are embedded and secondly, their relation to other competing or complementary concepts or theories. However, before saying more about these criteria, let me add to the point about subjective adequacy.

Above I was careful to say only that 'many' aspects of the notion of subjective adequacy are irrelevant to theoretician's concepts. There are other aspects of subjective adequacy which may or may not be relevant depending upon their intended purpose and the kinds of empirical phenomena that they are meant to indicate. In this respect theoretician's concepts may be classified in terms of the three I have already identified (behavioural, systemic and bridging) according to the phenomena they are designed to depict. For example, the notion of 'practical consciousness' is in some sense a behavioural concept in so far as it conveys something of people's lived experience. The typical distinguishing feature of theoretician's behavioural concepts is that they are usually highly abstract in nature – they attempt to depict the general nature of aspects of lived experience rather than specific and direct aspects. Other concepts may be of the bridging or systemic type and as such they will relate to the notion of subjective adequacy in the manner I have already indicated. That is, in general terms there will always be some connection with subjective adequacy since even purely systemic concepts contain residual references to the behaviour of the people living out their lives within the settings and contexts denoted by the concepts. It is a question of emphasis, as I have already suggested.

Although subjective adequacy has a variable role to play, there are two aspects of theoretician's concepts which often separate them in a fairly radical sense from the other concept-indicator links. Sometimes these differences are either ignored or overlooked. The first issue concerns the question of the extent to which social scientific concepts can be said to be absorbed by the lay community. Giddens (1984) in particular has argued that a distinguishing feature of social scientific concepts in general (as compared with the concepts of natural science) is that they are continually appropriated by ordinary common-sense usage. I think this is a serious exaggeration at best, and, at worst, simply incorrect. We only have to look at some of the concepts from structuration theory itself – 'the recursive nature of social life', 'the dialectic of control', 'the duality of structure', 'discursive consciousness' – to appreciate that many, if not most, concepts that derive from general theoretical systems have little if any chance of becoming the stock-in-trade of common-sense terminology. With very few exceptions it is far more accurate to say that theoretician's concepts are infrequently incorporated into everyday life even though many of them refer to aspects of lived experience.

This returns us to the criteria which do play a distinctive and crucial role in assessing the validity of such concepts. As I briefly mentioned above, these have to do with the wider context of the theory from which particular concepts are drawn and their relation to other competing or complementary concepts or theories. Both of these criteria draw attention to the distinctiveness of theoretician's concepts in that such concepts can never be assessed as if they stood simply in their own right as singular concepts. They always bear relations with other concepts through chains of reasoning either within the 'home' theory (or approach or school) or by comparison with other 'parallel' concepts drawn from other theories (approaches or schools). It is this discursive nature of the chains of reasoning and the wider contexts from which they are drawn that sets the terms under which validity must be assessed. This must include an evaluation of the links between concepts (their interconnectedness of meaning) and the range of questions/problems that are posed and answered within the remit of the different clusterings of concepts. For example, the concept of 'the dialectic of control' is just one aspect of Giddens's structuration theory and thus its 'meaning' is in part related to the theory as a whole. Although the concept can, in principle, be separated out and employed as if it was a singular, self-contained concept this is something of an illusion. Researchers must be careful not to overlook the 'extra baggage' of assumptions that are imported (from structuration theory) by the use of an individual concept. Conversely, significant 'damage' may be done to a concept if its wider connections and references are not properly taken into account. This is not a call to limit the use of such concepts. Quite the contrary. It is a plea to take serious account of the 'network nature' of general theoretical discourses.

Conclusion: some practical implications

As I pointed out in the introduction to this chapter, it is important to bear in mind the different levels at which concept-indicator links operate – as 'underlying' and 'surface' aspects of research activity. Of course it is important to be aware of the more surface features of these links, such as how do particular concepts like 'habitus' or 'emotional labour' match up to specific data, information or observable 'facts' in the empirical world. Being certain that there is a good fit between specific concepts and empirical indicators is essential for the production of sound research. However, my emphasis in this chapter has been on the more 'underlying' aspects of concept-indicator links, both because these are frequently neglected, and because by focusing on them they add another dimension to the analysis, thus making it richer and more dense.

The underlying aspects concern the status of concepts in relation to different features of social reality which lie behind their more empirically accessible 'surface' manifestations. As I have made plain, it is important to be clear about whether the phenomenon referred to by a particular concept is behavioural, systemic or bridging. This also involves judging the validity or adequacy of the concepts we use by rather different and more complex criteria than is usually the case. Very often methods texts view validity and adequacy as centring on the extent to which the researcher's account – a concept, an explanation, a set of findings – accurately represents the observed phenomenon (Silverman, 1993: 155–6). However, this account tends to presuppose two things: first, that the phenomenon is simply behavioural and secondly, that it is observable in the same sense as all human activity is potentially accessible and observable. This is because many methods texts view methodology from a 'humanist' standpoint (which includes interactionism, grounded theory, phenomenology and ethnomethodology) which does not acknowledge the partial independence of structural or systemic phenomena. Thus these perspectives are unable to conceptualize such phenomena or those that constitute 'bridges' between them and behavioural phenomena. Similarly, many perspectives (poststructuralism, postmodernism, structuration theory) deny that there are any real differences between behavioural and structural (or systemic) phenomena – sometimes for very different reasons (Layder, 1994, 1997). Thus these perspectives also are unable to deal with the very different aspects of social reality (agency-structure and macro–micro linkages) which underpin the empirical information and data that researchers analyse.

Moreover, many of these perspectives (structuration theory being a prominent exception) deny or devalue the importance of formal or general theory. They are unable to come to terms with the status and validity of theoretician's concepts and their important role in generating theory in the context of empirical research. It is important for researchers to be aware of social reality (social life) in a much broader – and deeper – sense than simply the immediate topic or area of interest. This makes for more sophisticated analyses both theoretically and empirically. Attending to the deeper ontological features of social life means moving beyond immediate substantive concerns in order to add to our understanding of them. Thus, awareness of these aspects of concept-indicator linkages aids both theory-generation from data analysis as well as the use of theory to guide data collection and analysis in the following ways:

1   It facilitates the generation of codes and concepts (provisional, core and satellite) for example, the concept of 'typification' as a bridging concept or 'emotional burn-out' as a behavioural concept.

2   By combining this awareness with the use of theoretical memos one is adding to the resources through which conceptual innovation may thrive.

3   Sensitivity and awareness of concept-indicator linkages contributes to a multi-strategy approach. Thus it generally enhances theoretical formulations when analysing data.

4   As I shall detail in Chapter 5, sensitivity to concept-indicator links informs the use of 'orienting' concepts and the subsequent choice of core and satellite concepts.

5   It helps to develop a sense of the different types of connection between concepts and social phenomena, thus fuelling the theoretical imagination.

6   It allows the researcher to gain insight into agency-structure and macro–micro interconnections in relation to particular substantive areas, topics or problems.

7   It allows the researcher to make connections between emergent theory and extant or a priori theory.

8   It contributes to the synergy between different elements necessary for adaptive theory (see Chapter 6). Specifically, it simultaneously aids the development of provisional theoretical models which guide and inform data analysis while allowing for the emergence of data and theoretical ideas which may lead to the reshaping (adapting or revising) of these provisional models.

CHAPTER 5

FROM THEORY TO DATA: STARTING TO THEORIZE

Before suggesting some strategies and techniques designed to help researchers generate theory, let me first give a provisional indication of the nature of theory and theorizing. First, theorizing involves the ability to think conceptually and analytically in order to be able to ask (and come up with) answers to how and why questions about social phenomena (including facts, data, information). In this sense theorizing is about providing *explanations* of social phenomena – accounts of why they exist and operate in the manner that they do and the form that they take in social life. This emphasis on explanation distinguishes theory and theorizing from other types of endeavour in social analysis, such as discovering or gathering information on people's attitudes or illustrating or describing social behaviour. Of course, the distinction between theorizing and these other activities is not always clear-cut. Providing explanations via the use of concepts and ideas often requires the deployment of evidence, elements of description, and so on in order to substantiate particular explanatory accounts. Conversely, a preoccupation with description often entails the use of relatively abstract concepts and other elements of explanation.

Secondly, in that theorizing involves thinking analytically and conceptually, it requires the application of logic and reason to tease out the relations between concepts and the empirical variables that they indicate. It also requires thinking through the relations between concepts and their dimensions or properties (for example, the logical relations between power and authority and the different forms that they take).

Thirdly, theorizing involves the ability to move from the concrete and particular (detailed observations or factual information) to more general and abstract concerns and ideas – that is, to shift to a concentration on the more general characteristics of the things one observes. This, in turn, involves a process of generalizing which requires the application of the same principles, standards and criteria across a broad range of situations and examples rather than limiting oneself to describing the details of particular situations, events or examples.

Finally, thinking theoretically involves tacking to and fro between different 'levels' of reality and analysis – the general and abstract and the concrete and particular. For example, in formal abstract terms the concept of power refers to the ability of a person or group to accomplish certain objectives and to get others to do things – despite any reluctance or resistance. However, theorizing requires the ability to grasp the connection (and thus to shuttle) between this formal definition and the particular instances or examples of power as they are manifested in social life – such as a bank robbery, the ability to purchase scarce goods or to give orders.

The use of orienting concepts

In a previous book (Layder, 1993) I refer to the use of 'background' concepts as a useful means of developing theory, although here I prefer the term 'orienting' concepts. Examples of these, taken at random from the sociological literature, are 'emotional labour', 'musical worlds', 'the dialectic of control', 'career', 'power and surveillance', 'organizational morality'. Two important features of orienting concepts are their '"two-sided" nature' and their reference to social processes. The two-sided nature of orienting concepts concerns their dual reference to objective and subjective aspects of social life. A concern with social processes focuses on their ability to trace social activity and events over time and space. I shall illustrate these in more detail later in the discussion. Here I want to focus on the fact that the use of such concepts can be used to 'crank start' the process of theory development in a piece of research.

First, let me say from where orienting concepts may be drawn in a broad sense (the kind of context from which they derive) and then go on to give some practical advice about how to choose one (or several) that may aid in the analysis and organization of data gathered during research. The first source from which they may be drawn is an existing body of theory – a theoretical framework or general theoretical perspective, such as Marxism, symbolic interactionism, feminism, structuration theory. This overlaps with another source – that of the work of particular authors who may be associated with the use of particular concepts (such as Bourdieu's concept of 'habitus') or particular meanings of concepts (such as Foucault's use of the concept of power). Clearly, these concepts may or may not be related to a wider body of theory. The point is that in either case particular concepts may be adopted from existing work and used as 'background concepts' to give direction and guidance in the initial stages of a new research project.

Finally, orienting concepts may be drawn from particular substantive or empirical areas of social analysis, such as suicide, medicine, education, occupations, class, and so on, in which particular concepts are routinely used in connection with particular topics. The concept of 'career' is a case in point. Normally 'career' is associated with careers in occupations, but, as various authors have shown, it can be usefully applied to a broad range of empirical phenomena. A useful distinction to bear in mind in this regard is that between 'practitioner defined' and 'sociologically defined' concepts. The former concern the sorts of labels and ideas that are used by the people who are the subjects of the research to define various aspects of their own activities – for example, Giallombardo's (1966) typology of women prison inmates. Socio-logically defined concepts are those constructed by the researcher, or previous researchers, in order to understand and organize the data they have collected on a particular group – for example the concepts of 'primary' and 'secondary deviance' or 'deviance amplification' (Lemert, 1962; Scheff, 1966). As such, these latter are more technically defined concepts chosen for their clarity, as well as their descriptive or explanatory powers.

Selecting orienting concepts

There are a number of strategies which may be employed that will help in the selection of orienting concepts that are appropriate for the area or problem under focus.

Consciously searching for concepts

Generally in searching for an appropriate concept one has to inten-sively scan the literature concerned with the topic at hand, and read it *with the conscious intention of looking for such concepts*. This is a very 'active' way of reading material in the sense that one is looking for something although one does not quite know at this point what it is that is being sought. It contrasts with the 'normal' mode of reading which involves the rather 'passive' absorption of information. I am not implying that reading does not generally engage the creativity of the reader – and in this sense the distinction between 'active' and 'passive' reading does not quite capture the point I am making. The important issue is that the search for an orienting concept entails an openness to unanticipated possibilities in terms of the objective of finding a suitable concept.

This further involves the ability to play around with received meanings by adapting or adding to them, or in some other way stretching their applicability beyond the range of empirical phenomena with which they are normally associated. It demands imaginative work and the channelling of creative energies in order to explore possibilities prior to the actual employment of specific concepts as orienting concepts. This is in direct contrast to a mode of reading which assumes that what is being read is a closed or finished product which is not amenable to reinterpretation or re-rendering in slightly different contexts of research or topic areas. This may sound rather abstract at present but it is an essential part of the process of theorizing or theoretical thinking and is an ability which (up to a point) can be acquired even if it is not a 'natural' part of the researcher's repertoire of skills. Throughout this chapter I shall be attempting to spell out in more detail exactly what is involved in these skills and how one might pursue the process of acquiring them.

Focusing on specific topics

One way of delineating an area which may yield background concepts is to focus on a specific topic such as patient care, racialization, mental illness, or deviance. Many such areas are already well established and researched and therefore will include an array of formal and substantive concepts relating to the accepted forms of theory and explanation as well as the body of evidence relating to the topic, group or context in question. For example, in the area of the sociology of mental illness there are a number of theoretical concepts and approaches such as 'labelling theory', 'residual deviance', 'primary and secondary deviance', 'deviance amplification', all of which have been used to explain various forms of mental illness (such as schizophrenia, paranoia, depression). Incidentally, these same concepts and approaches have been used and are applicable to other areas of deviance analysis, such as illicit activities of a sexual and criminal nature. Also, there is a large data base of information about the incidence of mental illnesses among various groups (such as men and women from different socio-economic classes) as well as their use of medical and other services in relation to these illnesses.

As I say, each established substantive area (like the sociology of mental illness) will typically have a body of concepts, approaches and information attached to it. However, it must be remembered that the 'area' in which the researcher is interested may not be defined directly by a neatly compartmentalized area of sociology. Research areas in the social domain are often diffuse and multi-faceted, and may be defined by a number of cross-cutting or complementary disciplinary interests, each with its own distinctive literature. In the above example the specific topic may be covered by several disciplines and the relevant literature may be found under community medicine, psychiatry, and so on. By surveying the whole range of literature pertinent to the area being researched, one will subject oneself to the main organizing principles, ideas and concepts which serve to give this area or topic its unique identity and coherence as a discrete body of knowledge.

In order to identify potential orienting concepts it is best to try to pinpoint the *key concepts* that define the area in question. That is, concepts which are recurrently employed in the literature as basic organizing devices in terms of tried-and-tested explanations and accounts of the behaviour, events and data that fall within the rubric of the area or topic in question. By identifying these concepts one has a provisional anchorage point in the search for a useful orienting concept. It may be a key concept itself (such as 'residual deviance') that may start the process of theorizing, but equally likely it may simply be the prompt from which one can derive more specific concepts and ideas. Later on I shall give some examples of the development of subsidiary concepts which have an organic relation with orienting concepts. The point here is that the key concepts in any particular area will not necessarily be formally defined or in a form which is 'already theoretical' – for instance, they may simply be words or phrases typically employed to describe particular aspects of data. That is, the background concept may not present as a formally defined idea ready-made for one's own specific purposes. All in all, the potential resource base from which a suitable orienting concept may be chosen will be composed of a rag-bag assortment of words, ideas, accounts, frameworks, phrases, and so on, which represent the established and recurrent ways of talking about the area in question. In this sense they are the key organizing principles of that substantive area.

Borrowing concepts from adjacent areas

The above comments apply particularly to those areas which have already been researched in a fairly thorough and systematic manner. However, even if the area or topic in question has not been researched before, it is possible to tap into a literature that may yield potential orienting concepts. This is because there will always be an *adjacent* technical – or other – literature (either within a particular discipline like sociology or from an adjacent discipline in the context of multi-disciplinary research) from which one can borrow orienting ideas and concepts. Although one may be starting research on a topic about which there is little or no existing information, the research topic or project has to be viewed in the context of a comparative outlook or perspective. By this means it becomes possible to understand how any and every topic is surrounded by 'adjacent' areas (within or between disciplines – in the case of multi-disciplinary work) which are intrinsically related to the focal area of one's own research. Thus the couching of initial ideas about a research project in terms of a comparative perspective is an essential ingredient of the theorizing process in general.

The following example highlights some of the issues involved here. In starting my own research on actors' careers I was faced with the fact that very little research had been done on the sociology of acting. However, by looking comparatively at this topic I could see that it intersected with a number of different but related areas, all of which had their own body of literature attached to them. For instance, there was a large body of literature on other kinds of occupational careers, particularly bureaucratic and managerial types of careers. There was also a large literature on the general sociology of occupations from which useful ideas could be culled about occupational organization as it contrasted with the acting profession. Furthermore, the notion of career is related to questions surrounding the sociology of labour markets, about which there was an extensive literature and body of theoretical ideas. I also found the area of formal organization studies to be a productive literature from which to borrow ideas and orienting concepts, as well as the more general areas of power and authority. Clearly, all these areas overlap with each other (some more than others) but, most importantly for my purposes, they represented satellite areas of established research and study surrounding my area of interest which in itself was largely unresearched and thus was largely without an analytic literature.

In this sense I was lucky to have such a wealth of adjacent areas to draw from, but the same principle could be applied to almost any other unresearched area. For instance, although a particular form of deviance (sexual, criminal or whatever) may not as yet have been subjected to study, other areas of deviance have generated a number of theoretical concepts and approaches. Also, it is important not to restrict one's comparative perspective to other 'similar' examples. In the case of deviance it is important to compare one's focal topic of interest not only with other similar ones – for example, say a particular form of 'perverted' sexual behaviour, with other kinds of sexual deviation – but also with others that are quite different. For example, comparing sexual deviance with, say, mental illness (considered as a form of deviant behaviour) will have the effect of broadening the flexibility and utility of concepts and forms of description 'originally' pertinent to a particular example. That is to say, the more dissimilar the points of comparison one can make, the more likely it is that one will begin to modify and create new ways of thinking theoretically about an area.

Searching non-theoretical and non-technical literature

As the above examples have indicated, it is crucial not to confine oneself strictly to ideas and concepts which already have a theoretical 'pedigree'. As I have tried to emphasize, sources of theoretical thinking are not simply limited to things which look promising because they already seem to have a theoretical 'feel' or 'look' to them. Words and phrases and straightforward empirical facts or information may be important sources of orienting concepts. In this respect it is also important to consult the bodies of non-theoretical and non-technical (sociological) literature as potential sites for orienting concepts. All manner of books (fiction and non-fiction), magazines, documents, videos, and so on, provide a more general literature on particular topics and may be sources of insight which have eventual theoretical significance. It is important not to rule them out simply because they do not have an apparent or formal connection with the sociological literature.

Of course, the literature I am referring to here will be directly related to the area in question and will have been chosen because of this, even though it may have no obvious connections with social research. Furthermore, sifting through this kind of literature should be a systematic and planned procedure rather than a haphazard and adventitious enterprise, otherwise much time and effort may be wasted. However, it is important not to underestimate the role of accidental factors in this kind of search. The principle of serendipity can play an essential part by producing the chance discovery of concepts and ideas, so the aspiring analyst must be constantly aware of the potential for such discoveries in literature (or even conversations) of every kind at any time and place.

Intuition, perception and sensitivity

As I said earlier, orienting concepts can only be identified as a result of deliberate choice through 'active' reading and sifting through information found in the relevant literature. In order for such concepts to suggest themselves – to impress themselves on your thinking – three things are required: intuition, perception and sensitivity or 'readiness'. Taken together, these three represent a predisposition to 'lock-on' to suggestive ideas and concepts. Intuition is an important means through which theoretical ideas and concepts can be detected. Very often such abilities are frowned upon by those who believe that social analysis and theoretical advance are entirely dependent on rational modes of thought. This is usually coupled with the view that only rational modes of thought are 'properly' scientific. Such a view is baseless. Scientific analyses rely on both rational and intuitive modes of thought and this insight must be incorporated into our general approaches to theorizing. Intuition is allied to the ability to perceive or apprehend useful orienting concepts and ideas, and this is a skill which can and must be developed and refined; it is not something that researchers automatically possess, even if they have a great deal of experience.

Perception involves homing-in on particular features of the world and excluding others. It involves identifying particular patterns or configurations of elements and thus viewing the world in certain ways. In the case of identifying orienting concepts, one is seeing the relevance of certain forms of description or explanation for the understanding of data, behaviour or research problems.

The combined effects of intuition and perception result in a general sensitivity or readiness to 'see' concepts and thereby to identify or discover them in one's reading matter. This, I cannot overemphasize, is an essentially creative enterprise in which one has to sensitize oneself to the possibilities. The concepts are not simply there in the literature waiting to be discovered, they are in a special sense 'constructed' by the person who is searching for them in that it is the researcher's willingness and ability to spot them that actually induces their discovery!

This leads on to a point which relates not only to the search for orienting concepts but also to the more general aspects of theorizing, particularly the development, extension, elaboration and refinement of concepts and conceptual frameworks about which I shall say more later. This connects us to the point about intuition and creativity as normal features of theorizing and concerns the issue of discontinuity or the experience of 'fallow' periods. There will naturally be periods in which little happens in the way of the development of new ideas or the spotting of fresh conceptual tools. Such fallow periods may be short-lived, temporary breaks but, conversely, a gap may turn out to be long and daunting. However long a gap, it is important to remember that such breaks in continuity are 'normal' features of the theorizing process. To experience such a gap does not imply that the ability to theorize has suddenly disappeared never to reappear; it just means that the whole process will be uneven and somewhat unpredictable.

As I hinted before, this is because theorizing is not simply a logical process dependent on rational skills which can be controlled at will, rather like turning a tap on and off. Although there is a good deal in theorizing which requires the application of formal powers of reasoning, the process also requires just as much intuitive, creative and imaginative skill. As I said in the opening section, theorizing involves the ability to shuttle between the general (abstract) and the particular (concrete) and this requires creativity. In other words, to be able to combine formal analysis with the handling of empirical material in ways that are likely to produce novel forms of explanation is very much akin to the creative imagination. In this particular sense, being able to theorize has more in common with artistic or creative activity rather than strictly with a rational, logical and formal scientific approach.

The analogy with artistic inspiration is a useful way of understanding the elements and skills that are involved in theorizing. Like painters and writers, the need for inspiration is an essential part of theorizing but by its very nature inspiration is not something that is constant and can be summoned up at will. Sometimes inspiration just runs out and it cannot simply be turned on again. At these times the researcher needs to be patient and diligent to carry her or him through these fallow periods. However, developing one's sensitivity and readiness and being prepared and predisposed to cues will help to ensure that the period of 'drought' will not be too prolonged.

The role of orienting concepts in research

Orienting concepts are most useful as *provisional* means of ordering data. By using orienting concepts one is able to deal with the problem of how to bring some provisional order to a mass of data or information. This can be a problem at different stages for different kinds of research. For example, with qualitative research on an area in which there has been little previous work and which is aimed wholly at theoretical discovery (rather than extension and replication), this kind of problem will often arise as the researcher gathers more and more data, say through in-depth interviews. It may be clear to the researcher which people she or he needs to talk to and the general sorts of topic she or he wants to cover. However, because this exploratory kind of research is not underpinned by a well-established body of theory or a sizeable research data base, it may be difficult to anticipate the relevant concepts that will help to shape and lend some order on the data that is being amassed. Indeed, instead of becoming clearer about what the data means, its steady accumulation may produce uncertainty and confusion as competing or contradictory bits of information come to light. In this sense the orienting concept enables the researcher to impose meaningful patterns on the data in a provisional way. Such an initial conceptual organization of the data allows the researcher to begin to code the interview transcripts, thus facilitating interpretation of the data and reducing their volume at the same time. As I shall go on to argue, the initial orienting concept may turn out to be a temporary means of imposing order on the data and may be supplanted or modified later on. Nonetheless, while in use it serves as a way of defining what is relevant and not relevant in the data.

If the concept, category or idea is dispensed with later on, it may be necessary to go back to the data and re-code it around different categories. In my own research I dropped the concept of 'positive type-casting' in favour of the concept of 'typification'. It can be appreciated that in this kind of research scenario the usefulness of orienting concepts is associated with the ongoing nature of the research once the data collection has begun in earnest. In areas which have already been well researched, the research process begins from an accredited body of knowledge, information and theoretical ideas. In this case (which, incidentally, more often requires quantitative materials as a form of supporting evidence), orienting concepts or conceptual schemes will be of use prior to the data collection stage since much of the data collection will be shaped around the theoretical questions that are being posed in the research.

At this point it might well be worthwhile to highlight the similarities and differences between what I have termed orienting or background concepts and what are known as 'sensitizing concepts' in the social research methods literature. Blumer (1954) introduced the term 'sensitizing concepts' in order to bring out a contrast with 'definitive' concepts. Such concepts are not as precisely defined as definitive ones and are not associated with a rigorous objective scientific approach (positivism) which is concerned with the formulation and testing of laws of behaviour. Instead, sensitizing concepts are more flexible and shape up to the variability and unpredictability that derive from the meaningful nature of human behaviour and which, as a result, does not conform to universal laws. Thus, the notion of a sensitizing concept is inherently wedded to the view that social analysis is a humanistic and interpretative endeavour (see also Giddens, 1984).

It is the flexibility of sensitizing concepts that indicates an affinity with orienting concepts. However, this flexibility is rather more pronounced than is the case with sensitizing concepts because orienting concepts are not tied to the idea that social analysis is exclusively about the analysis or interpretation of actors' meanings.

The notion of an orienting concept has a greater potential range of application than this in so far as it is associated with a vision of social analysis which is both about non-acting social phenomena, such as social systems, structures, cultural knowledge, and so on, as well as active, intentional and reflexive human agents.

This position is sometimes referred to as social scientific realism (Layder, 1990, 1993). This is not the place to elaborate on this view of social analysis but it does highlight the way in which a post-positivist (or post-empiricist) social science cannot be content simply to adopt a hermeneutic or interpretative stance as is the case with many modern schools of theory, including postmodernism and structuration theory. Most crucial to the realist position defined in these terms is the need to separate out the different but connected properties and effects of agency and structure (Archer, 1995; Layder, 1993, 1997).

In this sense, then, the notion of an orienting concept may refer to aspects of human behaviour ('lifeworld' in Habermas's terms (1984, 1987)) or of social structures ('systems' as Habermas refers to them) or both, and I have already dealt with an example of what I call bridging concepts. Another crucial difference between orienting and sensitizing concepts is the fact that the former are rather more to do with suggesting or indicating (although not forcing) patterns upon data as a means of dealing with the ongoing problems of data collection and interpretation. Sensitizing concepts have a much looser connection with the data in the sense that they either fit or do not fit the data concerned. The purpose of an orienting concept is primarily heuristic and suggestive of further lines of inquiry even if it is dispensed with in the long run. Also, once an orienting concept has withstood the test of confrontation with more and more evidence, its purpose is then to provide a centrepoint for conceptual extension and theoretical elaboration (see later comments). By contrast, sensitizing concepts tend to stand alone and thus have a less firm relation to the building of systematic theory.

In one particular sense, then, orienting concepts are more *directive* of theoretical inquiry than *indicative* of the fit between particular concepts and data. This directive function is related to what I have otherwise referred to as suggesting a pattern for, or ordering, the research data in some way – either before data collection as a prior conceptual framework, or as a continuous and emergent feature of data collection and analysis. Also, as I previously indicated, this should not and does not necessarily mean forcing the data into preconceived categories (see Glaser, 1994 for critical comments on 'forcing'). Imposing a pattern does not irrevocably commit one to a conceptual standpoint irrespective of feedback from data, and in this sense there is no unnecessary forcing of data into alien categories. Nonetheless, there is a need to get the theoretical imagination started by trying out provisional conceptual schemes. This is a basic flaw with the pure grounded theory point of view which seems to imply that it is possible to start theorizing from a completely atheoretical point of view (Glaser and Strauss, 1967; Strauss, 1987; Glaser, 1994).

It is better to be consciously aware and reflective of one's theoretical assumptions and prejudices than to imagine that a researcher starts afresh every time she or he begins a piece of research. Furthermore, it is surely sounder to suggest that theorizing, of necessity, has to be the outcome of both conceptual appropriation of data (deduction) as well as conceptual induction from data rather than to argue that data alone gives us our theoretical categories independently of the prior interpretative (theoretical) judgements of researchers. Anyway, as I shall go on to argue, to reject existing theory as a priori and thus irrelevant to research and to the anchoring and grounding of theory in the empirical world is a waste of extant theoretical ideas and concepts which have proven to be of lasting value.

Given, then, that orienting concepts are geared towards the imposition of a specific order on data, we can see that this has the effect of suggesting certain ideas. First, orienting concepts suggest forms of explanation of the data by providing specific descriptions and 'slants' on the evidence that has been uncovered. In short, the concept or idea will suggest that the behaviour, events or social structures under scrutiny occur for specific reasons. Secondly, such concepts suggest lines of empirical inquiry which are as yet untried. This may apply to the beginning of a research project by outlining a specific set of objectives or a plan of the research in advance of any investigative activity. However, it may also apply at various ongoing stages of the research in that the use of an orienting concept may suggest alternative lines of inquiry to those that have so far been pursued. More routinely, the use of orienting concepts in ongoing research has the effect of indicating which topics, areas and people should be investigated next.

Finally, orienting concepts are (hopefully) suggestive of further concepts that will feed into an emerging theory as the result of different mixes of deduction and induction. The latter implies that the emerging theory may be primarily the result of empirical inquiry (giving rise to the kind of grounded theory originally envisaged by Glaser and Strauss (1967)). Conversely, it may have been given its initial impetus from a concentration on the implications of various lines of theoretical inquiry. It has to be remembered that from the point of view of the argument offered here both of these options are not to be understood in pure terms. That is, there is no such thing as pure induction or deduction. There are only various mixes or combinations of the two – albeit sometimes weighted or skewed towards one side or the other of the empirical and theoretical equation. In my view, this is a matter of emphasis since all empirical investigation is replete with theoretical assumptions and directives. Conversely, all theory is in some sense 'grounded' in reality otherwise it would cease to be properly theoretical. What distinguishes different kinds of grounded theory is their level of empirical anchorage, their degree of abstraction and their explanatory power.

Although the point of orienting concepts is to suggest lines of inquiry and theoretical thinking, they have to be thought of as entirely provisional in nature. What they provide is a route into the interpretation and analysis of data at a relatively early stage of the research. The great virtue of their provisional nature is that as more and more data are gathered, the original concept may recede in importance and may be dropped altogether, especially if a more appropriate one is found. In so far as the original concept begins to recede in importance, this may be because it is evolving or transmuting in some way as a result of its 'measurement' against the emerging evidence. This transmutation may not be positive in that the usefulness of the concept may depreciate over time and thus have to be abandoned in the long run. On the other hand, it may be entirely positive, eventuating in new ideas and concepts with greater explanatory and descriptive powers better suited to the research task at hand.

It is also possible, of course, that the original orienting concept will grow in strength and gather importance as the research proceeds. It is therefore important to stress that flexibility means there should be room for it to grow both internally, as a development of its own properties and characteristics, and organically, with the research as a whole. Thus, the provisional nature of orienting concepts has to be understood in two senses. First, as potentially dispensable in the long run and secondly, as having no preconceived form which is fixed and immutable in the short run. In the second sense, one is referring to the inherent plasticity of the concept. On the other hand, although such concepts are intrinsically capable of being transformed or remoulded to suit modified circumstances, this does not mean that this will necessarily be the case. The growing importance of the concept during the unfolding of the research may indicate that much of the original form and explanatory power of the concept is progressively confirmed. Thus its growth in strength will result from an increasing sense of its extant credibility in the context of the research.

Whatever reason there may be for the persistence and continuing relevance of the orienting concept, it is of paramount importance that it (or 'they' in the case of several) should not dominate the analysis in a dictatorial manner. Orienting concepts must always be employed flexibly, with an eye to ongoing data collection or emerging theoretical ideas, and must not become 'sacrosanct' or part of an analytic dogma that has the effect of suppressing new ideas, concepts or lines of inquiry. The orienting concept will thus function as a provisional *core category* – an analytic unit around which coding and analysis of data will take place. However, unlike the meaning that Glaser and Strauss attach to the notion of a core category, I do not mean that this automatically becomes the central idea (concept, category) around which the rest of the analysis and other concepts revolve. A core category in Glaser and Strauss's terms is one which is arrived at only after a fair amount of data collection and provisional (open) coding and analysis. For them, the core categories emerge from ongoing data collection and analysis and this procedural sequence fits in with their idea that grounded theory must avoid using preconceived theory (or concepts) because it automatically presumes relevancies in the data in advance of data-gathering.

However, the whole thrust of the approach I am here advocating is to encourage this kind of presumption of relevancies in the data as a means of crank-starting the process of theorizing. The only way in which such a procedure may become a problem in terms of 'forcing' data is when the orienting concepts are used in a dictatorial and inflexible manner. Glaser and Strauss's insistence that theory should emerge strictly from data in order to claim that it is properly grounded amounts to a form of dogmatism in that it precludes other ways of proceding on a priori grounds. In particular, it refuses to confront the uncomfortable fact that it is only possible to begin analysing, theorizing and explaining aspects of social life if one is already in possession of certain assumptions and ideas about the social world. By avoiding this 'fact' one is surreptitiously importing underlying assumptions, values, prejudices and theoretical predispositions towards the social world into one's analysis, perhaps without even realizing it. The approach I advocate here treats seriously the philosophical premise that observation is always saturated with theoretical ideas and makes a virtue out of this fact by treating it in a systematic manner.

My approach reverses Glaser and Strauss's emphasis by insisting that we can start with preconceived theory in the form of orienting concepts and still claim that the theory is empirically anchored. I say 'anchored' and I would claim that this actually includes the notion of groundedness in data. However, it also has an advantage over the term 'grounded' (as in 'grounded theory') in that this seems to imply an exclusively empiricist position. Starting out with preconceived theory does not mean that it enforces a rigid or pre-determined explanatory grid on the data. Whether this actually happens really depends upon how the theory or concepts are used and whether the pitfalls and dangers of its dogmatic or dictatorial use are routinely attended to as part of the ongoing research and analysis. Glaser and Strauss's position has a great deal in common with other theorists of a humanist, interactionist or phenomenological persuasion who insist that prior theory (in the form of concepts or theoretical frameworks) should play no formal part in social research and analysis (Bruyn, 1966; Blumer, 1969; Becker and Rock in Rock, 1979).

But this attitude also overlaps with the work of both feminist and postmodernist authors who reject the notion of theory because of its alleged link with an inherently objectivist and scientistic approach which negates the authentic voices of those who are being studied (Stanley and Wise, 1983; Rosenau, 1992). Similarly, postmodernists like Foucault, Lyotard and Baudrillard eschew theory as an example of the illicit use of general theory or meta-narratives. In my view these criticisms are mistaken, misplaced, premature and forlornly inadequate as a means of coming to terms with a post-empiricist and post-positivist social science. My own position rests on a strong defence of the importance and efficacy of modern social theory as it is continuous with both the classic project of sociology and the empirical and theoretical traditions it endorses (see Layder, 1997). In this sense my position aligns itself with those of other critics of postmodernism and relativism (see Alexander, 1995; Archer, 1995; Bryant, 1995; Mouzelis, 1995).

To defend a moderate form of objectivism (see Alexander, 1995; Layder, 1997) as a means of coming to terms with the interconnections between lifeworld and systemic features of social life (including the intertwined contributions of agency and structure) does not entail the derogation of lay actors as Giddens (1979) claims. Nor does the use of formal and general theory suppress or negate the lived experiences or local narratives of research subjects, as postmodernists and feminist relativists are prone to claim. In fact, adherence to a moderate objectivism, coupled with the employment of general theory, opens up the range of applicability and the accessibility of knowledge by adopting a generalizing frame of reference. Such a frame of reference is capable of incorporating the meaningful, intersubjective worlds of people while simultaneously registering the social forms, structures, institutions, culture, knowledge, and so on, that stretch beyond and form a backdrop to elements of the lifeworld (Popper (1972) terms these 'World 3' phenomena).

To dismiss formal concepts and general theory is as much a waste of good extant theoretical ideas as is Glaser and Strauss's insistence that the only important or efficacious kind of theory is that which is grounded and generated from within specific research projects (and is thus restricted to registering the phenomenal worlds of people). Such stances lead to a disastrous waste of a wealth of theoretical materials because they overlook or simply ignore concepts and theoretical ideas that have, in the past, proven themselves to be useful explanatory devices. As such, the potential applicability of these concepts and ideas in contemporary research and analysis as ways of understanding, interpreting or organizing newly gathered empirical information is simply foregone. Also, proscribing the use of such extant theoretical materials means that their potential as fruitful feeders, pathways or conduits for the emergence and development of new theoretical ideas and approaches is ignored. For example, consider the following theoretical ideas taken (randomly) from the work of Marx, Durkheim and Weber.

- *Weber* – Bureaucracy; bureaucratic control; hierarchy; administratively defined statuses and careers; codified rules and regulations; rationalization.
- *Marx* – Relations of production; mode of production; economic infrastructure; class domination; class conflict; ideology; exploitation.
- *Durkheim* – Organic and mechanical solidarity; degree of integration; anomie; types and causes of suicide; collective consciousness; individuation; division of labour.

I point to these simply as convenient examples, but in principle one could draw up a fairly lengthy list of comparable concepts and ideas drawn from the work of more recent authors such as Parsons, Merton, Gouldner, Foucault, Goffman, Habermas, Giddens, and so on. I am suggesting that we should creatively use such prior theoretical concepts, frameworks and ideas in the guise of orienting concepts to see what they may yield in terms of what I shall term their 'expanded' explanatory domain and scope. By employing them as orienting concepts one is implicitly exploring the question of the extent to which they can help to explain research problems for which they were not originally designed or intended. That is, one is ascertaining whether they fit, or are suitable for, the analysis of new research problems and/or empirical areas, such as the 'adjacent' areas mentioned earlier. In this sense we are asking whether these ideas, approaches or concepts can be reformulated, expanded upon, amended or extended in relation to new empirical data or new topics of inquiry. Also, by making the analyst reshape concepts according to varying empirical circumstances, the received theory may undergo a process of metamorphosis and become recreated in an alternate form as different research conditions dictate. However, we can never know these metamorphosed forms unless we try out or apply the original concepts and ideas in the first place. Unless we test the flexibility of the preconceived theoretical ideas we shall never know what they can yield in terms of the transmutations they may undergo and the lines of theoretical and empirical inquiry that they may generate as a consequence.

My whole argument here is designed to augment the cumulative nature of sociological knowledge in general. I have suggested that only by joining together theoretical ideas in the context of research (and thereby encouraging fissuring and elaboration) can overall effort be concerted in a cumulative manner. Thus I have argued against both the atheoretical and anti-theoretical strands of postmodernism, feminism and relativism, as well as the anti-formalism of grounded theory, on the basis that they do nothing to help in the accumulation of sociological knowledge. This is principally because they sever social analysis from any basis in, or continuity with, 'tradition' in the form of an extant body of established theories, concepts and frameworks. Those anti-theoretical strands which eschew general theory simply make a radical break with all elements of sociological orthodoxy and tradition and are thus left with the insuperable problem of reconstituting sociological knowledge *ex nihilo*.

It is important to avoid these culs-de-sac and dead-ends by fashioning a continuity with the whole panoply of sociological thought. For researchers to cut off contact with both modern and classical thinkers and the extant theory that has shaped sociological consciousness is actively to facilitate the fragmentation of sociological knowledge. Thus as Merton (1967) pointed out some time ago, such a tendency creates respected little islands of knowledge rather than aiding the overall accumulation of theory and research. Although Glaser and Strauss are aware of this problem and stress the need to move from 'substantive' to what they term 'formal' theory, their overall approach rejects all forms of general theory and the use of preconceived theory. Such a position reinforces the fragmentation of sociological knowledge by privileging one particular form of theory-research connection.

Theory elaboration

Let me now move on to the question of how one may generate theory and concepts by the theoretical elaboration of orienting concepts. This leads into the development of conceptual frameworks and more inclusive theoretical ideas since very often adequate explanatory or descriptive accounts demand the employment of networks of associated concepts rather than the use of single concepts or a few weakly related ones. By elaborating from core orienting concepts and categories one is maximizing the strength of the links between the original concepts and the ones that emerge subsequently. The notion of a 'core' concept helps us think in terms of a web or network of interrelated concepts which radiate outwards from this core.

The point is to develop a primitive conceptual framework fairly early on in data-gathering and analysis. Some of the other concepts in the web may already be suggested or worked out in some way in the existing literature – for example, Weber's conception of bureaucratic organization is associated with a number of related concepts such as hierarchy, career, formally defined statuses, and so on. While these may help, there is a danger that they may encourage the researcher to fit or force the data into preconceived categories simply because they are already 'available' and therefore do not require further theoretical labour, so to speak. In this sense they have to be employed in their present form with caution.

More important for the development of theory and theoretical lines of thinking is the fact that cognate concepts can be generated and derived from core concepts in three main ways. First, they can be derived logically and deductively from the core concept (or concepts). Secondly, related or elaborated concepts may be derived from empirical work – the uncovering of data or information – and thus will rest primarily on an inductive procedure. It has to be emphasized that neither of these processes should be understood as purely inductive or purely deductive – there are always elements of both in any analytic procedure. What they refer to, then, is a situation where the weight or balance of emphasis in a particular example is on one or the other of these processes. Thus the third and perhaps most common possibility is where there is some relatively equal combination of both.

Primary elaboration

As I said, it is best to think of the core concept as the centre of a potential web from which the others extend outwards. Initially, how these other concepts relate to the core does not matter – this is where the creative element of theory development enters the equation. At the start all that matters is to identify a number of concepts that appear to be related to the core, concepts which could be described as satellites around the core. In practical terms this simply involves making a list of possible concepts by thinking through the rami-fications and implications of the core in a logical way. The best method to use is to think of them as further dimensions, properties and characteristics that are implied by the core.

For example, say the researcher had been influenced by Hochschild's (1983) study of emotional labour (particularly as it is

demanded in certain occupations, such as airline flight attendants)
and subsequently decided that the concept of 'emotional labour' was
to be a core analytic feature in a particular research project. By
carefully reading through Hochschild's study of flight attendants and
thinking through the implications of this concept in more general
terms, one could come up with a list such as the one below. First, one
could set out the general dimensions of emotional labour which I
have labelled as 'sources', 'consequences' and 'structural aspects' of
emotional labour. I have then gone on to list categories and concepts
that are related to each of these general dimensions.

- *Sources* – Company demands (for emotional labour); interactional
  (passenger) demands; social-psychological pressure.
- *Consequences* – Emotional overload; emotional burn-out; true
  and false emotion; true and false selves; self-projection and
  presentation.
- *Structural aspects* – Occupation, work (requiring emotional
  labour) gendered jobs.

I do not claim these are exhaustive or necessarily the ones that other
researchers would come up with, and therefore to some extent they
reflect my own interests and preoccupations. However, they are
meant to illustrate the theme of theoretical elaboration. To give
another illustration, if the core concept was 'career', then one could
list the following:

- *Signs of progress* – Benchmarks; status sequences (start-point, end-
  point); nature of progress (clearly defined or ambiguous and
  fuzzy); certainty/uncertainty of outcome; pace of progress (time
  and space).
- *Contingencies* – Momentous occasions; fateful moments; crisis
  points; turning points; changes in self-identity.
- *Control* – Who controls the career (doctors over the illness careers
  of patients, agents over actors); mode of control; balance of power
  (the career of a marriage or partnership).
- *Context* – Objective/subjective careers; formal/informal, market-
  defined/employer- or organization-defined (actors versus civil
  servants); continuity/discontinuity; multiple careers (work,
  illness, leisure, lifestyle, partnerships); overlapping contexts
  (number of); nature of interconnection.

By listing things in this manner one is teasing out the implicit
subsidiary concepts that are associated with the core concept of
career. There are two levels involved in this example. The main
dimensions of career analysis I have listed are signs of progress,

contingencies, control and context. Of course, as the list implies, the notion of career here has a wide range of applicability, being relevant to both occupational (or work) careers as well as a number of other kinds of social activities and involvements such as criminal or deviant careers, illness careers, careers of relationships, and so on. The concept applies to any social activity which involves sequences of status changes over time on the way to some definite end-point (or terminal status). The list, therefore, might function as an initial guide to help decide which general areas are to be taken into account in undertaking an analysis with 'career' as an orienting concept. The more refined listings alongside each of the main categories help in defining the more detailed characteristics and properties of these principal dimensions.

I have adopted some of these dimensions and properties from Glaser and Strauss's (1971) work, although I should point out that I have considerable doubts about their overall approach both methodologically and theoretically (see Layder, 1990, 1993, 1997). Because the area has been fairly well worked over, many of the dimensions and properties have been used before in some guise or other, and can be identified by a thorough search of the literature. However, in bringing them together in certain ways *and in relation to* specific research contexts, problems and objectives, one can begin to generate new perspectives on particular problems. Simply writing them down as a list prompts the theoretical imagination and the process of developing a network or webbing of interrelated concepts.

The development of such a network allows one to tackle questions which are fundamentally theoretical in nature. That is, such a starting point allows us to ask how and why questions about the area in question as well as to provide provisional answers to such questions. However, as I have just indicated, the whole dynamic of the process is fuelled by the application of this theoretical thinking to the empirical problem or area in question and it is the interplay between the two that generates the elaboration of (empirically) anchored theory. For instance, the dimensions and properties of emotional labour, as I have listed them above, relate primarily to Hochschild's study of airline flight attendants (mainly women). But the concept of emotional labour can be of relevance to a number of other research areas. School teaching or nursing require emotional labour in very different occupational contexts, while other facets of social life require other kinds of emotional involvements, such as partnerships, marriages, friendships – even relations between casual acquaintances or the 'unacquainted' (strangers), require variable levels of emotional commitment (or distancing).

Depending upon exactly which empirical problem or area one is focusing on, one can begin to group or cluster concepts around the specific empirical problem in question. For example, if school teaching was the focus, one could ask questions about the nature of the emotional labour involved. To what extent is it like or unlike that required of flight attendants? To what extent are there equivalents of 'company demands' on teachers? That is, do teachers' employers specifically concentrate on the development of emotion-work skills with children as they do with airline passengers? To what extent do commercial considerations play a role in the respective levels and types of emotional labour involved? Is this related to the issue of true and false emotions and the associated problems of feelings towards self and self-presentation? This sets up a hypothesis worthy of investigation; that is, one might surmise that there are fewer problems relating to sincerity of emotional expression and consequent feelings of 'inauthenticity' for school teachers as compared with flight attendants. This might be related to the extent of commercial pressure, the nature of the client group (adults versus children), the nature of the work task (servicing the material needs of passengers versus catering for the educational, moral, psychological and emotional needs of children).

These questions can then be cross-referenced with other questions, such as to what extent are the concepts of 'emotional overload' and 'burn-out' applicable to school teachers? If they are, are we dealing with exactly the same phenomena as compared with other occupations, say flight attendants or company executives? Again, for example, one might want to investigate the supposition that emotional overload and burn-out may result from pressure of work and the moral responsibilities of teachers rather than from pressure to be falsely sincere and friendly, which is seemingly more pertinent to the more commercialized contexts. In this manner, the exact empirical circumstances affect the sorts of questions that become pertinent and as a consequence these affect the manner in which the cluster or grouping of concepts begins to take shape. The concepts, dimensions and properties juxtapose each other in varying ways according to the empirical conditions in which they operate, but the very configuration that is formed out of their juxtapositioning has the effect of posing 'how' and 'why' questions and pointing to answers – or at least, suggesting lines of inquiry that might lead to such answers. That is, the very arrangement of concepts leads to the setting up of hypotheses that require testing and investigation.

If the original orienting concept had been that of 'career', one could begin to ask questions concerning the way in which control over status movements in the career is connected to the rate of progression of individuals or groups through the career in question. This will have theoretical or explanatory force when considered in relation to particular empirical applications such as the rate of progress of an illness career and the joint controlling influences of patients and various medical personnel. We can more easily understand the theoretical pertinence of this if we compare it with a career in which statuses are more clearly defined and progress is less easily masked or disguised by various parties, as is the case with managerial careers.

These control issues tie in with questions about the clarity of signs of progress and who legitimizes them (doctors versus patients over the rates of recovery from various illnesses). It also connects with issues concerning the levels of uncertainty and stability involved in promotion through a bureaucratic hierarchy versus market-based careers (as in the arts and sports) where upward career movements depend on the establishment of 'a market-place value which is reputation based' (Kanter, 1989: 512). Similarly, one could ask questions about how other dimensions or properties of career are related to each other, such as how does the experience of contingencies affect a careerist's progress and the direction of career movements or his or her decision to abandon or to switch careers? For example, a marriage may founder because of a serious argument (or a sequence of 'disagreements') and precipitate a change-over of partners. A similar psychological contingency, such as a sudden or gradual realization of a person's 'true' sexual preferences, may involve a switching of sexuality, as well as partners.

Secondary elaboration

Let me now go on to show how this kind of theoretical elaboration can be taken further by beginning to focus on one or more of the satellite concepts generated by this type of classification. For this purpose I shall stick to the example of career. Each dimension or property can in principle be treated in the same way as the original orienting concept by using it as a basis for generating another cluster or grouping of concepts, properties, dimensions and characteristics. In one sense this can be regarded as a sub-division of the original cluster but, depending upon the direction and flow of the research, the second cluster may take on greater importance and become the main focus of theoretical attention. For instance, the empirical example may indicate that the issue of control over career (status) movements is of particular importance and thus one could begin to investigate this idea more intensively by generating a further series of dimensions, questions, concepts and properties, as below:

- *The nature of control* – What does control entail?; self-control; control over others; control of one's (career) destiny; control over resources (property money, capital).
- *The forms of control* – Control by force of personality (charismatic control); control by manipulation of rewards (inducement) and punishment (coercion); control by possession of power, influence or authority (how do they differ? Are they connected?); direct and indirect (mediated) control.

After beginning with a general focus on the orienting concept of career it may be apparent that the research problem or question is related to the issue of control itself. Thus control, or some sub-division of it, may displace the original concern with career. In this respect the notion of career may be dropped altogether as the researcher homes in on emergent ideas and concepts. However, the original orienting concept will have served its purpose by providing a stepping stone to a new set of conceptual concerns. On the other hand, this is not an inevitability, since the concept of career (and its sub-properties and dimensions) may remain in the background as a *necessary* but essentially subsidiary concept. In this respect there would simply be a shift in emphasis whereby the various properties of control begin to occupy the foreground of the research focus.

Tertiary elaboration: drawing on general theory

The process of theory elaboration may proceed a stage further by pulling into the frame of reference various aspects of general theory. Again, like secondary elaboration, this is not an absolutely essential feature of all theory development but depends very much on the natural flow of the initial elaborations – the sense in which the logical and reasoning aspects work themselves out – and the specific circumstances of the research itself. Although it is not essential, I do want to suggest that whenever possible advantage should be taken of this option because it represents another route towards the general accumulation of sociological knowledge. That is, any attempt to trace connections between the formal and substantive theories associated with particular research areas or projects and more general theories and frameworks will help in drawing together what may otherwise remain disparate and fragmented aspects of sociological knowledge.

Making such links explicit is crucial to the overall growth of social scientific knowledge since there is an unfortunate tendency for the development of general theoretical ideas to be somewhat removed from substantive or empirical research. Of course there are always exceptions to this, but there is a general tendency for the complex division of labour in the social sciences to enforce specialist concentration on fairly narrowly defined areas. Thus applied researchers often focus on particular fields of expertise (for example, labour markets, health and medicine, stratification) and stick to knowledge of the (substantive) theories associated with their area of expertise. This can become a difficult problem in the context of funded research in which the funder's needs may restrict the parameters of the research itself. Alternatively, funders may insist on or 'suggest a preference' for the employment of particular perspectives or approaches, thus narrowing down the range of possible resources for theory construction. For example, this is reflected in the rather restricted bio-medical focus of much health-care research.

Conversely, general theorists are often so preoccupied with the development and elaboration of the internal conceptual logic and reasoning of their schemas that they fail to produce theories that bear some clear and direct relation to the empirical world of applied research. Sometimes they produce work which is so abstract and difficult that it is impossible for researchers or non-specialists to 'understand' its substantive implications or to translate them into research terms (see Bryant, 1995). As a result of the increasing trend towards disciplinary specialization and the exponential growth of knowledge in all these areas, the barriers to communication between general theory and research (substantive) theory are becoming more difficult to surmount. Thus, one way in which this can be tackled is to adopt the strategy of elaboration that I am endorsing here. As I say, there are sporadic examples of particular researchers or particular theorists whose work manages to overcome these difficulties, but they are by no means typical.

It is important to be aware of both the similarities and dissimilarities between this tertiary elaboration and primary elaboration using orienting concepts. There are definite connections in the sense that orienting concepts may be taken from the body of general theories just as they may be drawn from empirical findings or general descriptions of empirical data. However, the point about the use of such concepts is that they function as initial organizers of empirical data in a *partial* sense, as routes into theoretical elaboration. (This is in contradistinction to the importation of theories or theoretical frameworks *in toto* to organize the whole research process in a prior determinative sense. Such strategies usually have the effect of simply reaffirming what is already known and do not adequately 'test' theory or facilitate its advancement in any real sense.) The point of tertiary elaboration is rather different from the use of orienting concepts in that it draws on general theory in a more comprehensive sense in order to enhance explanatory potential. However, tertiary elaboration should be employed in such a way as to avoid the unthinking adoption of favoured theories which, perhaps unwittingly, operate as prior 'dogmatic' constraints on the analysis. The point is always to develop, test, modify or extend theory; it is never simply to reaffirm one's theoretical prejudices.

There are, then, three main modes of tertiary elaboration and they all correspond to different stages of the research process – before, during and after. They may occur either in conjunction with other types of elaboration or relatively independently of them. Let me take them in the temporal sequence just indicated and begin with the incorporation of general theory prior to the research. In this respect the researcher may have decided on the basis of a review of the literature in advance of the research that some general theoretical imput would be a useful way of organizing some of the data on the issues stemming from a particular research focus. Conversely, through reading general theory, a researcher may have been interested in looking at the empirical application of some aspect of the theory. For the sake of continuity with previous examples, let us imagine that the issue was about control and that the researcher had decided in advance that he or she was going to employ some aspect of general theory. Below I have listed three possible sources of general theory (there are many more) that might be pertinent in such a situation.

- *Weber on authority and domination* – Charismatic; legal-rational; traditional types of authority; forms of legitimation; distinction between authority and power; routinization of charisma; rationalization; bureaucracy; delegation of authority.
- *Giddens's theory of structuration* – The dialectic of control; the duality of structure; power as relational; authoritative and allocative resources; agency and power; importance of actors' reasons and motivations.
- *Foucault on power* – The nature of discourse, knowledge, power and the interrelations between them; bio-power; disciplinary power; the critique of sovereign power; power as a commodity or as possession by individuals or groups; power as productive rather than prohibitive.

I have not listed all the possible concepts and theoretical ideas that would be pertinent for each author since this is simply meant to give a flavour of the possibilities on offer. A researcher may, for example, simply adopt Giddens's notion of the 'dialectic of control' as a useful starting point for understanding certain aspects of the data at his or her disposal – the balance of power between certain groups or individuals as it shifts over time and in different contexts. On the other hand, the researcher might want to make use of the more inclusive propositions of structuration theory which form the wider theoretical context of the dialectic of control. Another researcher may be convinced of the insightfulness of Foucault's or Weber's views on power and draw in part, or more inclusively, on their theoretical formulations as a means of ordering the data in the initial phases of the research. In each case, however, the researcher must steer clear of the wholesale and 'prior' endorsement of the theoretical materials in question. The materials must be used in a spirit of scepticism about their potential applicability in relation to the information that is unearthed rather than as the imposition of a deterministic grid on the whole project.

The primary reason for using general theory in this manner is not to confirm or verify the theory in question, but as a starting point for theoretical elaboration and exploration. The purpose of elaboration is to extend and develop original or independent lines of inquiry by using extant general theory simply as a point of departure. If, despite attempts at elaboration (by exploring amendments, extensions and modifications of the theoretical ideas and concepts), the researcher is ineluctably drawn to the conclusion that the research confirms *in toto* the extant theoretical material, then this is perfectly in order. Such a conclusion is only illicit if it is arrived at as the result of a decision regarding the undoubtable validity of theoretical material prior to the research and which is subsequently ensured during the conduct of the research by the forcing of findings and data into 'inappropriate' categories and concepts.

The second kind of tertiary elaboration involves a decision to co-opt various aspects of general theory during the course of the research as a result of the unfolding nature of the research. Again, I shall stick with the example of control. To trace through the full implications of this let us imagine that, as in an earlier example, the concept of control had come to occupy the foreground of the researcher's focus of interest as the result of secondary elaboration (while the initial orienting concept of 'career' remained in the background). In such a case, the research topic or area itself may demand additional theoretical inputs to aid the process of theory elaboration – perhaps because the sources of theory-generation 'internal' to the research have run out of steam. As with the above example, various elements could be drawn from the work of Weber, Giddens or Foucault with a view to regenerating the impetus of theoretical elaboration. By utilizing ideas that are essentially 'external' to the specifics of the research one is attempting to introduce new lines of attack and new sources of creativity and inspiration to the explanation and interpretation of the data (as it is drawn from interviews, documents and observations). Thus, this type of co-option is employed in an ongoing sense. It proceeds in tandem with the unfolding of the research process itself and involves continual incorporation of various theoretical/conceptual resources. This is basically an improvisatory technique which trades on the synergy produced through a confrontation between the researcher's own analytic thinking, the unfolding character of research, and the analytic tools and ideas derived from an extant body of general theory. Such a triad of mutual influences hopefully produces new ways of looking at and interpreting the findings of the research.

For example, in studying interpersonal relations between partners, a researcher may be convinced of the importance of control or some aspect of control (such as the distinction between direct and indirect control), but may then be at a loss as to how to extend or refine the analysis to explain fully his or her findings. At this point the researcher might call upon Giddens's notion of the 'dialectic of control' in order to regain impetus. The dialectic of control emphasizes that there are continually changing balances of power in social relationships because those who are in subordinate positions (at any one time) always have some resources at their disposal to affect the behaviour of those who dominate. This insight might lead the researcher to focus on the kinds of resources that different people have at their disposal in conducting their day-to-day relations with their partners. In turn, this allows the researcher to begin to develop ideas about how people exert control over their partners by both direct and indirect means and how this feeds into a continually shifting balance of power between them. Again, this opens up a number of further conceptual possibilities, such as developing a typology of interpersonal strategies used for regaining or maintaining power in such relationships, or identifying situations in which the dialectic of control does not seem appropriate as a way of understanding interpersonal relationships.

Essentially, this kind of theory elaboration has two main functions and produces two sorts of effects. In the first case, general theory is co-opted for the purpose of reviving a flagging theoretical impetus by adding new issues and 'prompts' to existing ones. As a result one produces hybrid ideas and forms of theoretical thinking. In the above example this is reflected in the refocusing of interest on resources, direct and indirect control, and the development of a typology of control strategies (and the circumstances in which they are activated). In this sense one is using the dialectic of control (and associated concepts) simply as a bridge or useful means of developing new conceptual formulations. As a by-product of this one might also produce some suggestions as to how the dialectic of control may be modified or extended to cover the kinds of instances that are the subject of the research, but this would not be its main purpose.

Principally, with this strategy one is not interested in developing the general theory itself (or even bits of it). Rather, the interest centres on using it as a convenient means of developing original theoretical ideas.

In the second variant of this kind of elaboration the spotlight switches to the general theory. Again, however, the emphasis must not be on simple confirmation or verification unless the overall outcome of the research process suggests overwhelmingly that this must be the case. The emphasis is rather on extension, elaboration, modification and revision. In the above example this is reflected in the idea of identifying situations in which the dialectic of control is inappropriate for understanding control in interpersonal relationships. The conclusion that results from this kind of analytic scrutiny might be that the dialectic of control does not explain crucial aspects of control in interpersonal relations and therefore has no role to play in a general account or explanation.

On the other hand, the conclusion may be in the form of a suggested modification or qualification to the claims made for the concept (for example, that it applies to all power relationships) in order to preserve its viability and integrity as a concept but in a more circumscribed sense. Essentially, then, this kind of elaboration adopts an orientation which emphasizes testing the adequacy, viability, validity, and so on of the general theory in question. This questioning, 'dialogical' posture has the effect of developing and refining theory and is to be preferred over the verificationist approach which simply takes the validity of the general theory for granted. It hardly needs to be said that this latter approach cannot lead to theoretical innovation (either through refinement or by discarding elements). Rather, it can only lead to a circular form of confirmation and a stultification of theoretical development.

The final form of tertiary elaboration concentrates attention on the co-optation of general theory *after* the research process has been concluded – that is, after all the data and information have been collected. It may be that the research began rather more as a fact-finding mission on an area about which there was very little prior information. In this sense it might have been primarily 'problem'- or 'social policy-oriented' and thus not 'steered' by any specific theoretical problem. However, after the data has been gathered it may become apparent that certain theoretical ideas or concepts may throw light on the data, or, conversely, that the data directly highlight certain theoretical principles. A good example of this is Bloor and McIntosh's (1990) study of health visiting and therapeutic communities in the UK which focused on client–professional relationships. The main themes of their observations and interviews centred around the problems encountered by the professional health and community workers in monitoring the behaviour of their clients, and the ways in which the clients dealt with this by adopting various forms of resistance.

After completing the data-gathering, the authors realized that Foucault's (1977) work on power, surveillance and resistance was highly relevant to their data so in their final analysis they utilized some Foucauldian concepts and ideas to make sense of, and give some order to, the data. This is a case of the explanatory enhancement of data by employing aspects of general theory. Clearly, the researchers had already developed a typology of client resistance from their data (ideological dissent (both individual and collective), non-co-operation, escape or avoidance and concealment), but they geared up the level of their analysis and its explanatory power and refinement by linking this typology to Foucault's ideas on power, surveillance and resistance. The results of such elaboration cut two ways. First, they add to Foucault's analysis by providing unusual empirical materials by which to judge the explanatory usefulness of Foucault's concepts and ideas. Secondly, they also enhance the explanatory reach and power of the typology of client resistance in a manner which is somewhat independent of Foucault's general social analysis as a whole.

Another variant of this *ex post facto* form of elaboration concerns the conjunction of empirical materials (gathered perhaps for other or parallel purposes) and general frames of reference (or at least sizeable chunks of them) which bear some direct relevance to each other. In this respect the empirical materials allow one to test or check the adequacy or validity of the general theoretical elements. This is not simply a matter of either confirming or disconfirming the general theoretical ideas or concepts, but should be slanted towards the attempt to develop theory in the sense either of refining and extending the original theory or of moving away from its terms and conceptual ambit altogether.

An example of this is a piece of work undertaken by myself and two colleagues (Layder et al., 1991). The empirical area of study concerned young people's movements from school to work and the pattern of labour-market participation of young people from different social classes. Originally, the data-gathering and analysis were carried out as part of a much wider study of work, labour markets, employment patterns and social class. However, we realized that this same data provided very pertinent materials from which we could examine some of the propositions that formed central components of Giddens's theory of structuration. To this end we examined some aspects of the 'duality of structure', specifically the intertwining of activity (like job searches, the use of educational capital) and (macro) structural features (class origins, local labour markets, availability of resources) of social life. Among other things (including comments on the Giddens's notion of 'methodological bracketing'), we concluded that the notion of duality of structure was only partly supported by the empirical evidence and that certain reformulations of the relation between agency and structure needed to be adopted in order to understand and make sense of the data.

The exact pros and cons of our debate with structuration theory do not concern us here. What is important are the principles underlying the joint use of empirical data and aspects of general social theory. Despite the fact that the data were originally gathered for a rather different purpose, they did throw interesting light on some aspects of general social theory. Although we would not claim that we have provided cut-and-dried conclusions about the general viability of structuration theory (especially since the whole issue involves a complex debate at a number of levels), nonetheless we were able to engage in a form of theoretical elaboration by the conjoint use of empirical research and aspects of general theory.

Conclusion: theoretical elaboration and social research

Throughout this chapter I have emphasized the importance of the use of extant theoretical materials, even if the whole purpose of research is to develop new ideas and to unearth new empirical data. I began with a discussion of the role of orienting concepts in the development of theory and theoretical elaboration. Unlike 'sensitizing' and 'definitive' concepts, the purpose of orienting concepts is to produce an additive or incremental effect on one's conceptual and theoretical thinking. The usefulness of orienting concepts is connected to the initial need to crank-start the process and also to establish some terms of reference for the further elaboration of theoretical ideas. Although the emphasis has been on theory as the primary point of departure, I have continually indicated that the process of theory elaboration is closely tied in with data collection and the unfolding character of empirical research.

As an initial stimulus for theoretical rumination, the use of orienting concepts helps general conceptual thinking about the data that is being, or has been, collected and the empirical area from which it originates. Core and satellite orienting concepts (and the network of ideas they generate) set up specific puzzles in relation to the data and topic of investigation. Essentially, these puzzles pose 'how', 'why' and 'what' questions about the way things work or operate in the area in question (a classroom, a marriage, client–professional relationships, and so forth). These also concern questions about the effects or functions of typical activities on the social settings and contexts in which they occur, as well as the reciprocal effects and influences of these structural or systemic features on the activities themselves.

I have also traced the various stages of theoretical elaboration and their implications. Although the use of orienting concepts represents a primary form of theoretical elaboration, I have emphasized the significance of secondary elaboration, which involves making explicit links between networks or webs of concepts which map the relations between 'core', 'satellite', 'derived' and 'subsidiary' concepts and categories. I have stressed the crucial role that general theory can and should play in facilitating closer links between social research and theoretical development. I have referred to this as tertiary elaboration simply to distinguish it from the others. However, this should not be taken to imply that it must come at the end of the temporal sequence. The use of extant general theory, in part or as a whole, can enter into research calculations at any point (including before and after) the research process. It can also be either concurrent with the employment of other modes of theoretical elaboration (including the use of typologies) or relatively independent of them.

Whatever overall configuration of elaborative strategies and techniques are utilized, a central thrust of my argument has been that the incremental effects of theory elaboration should not produce a network of concepts that functions as a closed net representing some terminal point in the process. My argument is that theory should never be like this, although some practitioners (and approaches such as positivism) have encouraged us to think this is the case. The cluster of concepts which reflects the 'latest' stage of elaboration should always be regarded as potentially revisable in the final stages of research. Even more importantly, the conceptual framework which supposedly represents the 'finished product' of a specific sequence of elaboration must be regarded only as an 'interim' finished product since it too must be regarded as potentially revisable.

This should not be taken as advice designed to undermine confidence in the labours of one's research and its theoretical fruits. Quite the contrary. It is an attempt to be more certain and secure about its status and validity by defining its epistemological basis. Emphasizing the lack of absolute fixity of the knowledge produced in this manner (its future revisability) is not a call to be unduly tentative about the results or conclusions of one's research. Nor should it be taken to imply that the research process is never-ending and increasingly uncertain in terms of outcome. Hopefully (although this can never be fully guaranteed), as the research and theory elaboration progresses, one becomes more certain of the soundness of the core categories and conceptual network that form its basis. The very openness of the form of knowledge and analysis I am advocating ensures that the interactions between theoretical reasoning, logical analysis and empirical 'fit' should allow the researcher to test or check out the adequacy of the theory and conclusions as the research unfolds.

CHAPTER 6

TOWARDS ADAPTIVE THEORY

In this chapter I want to expand on my overall vision of the kind of theorizing that both informs, but also follows from, the sorts of strategies and practices that I have previously outlined. I concentrate on questions concerning the nature, scale and philosophical under-pinnings of the kind of theory-research relation that I have so far advocated. I describe an approach that I term 'adaptive' theory, which falls somewhere between what are variously referred to as 'theory-testing' or hypothetico-deductive approaches on the one hand, and grounded-theory (or theory-constructing) approaches on the other. Adaptive theory also parts company with those approaches (including postmodernism and various forms of interactionism and phenomenology) which stress an anti-theoretical stance in which cumulative, general or systematic theorizing are no longer thought to play a role in social analysis and in which conventional canons of objectivity and research protocol are considered to be 'outmoded'.

I have already introduced some key components of adaptive theory, although I have not done so in any systematic way, nor have I suggested that the elements I have mentioned may be combined to form an overall strategy which can be used in research. I have dealt with issues of theory-construction and testing which draw upon sensitizing concepts, orienting concepts, elaborative techniques, typology-building, and so on, and all of these are essential aspects of adaptive theory. In this chapter I incorporate the features I have already dealt with in a discrete manner as part of an overall coherent approach to theorizing and research. In order to do this I have to place the separate strands of my argument in a wider context of supporting arguments which draw upon general theory, the philo-sophy of social science and research methodology. The discussion will proceed as follows. First, I shall outline eight key points which I take to represent the overall parameters of the adaptive theory approach as I see it. I shall then discuss these points in greater detail.

The Nature and Scale of Adaptive Theory

1   Adaptive theory is a synthetic approach which borrows from a number of others but also provides a distinctive alternative to them.

2   Adaptive theory is 'middle-range' in terms of immediate focus but has an 'open-ended' relation with larger-scale or more inclusive theories or types of research.
3   Adaptive theory both shapes, and is shaped by the empirical data that emerges from research. It allows the dual influence of extant theory (theoretical models) as well as those that unfold from (and are enfolded in) the research. Adaptive theorizing is an ever-present feature of the research process.

The Philosophical, Methodological and Theoretical Context

4   Adaptive theory uses both inductive and deductive procedures for developing and elaborating theory.
5   It rests upon an epistemological position which is neither positivist nor interpretivist.
6   It embraces both objectivism and subjectivism in terms of its ontological presuppositions.
7   It assumes that the social world is complex, multi-faceted (layered) and densely compacted.
8   It focuses on the multifarious interconnections between human agency, social activities and social organization (structures and systems).

To give the discussion a pragmatic feel and to centralize the importance of the practical strategies involved in the employment of adaptive theory, I shall deal first with the philosophical and methodological context in points 4–8 and then concentrate on the more practical details of adaptive theory itself (points 1–3). Of course, in doing this it is important to bear in mind the implications of points 1–3 (even though at this stage they are fairly sketchy in form) since the central purpose of establishing a wider methodological and theoretical context is to highlight the practical, user-relevant aspects of adaptive theory. A cursory glance at points 1–3 may give the impression that they stand alone as guidelines to research practice which have no need of further justification. However, what is at stake here is not just the depiction of a set of guidelines or practical 'rules of thumb' for research practice, but also the establishment of a new set of methodological rules for sociological analysis in general.

I shall expand on this in the concluding chapter but in an effort to forestall possible misunderstanding I should comment briefly on what is *not* implied by this statement. First, in saying that I am attempting to formulate a new set of rules of sociological method I am not suggesting that they should somehow replace all existing rules and methodological approaches and thus render them redundant. In general, my view of the practice of social research should be broadly conceived and must be flexible and open to a wide range of influences. No one approach or set of rules could possibly represent the infinite diversity of social reality and thus no fixed and rigid approach should be allowed to monopolize research practices. In this sense, in proposing 'new rules' I am implying that they should be understood as lying alongside conventional or established approaches – in some instances as a radical 'alternative' but in other cases as a complement to existing rules of method.

To this end the epistemological foundations of particular research protocols and the wider implications for general theory have to be addressed. Primarily this is because methodological issues (including epistemological and ontological questions), as well as those relating to general theory, are sometimes regarded as being 'independent' of or 'irrelevant' to research practice – particularly in books about research methods and data collection techniques. My position here is that this view is completely erroneous. All claims to the validity of knowledge (even those that insist on immunity from such claims) are underpinned by epistemological assumptions, thus they must be examined and justified as part of the ongoing adjudication of claims by the research community. Also, wider theoretical assumptions about the nature of society and social activity and how we are best to account for them are intimately bound up with questions about the best way to conduct research. These questions are therefore closely interwoven.

The use of deductive and inductive procedures

In social research, deduction involves using a set of general assumptions in order to formulate empirically testable propositions about a phenomenon (say suicide or the use of community resources) whereas induction relies more on the initial gathering of empirical data as a means of developing a more general (theoretical) understanding. Adaptive theory employs both deductive and inductive procedures – although the exact blend will depend on the circumstances – in order to formulate theory. However, this must not be confused with similar but ultimately cosmetic or 'surface' claims made by authors operating from within specific approaches or schools of thought. Such authors typically suggest that their favoured approaches or positions routinely employ both induction and deduction. In this sense all research practice is thought to comprise a dash of both induction and deduction (and hence also the empiricist and rationalist theories of truth on which they are based – see next section). However, on closer scrutiny these claims are often premised on very narrow defintions of these terms while the larger or more encompassing assumptions of their approaches actually prohibit, favour or privilege one or the other of these positions.

For instance, Strauss (1987), clearly working from within a grounded theory tradition, states that his position utilizes both deduction and induction. However, the underpinning assumptions of grounded theory only allow for this within the overall context of an overwhelmingly inductive procedure wherein legitimate or valid theory is thought to emerge in an ongoing fashion from the data of research and is not 'imposed on the data' as Glaser and Strauss (1967) claim. (I shall later argue that the idea of theory being imposed on data is a fundamental misconstrual of deductive (middle-range) and general theorizing.) In the case of grounded theory, it is clear that deductive methods are only tolerated within the confines of a master framework of assumptions about the fundamentally inductive nature of theorizing from research data.

Similarly, Merton's (1967) vision of research and middle-range theorizing is set within the confines of a largely hypothetico-deductive approach. This insists that theory must be developed or constructed via a set of abstract assumptions from which a set of testable research hypotheses may be deduced. Within the terms of this injunction Merton also envisages inductive elements, such as generalizing from empirical observations, or the discovery of par-ticular facts which necessitate a reformulation of existing theories (Merton, 1967). But again this is a narrowly conceived view of inductive procedure which is only permissible in a wider context of the deductive formulation of theory. These views are based on a narrow definition of either induction or deduction such that both are seemingly allowed within the terms of the wider set of assumptions. However, it is clear that this wider set of assumptions also prohibits and restricts more important meanings of the terms and their usage in social analysis and research. So the ostensible freedom of usage and operation is much more apparent than real.

It is exactly this kind of underlying epistemological restriction that I am concerned to avoid with my insistence that adaptive theory employs both deductive and inductive procedures. This has to be understood as an attempt to combine what may on the surface be regarded as 'incompatible' premises or underlying assumptions. Adaptive theory tries to steer clear of this incompatibility by avoid-ing extreme, rigid or dogmatic definitions of induction and deduc-tion and by conceiving of them as potentially 'open' discourses.

Thus, my usage of these terms does not invoke the idea that *in the final analysis* theory has *either* to be produced exclusively in a deductive manner *or* solely within an inductive frame of reference. In terms of adaptive theory both forms of theory-generation, construction or elaboration are permissible within the same frame of reference and particularly within the same research project and time-frame. In this sense both of the more encompassing meanings and definitions of the terms are allowed to come to the fore and to play a role in theorizing in research which involves the collection of primary data.

Also, with regard to these more encompassing definitions, I regard induction and deduction as frameworks of ideas – discourses and the practices they embody – which are potentially open to each other's influence. Thus it is not only a matter of allowing their dual influence on theory-construction, but also of allowing their mutual influence on each other. Moderate (rather than extreme) definitions of these terms will allow for this. As epistemological anchorages, neither induction nor deduction can be understood as prior or privileged in terms of their influence – neither must have a fixed starting point as the most basic premise of knowledge production. Induction and deduction must be conceived as equally important and mutually influential approaches to knowledge, according to different empirical and theoretical circumstances. These latter will reflect the ongoing nature of particular research projects. In this sense adaptive theory adapts to unfolding circumstances both in terms of emerging data and theoretical forms of explanation (models, concepts and frameworks). Thus an explanatory model (say, of types of suicide, or of the different modes in which prostitution is economically organized) will simultaneously shape and be shaped by the ongoing collection of data (such as interviews and documents).

In short, in terms of adaptive theory the question of whether one makes inferences from general assumptions to empirically testable propositions (deduction), or whether one begins from particular 'empirical' instances and works up to a general conceptual understanding (induction) depends upon the play of circumstances that are contingent features of the research process. That is, particular projects will produce a unique set of circumstances in terms of the practical and conceptual problems they pose and the practical and conceptual solutions that they bring forth. The exact roles that inductive and deductive procedures play with respect to each other will be dependent upon the unique and unfolding dynamics of the ongoing research. However, irrespective of the exact degree of influence of the two procedures in any particular research project, in all (or most) circumstances there will be a mutual interplay of influences rather than a single directional flow.

Theories of truth: empiricism and rationalism

The issue of induction and deduction also relates to and overlaps with another debate which is relevant here and which concerns the nature of knowledge production in social analysis and research – that between the respective claims and merits of empiricism and rationalism as theories of knowledge (epistemological premises). Empiricism insists that valid knowledge can only be based on sensory experience – in short, on the observed features of the social world as they present themselves to our senses. On the other hand, rationalism puts its faith in a priori knowledge – knowledge independent of experience and which is the result of various forms of argument and reasoning. Traditionally, empiricism has been associated with a 'correspondence' conception of truth in that theory and concepts are thought to 'correspond' in some direct (almost 'photographic') manner to the 'facts' or 'empirical data'. Likewise, rationalism has often been associated with a 'coherence' conception of truth in which the internal relations between concepts in a theory are thought to be decisive in shaping the terms in which we understand the phenomena to which the theory refers.

On the surface it might seem that this mirrors exactly the debate about induction versus deduction with empiricism being concordant with induction and rationalism having more in common with deductive methods. However, it is not as simple as this for it does seem that most approaches to 'empirical theorizing' have stressed empiricism as the most secure and fundamental basis of knowledge. For grounded theory this is clearly the case with its insistence that theory must emerge through observation and faithful rendering of the lives of the people whose experiences it attempts to represent. In this case any independent role given to forms of reasoning and theoretical argument are deemed to be at best ungrounded, speculative abstractions (Glaser and Strauss, 1967; Strauss, 1987; Strauss and Corbin, 1990) and at worst illegitimate reifications of social life (Blumer, 1969; Becker in Rock, 1979). On the other hand, Merton's (1967) highly influential vision of empirical theory would apparently seem to allow a role for rational forms of knowledge with its stress on deducing empirical hypotheses from logical assumptions and premises. However, closer scrutiny reveals that the role of rational knowledge in empirical theory is severely limited by the overriding importance that Merton attaches to empiricist criteria in two important respects. In the first place, Merton suggests that although empirical theory only becomes theory proper by being placed in the context of a set of abstract assumptions, the initial groundings of the theoretical problem are defined in and through empirical generalizations based on observations (such as rates of suicide or deviance). Thus, for example, according to Merton, Durkheim's famous theory of suicide was initially prompted by the observation that suicide rates are lower in predominantly Catholic countries than Protestant ones. The empirical generalization derived from this observation determines the nature of the theoretical problem – why are suicide rates lower in Catholic countries and higher in Protestant ones? – that is ultimately to be solved via a deductive procedure. Secondly, Merton suggests that after the theoretical problem has been properly formulated by being placed in the context of a set of abstract assumptions (which provide an explanation for the empirical observations and generalizations), the validity of the hypotheses so formulated have to be judged in terms of empirical testability, and their concordance or otherwise with empirical findings and evidence.

Therefore, on two counts Merton's notion of middle-range theory is heavily dependent upon empiricist criteria for the evaluation and production of legitimate theory or 'theory proper' as Merton phrases it. As with Glaser and Strauss, Merton tends to discount any theory which does not defer to the greater authority of the empirical world as it appears through sensory experience (such as observation and measurement) because it is deemed to be adrift from the empirical world. Thus, even though this approach employs a deductive method at various junctures, the decisive shaping and production of empirical theory is arbitrated by the world of empirical evidence, testability and other sensorily observable phenomena. In this sense the influence of rationalism is completely neutralized by the overwhelming influence of empiricist criteria of validity. Thus both grounded and middle-range forms of empirical theory endorse empiricist underpinnings rather than rationalist ones.

At worst, the effect of this has been to sever the important connection between empirical research – and the 'empirical' or 'substantive' theory to which it gives rise – and general theory in sociology. At best, it has had the effect of creating a buffer between them. This is because general theory has always retained some commitment to rational forms of proof, validity and explanation. Now while it may be argued that this leaning towards rationalism has extended too far in some cases, eventuating in almost wholly self-referential theories which eschew the validating authority of empirical evidence, it is also the case that general theory has never completely jettisoned its links with rationalism. In my view this important connection, which was present in the work of the classical sociologists, must be regenerated in the context of a *rapprochement* between empirical theory and general theory. It is precisely this linkage that adaptive theory seeks to secure by ensuring that rational forms of proof, demonstration and validity have a continuing role to play in empirical research and in the theorizing that results from, or feeds into, empirical (primary data-gathering) research. In this sense the emphasis on deductive modes of theory-generation have to be positively undergirded by rationalist criteria of evaluation.

However, as with the issue of the relation between deduction and induction, empiricism and rationalism must be understood as discourses which are potentially open to each other's influence and which are capable of producing positive and constructive interactions – rather than incompatible and incommensurable epistemological starting points. An important aspect of this (which I have already intimated in the preceding paragraph) is the theories of truth upon which rationalism and empiricism are based. While recognizing that both have something to offer, it is important to avoid either the extreme coherence or the extreme correspondence theories since they both lead to exaggerated and (thus) erroneous claims about the better hold on the truth (greater explanatory power). In order to look for the most adequate and powerful forms of explanation, adaptive theory draws upon both theories and occupies the intermediate ground between them in an effort to transcend the limitations of both.

The nature of social science and social reality

Adaptive theory adopts a position on the nature of social science which is neither positivist or interpretivist. Traditional positivism fails to recognize that the social world is constituted by the actions of meaning-conferring human beings whose behaviour is quite unlike that of the inanimate phenomena of the natural world which is law-like, predictable and generalizable. The behaviour of people and the operation of social structures and social processes are often unpredictable and never determined by universal principles; nor can they be described in terms of law-like generalizations. In this respect the interpretivist (or humanist) vision of social analysis correctly insists that a subjective point of view is of paramount importance in understanding social life. Social analysis must be about the attempt to understand the social world from the point of view of the people who are the subjects of research at any one point in time. One of the principal problems with interpretivism is that it tends to take this view to the extreme and envision the social world as entirely composed of intersubjective meaning and communication. This leaves out of account many features of social life, such as social structures and systems, forms of domination, cultural symbols, ideology, which cannot be understood solely in this fashion.

Adaptive theory attempts to reconcile the idea that many features of social life must be explained in terms of actor's meanings and subjective understandings with the fact that other aspects of social life have more in common with natural phenomena and must be explained in more 'objective', scientific terms. Social phenomena, like structures, processes, settings and resources (as well as the mechanisms that facilitate them), must not be confused with human behaviour and activity even though they are directly implicated in it. Such phenomena are often more accurately understood as generative or causal in nature and as underlying the observable surface of social life and helping to shape it. Thus, in themselves, phenomena such as class structures or forms of domination may not be amenable to direct observation and measurement. However, their effects on social life may be clearly detectable – as in social class variations in the distribution of resources or the presence of speech codes (Bernstein, 1973) or with the existence of various kinds of oppression and control which accompany domination.

Thus, although adaptive theory rejects positivism in general, it does not reject the view that there are phenomena in the social world which bear some similarities with those in the natural world. It is a mistake to think of these features of the social world as being simply aspects of intersubjective meaning and interactive processes. Instead, these phenomena must be understood as having their own 'emergent properties', which distinguish them from human behaviour and social activity, while at the same time possessing an intimate and indissoluble tie with the world of social interaction. Thus these social phenomena must be treated as relatively 'impersonal' and as possessing an objective or 'transpersonal' and transituational character.

To accommodate this, adaptive theory endorses an epistemological position which incorporates both the 'internal' subjective point of view of social interaction while simultaneously appreciating that such activity always takes place in the context of wider social settings and contextual resources. The latter exist externally to particular individuals, groups and situations, and thus have to be understood from an 'objective observer's' point of view (Habermas, 1987). This objective observer's point of view has nothing to do with positivist notions of objectivity involving claims about a privileged access to the truth – by dint of the elimination of subjective ideas, feelings, experience, and so on. It simply denotes a shift from the actor's perspective to an alternate vantage point in order to reflect the emergent properties of social settings and contexts – their 'systemic' features. Such an alternative viewpoint does not claim better access to an 'equivalent' truth. Rather, it indicates a different mode of access to parallel orders of social phenomena and the truth claims with which they are associated.

If these epistemological assumptions about the nature of social scientific analysis distinguish adaptive theory from those of positivism and interpretivism, then its ontological commitments – how it conceives of the nature of social reality – flow from these. Adaptive theory's embracement of subjectivism and objectivism means that it conceives the social world as including both objective and subjective aspects (and diffuse mixtures of the two). Both the world of social interaction (the 'lifeworld' in Habermas's terms) and the world of social settings and contextual resources (social 'systems' for Habermas) are considered to be real and connected features of the social world. However, I have suggested elsewhere (Layder, 1997) that these 'domains' are constituted in different ways and have their own partly independent properties and characteristics which cannot be reduced to each other.

In this sense adaptive theory endorses a moderate form of objectivism which must not be confused with those 'versions' that have come in for so much (and often unwarranted) criticism. For example, Giddens (1984), along with other humanist writers such as symbolic interactionists, ethnomethodologists, phenomenologists, and so on, vehemently opposes objectivism in all guises. Such a dismissal of objectivism is premature and unwarranted in so far as it fails to recognize that some form of objectivism is necessary since it is the only possible way of registering the distinctive and partly independent characteristics of systemic phenomena. In this respect the moderate form of objectivism that I propose is not associated with or identical to determinism, functionalism or positivism (as Giddens claims – see Layder, 1997). In the present context it is important to counter the incorrect attribution of determinism of social agency (activity, action) by social-structural or systemic phenomena as the allegedly 'logical' consequence of the adoption of an objectivist position.

The moderate version of objectivism merely assumes that social reality is composed of both subjective and objective aspects and that they both condition and influence each other since they are deeply interwoven. That is, social activity is conditioned and significantly shaped by systemic phenomena (values, ideology, power, money, and the socially organized settings in which they are embedded) while simultaneously activity itself serves to reproduce, sustain or transform these social systemic features and social arrangements. Importantly, such an objectivist position dispenses with a naive subjectivism which cannot envisage a world beyond the intersubjective realm, or beyond the motives and reasons that actors give for their behaviour. The idea that the social world comprises both objective and subjective features and various 'mixtures' or amalgams of their effects and influences means that for research purposes adaptive theory assumes that the social world is complex and dense. Furthermore, it also assumes that the texture of this complexity and density is formed from the multifarious interconnections between agency and structure.

Complexity and agency-structure relations

To acknowledge the density and complexity of the social world (principally its layered and multi-faceted character) is not in the least to deny the existence of, or to abandon the search for, various kinds of 'best approximations' to the truth. Indeed, the existence of complexity and density simply confirm that social inquiry be ever more attentive to the need for veracity in the explanations and findings that it offers, rather than to abandon the quest for more certain and adequate knowledge. Thus, while adaptive theory does not cling to any positivist notions of absolute certainty or the complete objectivity of the knowledge which constitutes the findings and outcomes of social inquiry, it does not relinquish the idea that the purpose of social inquiry is to produce ever-more adequate knowledge. In this respect the adequacy or validity of knowledge is reflected in two ways. First, it is reflected in the attempt to produce an enhanced or more accurate rendering of the nature of social reality under scrutiny (a particular group, a milieu, a social situation, a social policy issue) than that which has gone before. Secondly, the adequacy of knowledge is reflected in the formulation and presentation of ever-more powerful explanations of social phenomena. That is, explanatory forms which include more within their terms of reference than previous or extant ones.

These criteria and the overall search for greater adequacy are in direct contradistinction to the positions that postmodernist and poststructuralist schools of thought have adopted as responses to the problem of complexity. These include a thorough-going relativism, which may or may not also include the idea that all forms of knowledge are equally valid (irrespective of any concern with notions of accuracy or truth). The abandonment of the search for 'order' in an overwhelmingly complex social world is accompanied by a methodological injunction that 'anything goes', irrespective of canons of procedure and protocol. While some versions of the 'abandonment of method' thesis (Feyerabend, 1978) are acceptable as far as adaptive theory is concerned – particularly the idea that formal and epistemologically constricting aspects of methodology must be relinquished – the anarchic or completely unprincipled abandonment of methodological procedure and protocol is simply a denial of responsibility, standards of judgement and morality. Likewise, the adoption of a theoretical agnosticism, or the insistence of a proscription on general or systematic theorizing as a reponse to acknowledging the infinite complexity of social reality, is an abnegation of the researcher's duty to make clear his or her analytic presuppositions and the assumptions which underlie forms of social inquiry. It goes without saying that such fudging of explanatory responsibility and eschewal of canons of validity and reliability are totally antithetical to the aims and concerns of adaptive theory.

Let me now shift the focus of the discussion away from the question of the most appropriate ways of dealing with complexity and density, and move to the issue of how those aspects are constituted in the first place. While the social world is constructed in large part by the meanings, motivations and reasons that people give for their behaviour, this in no way exhausts the fabric of the social world. Thus complexity and density do not refer solely to the compaction and interpenetration of these phenomena. In this respect the idea that the social world is a purely intersubjective phenomenon must be rejected along with the interpretivist idea that social research must be exclusively concerned with these things. On the other hand, the idea that the social world is solely populated by social structural or systemic variables (such as class, status, income, occupation, religious affiliation, role expectations, and so on) must likewise be rejected on the grounds that they represent only a fraction of the possible phenomena which constitute social reality as a whole.

As I say, it is not that structural variables or intersubjective meanings are not important for our understanding of the social world. Rather, it is the imputation that either of these should be regarded as the exclusive focus of social analysis. Adaptive theory insists that such a view must be supplemented with a concern with systemic and structural forces, mechanisms and generative processes. In particular, adaptive theory focuses on phenomena that subsume these diverse elements and which represent the 'ligatures' which bind lifeworld and system elements together in a general sense. In other words, it targets the multiplicity of forms of interconnection between social agency and social structure (or system elements). These elements are tightly bound together to form a complex and multi-faceted social reality. Adaptive theory attempts to abstract from this tightly compacted complexity to identify specific forms of connection (between agency and structure/system). It also attempts to temporarily 'disembed' them (in a methodological sense) from their immediate context in order to analyse them.

In so far as it focuses on the joins or interconnections between agency and structure, adaptive theory is therefore most useful to research which is concerned with a similar focus. That is, adaptive theory is most pertinent to research which attends to the inter-weaving of system elements (settings and contexts of activity) with the micro-features (interpersonal encounters) of social life. It is less useful to research which focuses either exclusively on collective social phenomena (class, collective action, institutional and organizational features of society), or on the analysis of intersubjective meaning. In this sense the adaptive theory approach requires a concentration on both.

Such a view also necessitates a break with certain strands in modern social theory, particularly those that seek to dissolve the distinctive contributions of agency and structure into a seamless synthetic unity. Giddens's structuration theory (1984) has been very influential in this regard, and although it attempts to combine struc-ture and agency it does so by relinquishing the distinctive features of these aspects of social life as well as their different contributions to the shaping of activity and the reproduction of social structures and systems. One reason for this is that Giddens rejects objectivism in all guises (as do symbolic interactionists, ethnomethodologists, phenom-enologists and others committed to the same epistemological and ontological premises).

An important consequence of the rejection of objectivism is that it means that one is unable to trace properly the interconnections between subjective and objective features of social life. For example, for Giddens, social systems do not have any independence from intersubjective phenomena. For him, systems only exist in so far as they are directly implicated in actors' reasons and motivations. As a result, the predominant slant of structuration theory is towards a privileging of subjectivism and intersubjective phenomena. The result is a lopsided analysis and research focus which cannot properly register the partly independent contributions of lifeworld and systemic phenomena and thus is unable to trace adequately the interconnections between them. This is reflected in two of the 'new rules' of sociological method introduced by Giddens (1976).

In the first of these Giddens stresses that there are no 'pre-given' objects of social inquiry and that the social world is 'one which is constituted or produced by the active doings of subjects' (1976: 160). Adaptive theory, and the theory of social domains upon which it rests (Layder, 1997), rejects such an assumption since it leads to the lopsided focus on activity, meaning and motivation alluded to above. The theory of social domains insists that while there are no pre-given aspects of social reality which are completely independent of human agency, there are major features of society that are preconstituted and historically emergent. These represent ongoing 'external' conditions which confront people in their daily lives.

Such external conditions have an intrinsic link with the internal micro-world of the interpersonal encounters that contribute so much to the routine features of everyday life. Thus there are many aspects of the social world which are preconstituted (systemic phenomena generally) that exist in tandem with, and bear a complex relation to, the active doings of subjects in their situated encounters. It is also the case that structuration theory (Giddens, 1987) fails to recognize that situated activity (what Goffman (1983) calls the 'interaction order') has properties of its own which are not identical to institutional reproduction in the constitution of social life. Recognizing the partly independent character of situated activity complicates the productive and reproductive effects of social activity in general – and remains unacknowledged in structuration theory (see Layder, 1997).

The second methodological rule that Giddens (1984) suggests is contained in the notion of 'methodological bracketing'. This notion is a rather strange one, considered in the context of structuration theory as a whole, since a principal objective of structuration theory is to combine elements of agency and structure through the concept of the 'duality of structure'. By contrast, 'methodological bracketing' enjoins the researcher to 'bracket' (or hold to one side) elements of either 'institutional' or 'interpretative' analysis while focusing on one or other aspects of the empirical phenomenon under investigation. This holding apart is deemed necessary because of the supposed practical (and methodological) difficulties of examining them at the same time. Although Giddens says that in principle both interpretative and institutional analyses should be employed together, the practical difficulties involved mean that they have to be dealt with 'independently'. Curiously, this injunction has the effect of underlining the distinctiveness of lifeworld and systemic elements rather than emphasizing their interdependence.

While there are no doubt difficulties raised by the attempt to trace simultaneously the links between agency and structure (lifeworld and system), it is surely wrong deliberately to emphasize a gulf between them. The whole point of a focus on the relations between agency and structure in research is to underline their simultaneous implication in each other – to trace their actual interpenetrations and linkages – and not to abandon this task because of a methodological 'problem'. In any case, the methodological 'problem' only arises in its most acute (not to say 'insuperable') form if the distinctive characteristics of agency and structure are denied in the first place. This is precisely the problem that arises with Giddens's notion of the 'duality of structure' wherein the independent contributions of agency and structure are dissolved into a seamless unity with a 'dual nature' (as opposed to distinctive forms merged and interrelated in various complex ways). Thus the very conceptualization of the 'duality of structure' renders Giddens's structuration schema unable to 'unpack' agency and structure and thus to engage in interpretative and institutional analyses at the same time.

By adopting the alternative view of domain theory the researcher is encouraged to examine the nature and interconnections between lifeworld and system elements – rather than to hold them apart methodologically – while involved in particular research projects (Layder et al., 1991). An important feature of such an analysis is to attend to the epistemological status of concepts which refer to different aspects of social reality. I have dealt in some detail with many of the associated issues in Chapter 4, and so I shall not repeat them here. The point is that given the different types of concept I have identified (behavioural, systemic, bridging and theoretical), it is important to bear in mind the different functions that they perform and their different emphases in relation to an overall explanatory account of the research problem under scrutiny.

Particularly pertinent is the role of bridging concepts as a means of focusing on the ligatures that bind together lifeworld and system elements. However, it must also be borne in mind that although bridging concepts provide a seemingly more focused target of this problem, behavioural, systemic and theoretical concepts also play a crucial role. In this respect they are best understood as containing different 'weightings' of reference to lifeworld and system elements. This epistemological and ontological consideration is crucial to understanding the way in which concept-indicator links may buttress each other in their attempt to 'represent' a complex multi-faceted social reality.

Practical aspects of adaptive theory

Let me now leave the discussion of the philosophical, methodological and theoretical context and concentrate on the practical implications of adaptive theory. First, adaptive theory draws on a range of different approaches, paradigms and epistemological positions in social analysis (critical theory, general theory, grounded theory, middle-range theory) but is not reducible to any of them. In this respect it draws only upon those parts of other approaches that are consistent with its own assumptions. In particular, adaptive theory attempts to overcome the paradigmatic differences between some of these approaches by radically altering their epistemological context. Only in this manner is it possible to forge links between different approaches and to facilitate inter-paradigm communication.

For instance, although adaptive theory does not deny (and even attempts to absorb) some of the features of Merton's vision of middle-range theory, it rejects its commitment to an empiricist epistemology and the consequent limitations on social research and analysis which that entails (the rejection of certain kinds of general theory, and a proper grasp of intersubjective meaning). Likewise, although adaptive theory applauds the 'organic' nature of the grounded theory approach, it rejects the limited notion of what is permissibly entitled 'grounded theory' and thereby endeavours to extend its terms of reference (Layder, 1993). Similarly, while adaptive theory draws from general theory (including elements of critical theory), it seeks to go beyond the confines of purely theoretical analysis or the analysis of discourse in order to engage with questions about applied empirical research and primary data-gathering. In this respect adaptive theory engages in a constructive dialogue with a number of approaches or paradigms which may otherwise be construed as incompatible or as competing with each other. By firmly grounding itself in a coherent epistemological and ontological basis, adaptive theory avoids the charge of random or unreflective eclecticism. Instead, it seeks to be eclectic in a positive or constructive sense by collecting together hitherto isolated or disparate research strategies within the same fold. By then reformulating and reconfiguring their internal and underlying elements adaptive theory attempts to capitalize on their synergy and composite strengths. Thus while the adaptive theory approach is both eclectic and synthetic in nature, it also provides a systematic alternative to the approaches it draws upon.

Critical theory is a case in point here that I have not dealt with so far. Adaptive theory has an affinity with critical theory as it is traditionally conceived in so far as it centralizes the importance of the analysis of power and domination in society as an essential part of the endeavour of social research. Although I have not spent a great deal of time specifically on this question (see Layder, 1997 for a detailed analysis of power), such an emphasis is implied in the importance I accord to the analysis of systemic phenomena and the interrelations between lifeworld and system elements (agency and structure). It goes without saying that the analysis of power and domination opens up questions about the morality of various forms of oppression, be they of individuals or groups, as well as resistance to forms of domination and oppression.

Similarly, questions to do with giving voice to oppressed groups and the redistribution of power or the empowerment of relatively powerless groups and individuals all naturally spring from an interest in the analysis and 'critique' of malignant or exploitative forms of power. Adaptive theory draws on critical theory in as much as it focuses on many of these issues in the context of social research and analysis. However, it rejects many of the assumptions of those versions of critical theory which have derived from poststructuralist or postmodernist schools of thought. First, adaptive theory rejects the notion that the agency-structure debate has been transcended or overthrown and must thus be disregarded. Quite the contrary, and as the previous discussion has emphasized, tracing the ligatures and interpenetrations between agency and structure is an absolutely pivotal issue. Secondly, adaptive theory rejects the notion (deriving mainly from Foucault and his followers) that power is inseparably coupled with discourse – in short, that power is coterminous with discourses since discourses themselves have power effects. Without denying that discourses have power effects, adaptive theory rejects the imputation that this exhausts the analysis of power in social life. The theory of social domains underscores a multi-form notion of power which has to be understood in terms of complex relations with social agency, psychobiography, situated activity and systemic phenomena – as well as discourses. Subjective experience ('subjectivity') and social reality are not solely contained within discursive parameters, and as such they are infinitely more complex, variegated and textured than poststructuralism and postmodernism allow. Apart from these, adaptive theory rejects the presumption of many versions of critical theory that understanding everyday life is coterminous with the analysis of ideology or of formal power structures of social systems, although of course the analysis of ideology and domination is also an essential ingredient of social analysis. Everyday life must be conceived as subject to the partly independent influence and conditioning of the interaction order, as Goffman has termed it, and thus it must be treated as a domain in its own right.

The range and scope of adaptive theory

Adaptive theory is 'middle-range' in terms of its immediate focus. That is, its primary focus is on a set of activities (or events) and the social relations and organization which constitute its immediate environment. Thus a focal set of activities is understood as enmeshed in various social settings, such as formal organizations, labour markets and the forms of power and domination that underpin them. It is this set of agency-system linkages that provides the 'hook' of the research focus and problem-orientation. The questions that drive the research concern how and why particular configurations of behaviour, activities and events interpenetrate with their environing forms of power and social organization. However, within the parameters of this kind of focus there is a wide range of possibilities. For example, investigating the nature of emotional labour in the teaching profession provides an instance of an organizational setting in which formal positions of authority impinge upon teachers' abilities to employ emotional labour in various guises while teaching.

By contrast, research into actors' careers immediately spotlights a work setting – the acting profession as whole – which is much less formally organized. Short-term contracts (for a play, a film, a television performance), chronic unemployment and overcrowding of the profession mean that careers are underpinned by the volatility of supply and demand in the labour market for acting work. However, in both these examples the manner in which the everyday worlds and social activities of teachers and actors are reciprocally linked with systemic factors – such as the nature of the social relations (including power and authority), the organization of the work settings and its wider contexts – underpin the problem-focus of the research. Research into prostitution provides another contrasting example of a setting and context but with the same problem-focus on the interweaving of agency-structure or lifeworld–system linkages and influences.

O'Connell Davidson (1998) has demonstrated how the 'organization' of prostitution is diverse, ranging on the one hand from financially successful entrepreneurial adult prostitution through forms in which the prostitute is directly or indirectly employed and controlled (involving third parties such as pimps, procurers, escort agencies) to the other extreme of 'enslavement', as in the case of debt-bonded children. The everyday lives of the prostitutes and their relations with clients are significantly conditioned by these forms of domination and control and this is the typical kind of problem-focus that the adaptive theory approach emphasizes. However, although this is the immediate focus, it does not mean that it always remains limited to, or 'circumscribed' by, this initial focus or point of contact. In this respect adaptive theory is a flexible instrument in terms of its potential application and its overall purview of related issues and interests. Thus it may stray beyond middle-range concerns in the sense that it might include inputs from general theory of all kinds – theories of action or systems or theories of development, for instance.

Also, there is no reason to suppose that the interests of adaptive theory must remain centred exclusively on the intermediate level of social organization, even if this is a frequent starting point. The attention of the researcher or analyst may shift towards either the activity/behavioural side of things (the nature and modes of social interaction and relationships, and so on) or to the system side with a relative emphasis on settings and contexts (institutions, organization, reproduced social relations, power and ideology). Importantly, however, the shifting of focus to one side or the other should only take place as a temporary analytic device at particular junctures of the research in order to confirm or establish particular features and locate specific information. A tilt towards one side or set of issues should be immediately balanced by a concentration on the complementary set of concerns and should involve a systematic attempt to trace the links and interdependencies between lifeworld and system factors. Thus, an overall analysis will take place against the background assumption that agency and structure are instrinsically linked and that neither side of the equation can be properly understood in isolation. Crucially, both the inclusion of elements from general theory and the notion of a continual tacking between behavioural and systemic phenomena allows one to stray beyond the normal remit of middle-range concerns as they are defined either by Merton's (1967) or Glaser and Strauss's (1967) ideas.

What is adaptive about adaptive theory?

Let me concentrate on the term adaptive theory and try to explain what it denotes in a specific sense. There are two main meanings that are attached to the term. First, the word 'adaptive' indicates that the theory which is its focus is sensitive to, and registers the inputs of, the world of empirical phenomena as they are manifest in the primary data of research (interviews, observations, textual or documentary interpretations). In this sense adaptive theory is capable of adjusting to, or being altered or modified to accommodate the analysis and interpretation of data which is being collected in an ongoing fashion. (As such it preserves a residual 'core' of grounded theory, but stripped of its empiricist limitations.) Secondly, the word 'adaptive' suggests that some elements of relevant theory (such as theoretical models) exist prior to, and in tandem with, the collection and analysis of research data. Indeed, it is these extant theoretical elements which are the subject of 'adaptive' responses (adjustments, modifications) to newly emerged data and their interpretation.

So the adaptive part of the term is meant to convey that the theory simultaneously contains two fundamental properties. First, that there is an existing theoretical scaffold which has a relatively durable form since it adapts reflexively rather than automatically in relation to empirical data. Secondly, this scaffold should never be regarded as immutable since it is capable of accommodating new information and interpretations by reconfiguring itself. Thus, although the extant 'theoretical elements' are never simple empiricist 'reflections' of data, they are intrinsically capable of reformulating ('adapting' or

'adjusting') themselves in response to the discovery of new information and/or interpretations of data which seriously challenge their
basic assumptions. Such reformulations may involve only minor
modifications (such as filling out the details of an existing category or
concept such as 'third party controlled prostitution' or 'emotional
burn-out'), but they may also require fundamental reorganization,
such as either abandoning an existing category, model or explanation, or creating new ones, depending on the circumstances.

This depiction of adaptive theory underscores two essential ideas
about the nature of social analysis and its relation to the social reality
which is its object of analysis. These epistemological and ontological
principles underpin and govern the working philosophy of the
adaptive theory approach and flow logically from the methodological
issues discussed in the preceding sections. The whole approach sides
with the view that there is order in the world itself and that it is this
order which social analysis seeks to appropriate or capture in terms
of our knowledge (but not in some 'detached' positivist sense). Thus
social analysis seeks to 'represent' this reality in its theories and
explanations, although not in the form of a direct 'correspondence'
with the reality of this world. This view suggests that there is a world
which is independent of, and indifferent to, any particular person's
attempts to 'know' or appropriate it in various ways (such as
building models of it).

However, crucially, this position suggests that although social
reality has intrinsic properties (which are partly humanly constructed), when we analyse it we naturally impose various kinds of
linguistic orderings upon it (descriptions, conceptualizations,
theories) in attempting to make it comprehensible to us. Thus, in
coming to know this reality through research or analysis, we also
attempt to impose order upon it via the linguistic meanings we
assign to it. Adaptive theory attempts to yoke these two insights –
that there is order in the world which we attempt to contact and
capture and that we simultaneously impose various kinds of
ordering on the world as we analyse and interpret it. From the
viewpoint of an adaptive theory approach there are two main
problems which flow from this position and need to be tackled.

First, we have to be sensitive to (and hence as far as possible
avoid) the possibility that our impositions may seriously override
and do violence to the 'intrinsic order' manifest by social reality (the
problem of extreme rationalism or a coherence theory of truth).
Secondly (and conversely), we must not assume that social reality
offers its own explanation of itself. In other words, that its structure
gives us our knowledge of it independently of the linguistically
mediated social meanings which we impute to it. This is the problem
associated with extreme empiricism and correspondence versions of

truth. The difficulty therefore is to apprehend both the immanent order of social reality as well as to impose order on this reality at different (and appropriate) junctures in the research process.

We can see the practical implications of this in relation to the use of models in adaptive theory. Practically, adaptive theory is about the generation of theoretical models of the social reality that is the subject of the research. That is, it attempts to trace those conjunctions of forms of activity and the social relations and modes of organization in which they are embedded. An example of this would be the relations between prostitutes and their clients as they are conditioned by the mode in which the prostitution is socially organized and the forms of power and control inherent in these relations. The models are generated via a number of routes, including collecting and analysing data, generating emergent concepts and thinking through the theoretical implications of extant theory and bodies of knowledge (including focal and adjacent substantive areas – see Chapter 3) and engaging in theoretical elaboration.

Thus, the adaptive theory approach works to ensure that at some point during the course of a specific research project a theoretical model of agency–system interlocks will emerge (either nascent or more clearly formulated) which will provide an indication of what is going on and why. As this model (for example, of the social organization of prostitution, or of differences in occupational career structures, or of the causes of emotional burn-out) begins to emerge, it will come to play a significant role in ongoing research and the overall explanations and interpretations of the data unearthed by the research. The model will begin to feed into the research in the sense of imposing order on it, while at the same time the model itself will be constantly open to the possibility of reformulation via the orderings of social reality which manifest themselves during the uncovering of research data.

The logic of the process depends heavily on the early development of theoretical models (which may be provisional in nature) which then function to order data. Thus they stand as templates against which data is evaluated and fitted into a conceptual scheme (the model). In this manner, I developed a model of the stratification of the labour market in acting and the mechanisms that serve to reproduce it. This first began life as I scrutinized survey data on actors' employment and earnings, but subsequently the model was developed and refined in conjunction with the collection and analysis of interviews with actors, agents, casting directors, and so on. This elaboration and refinement occurred in two principal ways. First, the idea that the labour market was stratified and segmented in terms of the bunching of incomes and employment suggested certain patterns of interpretation for the analysis of interview data with key gatekeepers such as personal managers/agents and casting directors. Secondly, the interview data themselves fed back into the elaboration of the model and provided clues about the social processes that underpinned it, clues which could not be gleaned from, or suggested by, the initial model itself.

New concepts and theoretical ideas may also emerge in this way as data is collected and analysed, and complements or adds to the nascent model (by suggesting minor reformulations or reconceptualizations). However, if the data is not easily absorbed into the conceptual scheme – that is if it poses a significant challenge to the existing framework by either suggesting radically different sorts of concepts and explanations or, if new findings appear which contradict some of the basic assumptions of the model – then the analytic task is to refine the scheme, or those aspects of it, in order to accommodate the data. This may in fact necessitate the abandonment of certain concepts or categories (such as types of prostitution) or the creation of new ones (for example, by generating new categories relating to emotional overload or burn-out). Whichever is the case, this general use of models makes the adaptive approach very different from that of grounded theory which insists that theory is continuously emergent and that no elaborated conceptual scheme stands prior to data collection at any point in the unfolding of the research process.

The reasons for this difference are important in defining the distinctiveness of the adaptive theory approach. Partly, the differences arise because, as I have just intimated, grounded theory abandons the notion of prior conceptual schemes and the use of extant general theory because they are thought to stand in the way of generating new theory and conceptual ideas. By contrast, adaptive theory centralizes the idea that prior theory plays a vital and constructive role during theory-generating social research. Although new data and their analysis have the important role of suggesting refinements of the theoretical models that one is working with, they do not inform the models *in toto*. Nor are the models infinitely responsive to the demands of newly emerging data or information. Instead, they are selectively and reflexively responsive and hence they are accommodative of the empirical world rather than the result of an automatic and plastic response to it. In this sense the very existence of prior theory effects an organic link with newly created theory and exists in a reciprocal and dialectical relationship to it. It both prompts the emergence of new theory and limits it at different moments and junctures of analysis and the research process.

Another reason for the distinctiveness of the adaptive approach lies in the fact that grounded theory prioritizes elements of the life-world (forms of interaction, communication, meaning, and so on) in its theoretical deliberations and representations and simultaneously excludes a consideration of social structural or systemic phenomena. By focusing exclusively on lifeworld phenomena, grounded theory concerns itself with the details of interpersonal relations which are in principle infinite. Coupled with the injunction to produce as many codes as possible (see Chapter 3), this has an individualizing effect that encourages the researcher constantly to produce new concepts which represent behavioural features manifested in the data.

Behavioural features – especially those of participants as opposed to the observer's concepts – are potentially inexhaustible because there are as many meanings that can be attached to a person's behaviour as there are facets of that person's personality and social dispositions. This is, of course, further magnified when one considers the behaviour of people in interaction with each other. Although the analyst selects from this infinitude of possibilities, there is always the temptation to 'add-on' further descriptive concepts so as not to miss out any which may be representative or analytically important. Thus the number of possible candidates for the generation of new concepts multiplies exponentially.

Unless there is some attention paid to systemic phenomena (forms of power relation, social organization, resources, ideologies, and so on), then there are no natural brakes to be applied to the constant collection and accretion of behavioural concepts. However, such continuous accumulation does not necessarily add to the explanatory features of the theory; it merely produces a diverse array of concepts which may or may not be important for the theory in the long run. This is one of the main problems of the grounded theory approach – there is no real discriminating factor which can arbitrate between 'decorative additions' to a conceptual framework and essential components of the conceptual schema or theoretical model. By contrast, although adaptive theory pays attention to behavioural phenomena, this is simultaneously complemented by an awareness of, and concentration on, systemic phenomena. This has the effect of applying the brakes to the 'saturation' or 'carpet' generation of theoretical concepts because it intervenes in the theory-generation process as a whole. In particular, it allows the analyst to decide on the salience of behavioural concepts by 'measuring' them against their relevance to the social systemic forms in which they are intertwined. Thus, the generation of behavioural concepts is limited by their relevance to (and the extent to which they throw light on) systemic phenomena and vice versa. Once a basic array of behavioural concepts have been generated and 'tested', and serve as the core of the analysis of behavioural system interlocks, then there is no real need to generate more behavioural concepts. Of course this is not to suggest that there is some absolute prohibition on developing more and more behavioural concepts. But it does point to the fact that these are often unnecessary in that they do not add anything further to the analysis and/or explanation of the links between lifeworld and system phenomena.

The converse effect plays a role here in that the nature of lifeworld–system interlocks place reciprocal 'restraints' upon the development of system concepts. However, the analytic problems posed in this respect are not as acute as they are with behavioural concepts because the possibilities for 'unconstrained' generation of system concepts is never of equal scope or of the same proportions as they are with lifeworld and behavioural concepts. This is because a concentration on systemic phenomena in itself has an inherently generalizing effect rather than a concern with the concrete and particular – as it is with behavioural concepts. Systemic concepts are analytic concepts which are concerned with the general parameters of social organization and social relations. As such they deal with a limited number of possibilities of social-systemic forms (for example, occupational organization, types of prostitution, sexual scripts played out between prostitutes and their clients (O'Connell Davidson, 1998)). Systemic concepts are, by definition, non-behavioural (although they are related to behaviour) and therefore do not describe or depict aspects of an infinity of possible behaviours. They deal with general features of social relations and organization which cut across and transcend the particular examples of behaviour which are played out within these social forms.

Thus, the major difference between the adaptive approach and that of grounded theory is that the latter concentrates exclusively on the behavioural dimension of social life while the former deals with both the behavioural and systemic aspects. By dealing with the dual inputs of these phenomena, the adaptive theory approach possesses a number of features which endow it with advantages over grounded theory. First, it allows, and indeed encourages, a dialogue between prior theory (including conceptual models) and conceptual elements which are embedded in data and emerge as an adaptive response to data collection and analysis. It is the synergy produced by this interchange that creates the organic nature of the theory – it is 'alive', 'emergent' and continually unfolding according to the changing circumstances of the research and of social life. Secondly, it attends to much larger tracts of social life, particularly those areas which are stretched over time and space, such as reproduced social relations and forms of social organization which 'aggregate' reproduced social positions, practices and relations. Thirdly, the twin focus of adaptive theory enables it to define the relevance of emergent concepts more closely and in a controlled manner – irrespective of whether these emergent concepts derive from data collection or theoretical elaboration.

In many respects these features also distinguish the adaptive approach from that of deductive theory and middle-range approaches. The key feature of adaptive theory is its continuously accretive nature. It is an organic entity which is constantly developing and reformulating itself as a result of the interchange and dialogue between emergent (data-embedded) theory and prior theory (models concepts, frameworks). In this respect adaptive theory provides a sharp contrast to approaches which limit theory development to particular segments or stages of the research process, such as the beginning (conceptual framework) stage or the end (analysis and conclusions stage). These approaches view theorizing as if it were a discrete and rather static 'application' of analytic principles and procedure rather than an ever-developing, organic 'entity' which forms an intrinsic and continuous part of the processes of research and analysis. While adaptive theory draws on some elements of these approaches to theorizing, such as deductive principles and an attention to social-structural features beyond social interaction and symbolic communication, it parts company from them over the issue of the continuity of theorizing as an ever-present aspect of research.

The empirical and theoretical focus of adaptive theory

The aspects of social life that adaptive theory is most suited to in terms of a research focus are those that concern the interweaving between what I call 'social settings' and the 'situated activities' that take place within them. It is a focus on the interweaving of these two facets of social life that is important because they are tightly bound together and cannot in any sense be understood as entirely separate from each other. However, although settings and social activity are intimately related, it must also be recognized that they are dissimilar in that they possess independent characteristics. It is very important to continue to bear these distinguishing features in mind (as well as the interconnections between them) and resist the temptation to understand them as somehow neutralized, fused or dissolved as a consequence of their interrelatedness. This latter mistaken assumption has the debilitating effect of overlooking the independent contributions that each makes in its effects upon the other. This error is common to a number of approaches which are otherwise very different in terms of their general theoretical and research implications, including structuration theory, structuralism, poststructuralism, postmodernism, discourse analysis, symbolic interactionism, phenomenology, figurational or process sociology.

In common-sense terms it is also all too easy to overlook the significant distinguishing properties of settings and social activities since they seem so closely united in specific instances. In this respect we are more conscious of (and thus tend to make) distinctions between the many different kinds of settings we encounter in social life rather than distinguishing between them and our behaviour. Thus when we consider the many diverse settings of social life – such as coffee bars, restaurants, schools, universities, factories, stores, army barracks, monasteries, breakfast-room tables, court rooms, committee meetings, elevators, public transport, city streets – we hardly think to make a distinction between them and the activities which take place within them. Our common-sense way of thinking elides such distinctions and we tend to think that settings *are* the social activities which are displayed in a specific location and at a specific time. Conversely, we assume that the behaviours on display at any point constitute the very fabric of the setting we are in.

However, in order to understand the nature of social life and the implications this has for social research it is important not to lose sight of the different properties or characteristics of settings and activities which are simultaneously enfolded within the intimate bond between them. For analytic and research purposes it is therefore important to stress that they should not be regarded as the same (identical) even though they do not exist entirely independently of each other. Settings depend upon people and their social activities in order for them to have some continuity or persistence in social life. Thus it is social activity (in general) which both produces (in the present) and reproduces (over time) social settings in which this activity takes place. Conversely, social activity *always* takes place within the immediate environment of social settings (and a wider social context) and has no existence outside them.

However, there are two senses in which activity is partly independent of and distinguishable from social settings (and contexts). First, settings are different from activity in so far as they are the social locations of activity and as such represent the reproduced social conditions (relations, practices, resources, control, discourses, ideologies, and so on) under which specific social activities operate. That is, social settings and contexts represent the pre-existing social circumstances which have developed historically and condition and influence contemporary (ongoing) activities. Contemporary activity, on the other hand, is always predicated on the existential 'thereness' of the participants and is punctuated by their arrivals and departures (Goffman, 1967). Situated activity has its own inner dynamics to do with specific participants and the meanings and reality constructions they negotiate which are different from the reproduced social positions, practices and relations which are aggregated to form the basic structure or organization of the setting in question.

It is the manner in which the inner dynamics of situated activity intersect and intertwine with the reproduced positions, relations and practices of settings to transform, modify or maintain their organizational characteristics which is the main focus of the adaptive theory approach. Important sub-features of this concern the differences in organizational form of different settings, how they impinge upon social activities and how different types of situated activity impact upon the settings and their wider resource contexts (Layder, 1997). Social settings themselves vary considerably, as do the wider class, gender and racialized contexts of these settings and the material, power and ideological basis of resource allocation which impact upon them. However, settings themselves range from highly formalized, defined and crystallized forms reflected in bureaucratic and hierarchical organizations – as in some factories, military and religious organizations, and so on – to the very informal and personalized relationships that subsist in families, friendships, personal and sexual relationships, through to the uncrystallized, rather diffuse settings of street life, 'underground' criminal activities, public transport, and so on. The nature of the reproduced relations, practices and social positions in these different settings vary considerably and have entirely different implications for the people and behaviours they are influenced by and also help to shape. Conversely, face-to-face relationships and situated activities are in themselves multi-faceted and impact upon the settings in a multitude of ways. In short, the important problem-focus for adaptive theory is the manner in which specific activities impact upon and shape social settings (and contexts) and the manner in which these reproduced relations, practices, powers and discourses in turn shape and condition social behaviour and activity.

The elements of adaptive theory

As the above discussion has attempted to show, adaptive theory centres on descriptions and explanations of the interconnections between settings and the social activities which both sustain and transform them. Given this background of substantive concerns, the exact form that adaptive theory can take as it emerges or is developed from particular research investigations is variable. The main dimensions of these variations include: the sorts of conceptual and theoretical elements that it contains; the extent to which different elements are used within the same theory; and the manner in which

Table 6.1   *The main groupings of theoretical elements in adaptive theory*

Concepts	Basic building blocks for theorizing types: sensitizing; orienting; core; satellite; behavioural; systemic; bridging; embedded; extant.
Conceptual clusters/ networks/frameworks	Clusterings of related concepts covering a range of phenomena: general theory; substantive and formal theory; grounded theory; middle-range theory (open or closed, tight or loose integration).
Typological models	A connected series of models of a range of related phenomena which identify similarities and differences between them: behavioural (action) typologies; systemic (structural) typologies.

different elements are connected within the same theory. I have dealt with these different kinds of theoretical elements in a scattered manner throughout this book but here I shall bring them together in a systematic fashion.

In broad terms, there are three main groupings of theoretical elements which are of concern in adaptive theory: concepts; conceptual clusters, networks or frameworks; and typological models (see Table 6.1). Concepts are of course the basic building blocks of any theory since they provide us with general abstract definitions which group objects or social phenomena together in terms of a combination of aspects. Concepts, as I have discussed them, may be 'borrowed' and/or developed (through theoretical elaboration) from existing bodies of theory or conceptual frameworks. Alternatively, they may be developed from codes used to order empirical data such as interview transcripts, reports of observations or documents. Concepts have an important role to play in establishing the relationships with empirical indicators and thus of setting up specific concept-indicator linkages. As I have pointed out, concepts in adaptive theory have several different forms: sensitizing, orienting, core and satellite, behavioural, systemic, bridging, and so on. In general concepts label and classify small slices of social reality and as such they furnish us with the building blocks from which larger and more complex orderings of reality are possible.

In Table 6.1 what I have termed conceptual clusters, networks and frameworks represent the grouping of concepts together into wider configurations. These in turn can be sub-divided in terms of the kind of theoretical universe to which they belong. For example, whether they derive from general theories, substantive theories, grounded theories or middle-range (hypothetico-deductive) theories. Also they may be classified in terms of the extent to which they may be characterized as 'tightly' or 'loosely' integrated, and as being 'open' or 'closed' in terms of their boundaries with other frameworks and concepts. For instance, many general theories (like Parsons's, Foucault's or Habermas's) are tightly integrated and rather 'closed' in nature – from the point of view of other general theories – since they aim to be comprehensive and are to some extent in competition with them. On the other hand, substantive theories (of occupations, deviance, sexuality, and so on) are often more amenable to absorption into the more general types. We can also distinguish between 'extant' or 'emergent' clusterings, as well as various combinations of these characteristics (see Chapter 4). These variations point to the fact that not all individual concepts that constitute a framework will fit into the 'home' clustering to the same extent or in the same manner. For example, some may be tightly integrated with the others and occupy a 'core' position within the group, while other concepts may seem to have an uneasy or uncertain association with the rest of the group, while the main group itself seems to exhibit closer cohesion and integration. However, notwithstanding these internal variations, the principal differences between single concepts as conceptual building blocks and the more inclusive clusterings and frameworks hinge around the following issues.

First, single concepts may serve a wider function, such as providing a temporary ordering or depiction of a phenomenon which may later be substantially revised, abandoned or simply fade in significance – as in the case of orienting concepts (see Chapter 4). Secondly, some single concepts may have recently emerged either from data analysis, theoretical elaboration or some combination of the two, and as such *may* not yet clearly belong within a broader grouping. This of course may or may not happen later in the proceedings, depending on how the concept begins to shape up further along the line of analysis and elaboration. Thirdly, and almost by definition, a broader grouping of related concepts in itself covers a wider range of social phenomena than that indicated or depicted by an individual concept. That is, instead of simply referring to a small slice of reality, the inclusion in a wider grouping means that much 'larger portions' of reality can be referred to since the single concept is now a conduit to a more embracing network of concepts.

This therefore leads to the fourth difference between single concepts and related clusters. The complexity and range of meanings which a concept refers to is increased by its incorporation into an established grouping or cluster since this will imply that the meaning of the concept itself is now also related to the meanings of the other concepts in the group as a whole. An appropriate analogy here is that of vocabulary items compared with grammar in language. On their own, single words have a restricted range of meaning, but when combined through grammatical rules to form sentences, their capacity to generate meaning is vastly increased.

The final theoretical elements associated with adaptive theory are theoretical and typological models and both sorts draw upon the different types of concept and conceptual clustering that have already been discussed. However, before moving to typological models and regarding them as somewhat distinct from conceptual clusters, it is interesting to consider the role played by theoretical models in general. In this respect some models have more in common with conceptual clusterings in general. For example, many general theories (either of particular authors or of general approaches) contain theoretical models of particular aspects or features of the social world. These may be models of social behaviour or interaction (as in symbolic interactionism), or local practices (ethnomethodology), or they may be models of basic features of social life (as in Foucault's vision of the connections between discourses, practices and power). Of particular importance for the present discussion are those models of the linkages between intersubjective phenomena and social institutions which have been variously referred to as lifeworld and system (Habermas), or agency and structure (Giddens), or the interaction order and the institutional order (Goffman).

The specific model of the linkage between the two major aspects of social life that I have proposed at various junctures in this book is taken from my own theory of social domains (Layder, 1997). This provides an example of how theoretical models deriving from wider clusterings of concepts may become part of the organic growth of new theoretical thinking or the development of extant ideas as a result of their strategic deployment in particular research protocols – in this case of adaptive theory. Such models derive from, and are integrally connected to, more general theoretical systems of thought, although my argument here is designed to encourage (where appropriate and with due attention to the attendant problems) the use of theoretical models (or aspects of them) with varying degrees of detachment from their 'home clustering' for purposes of theory-generation in different contexts. In this respect theoretical models can take several forms – as Weber's famous ideal-type models of authority, bureaucratic organization, and the capitalist work ethic clearly demonstrate. In developing ideal types, Weber accentuated and exaggerated features found in empirical reality but common to the specific phenomenon under investigation, and this enabled him to develop general abstract models.

The notion of ideal types is closely related to the development of typological models (or 'typologies') of social phenomena. Ideal types concentrate on modelling the typical features of a specific phenomenon, say a bureaucratic organization, in order to build a picture of its generic characterisitics. Typology-building goes a step further and focuses on the range of phenomena falling within a similar class – say the range of types of formal organization that are possible and how they depart from, or correspond to, the bureaucratic model.

Thus typology-building utilizes a series of ideal types in conjunction with each other to examine the range of variation within the group. Building and using typologies helps to generate and stimulate theoretical thinking by encouraging the researcher to make comparisons between phenomena which are similar as well as different from the one under scrutiny. The questions 'why and how is this different?' and 'how or why is this similar or the same?' have the effect of generating codes, categories and concepts around such issues and thus stimulate further conceptual analysis and linkages.

I have emphasized, in Chapter 3 and elsewhere (Layder, 1993), the importance of distinguishing between behavioural (or action) and systemic (or structural) typologies in order to register and depict the very different social domains from which they derive. I have also emphasized the utility of developing both types simultaneously with a view to generating conceptual density when modelling the inter-linking of lifeworld and systemic phenomena. This is particularly important in that the literature on fieldwork methods often emphasizes action or behavioural typologies and, as a result under-represents the social systemic aspects of social life in and around the activities which are the focus of analysis. Of course, it is not always feasible, appropriate or possible to concentrate one's analytic attention on both at once, and therefore a certain amount of selective focusing is necessary. However, this is a matter of emphasis and should not prevent overall analytic attention from focusing on lifeworld or system phenomena. Two strategies are helpful in this regard. First, although one might have a 'primary' interest in the detailed development of either a behavioural or a systemic typology, it is always useful to work with a 'schematic' or rudimentary (and provisional) typological model of the 'other' aspect as a complementary balance to one's primary interest. Also, searching for bridging concepts helps in this regard by tying-down one's focus to the over-laps and interconnections between the two meta-domains.

The raw materials of adaptive theory

The conceptual and theoretical products of the adaptive approach derive from several sources which can be broadly classified into four groupings, two of which are theoretically based resources, and two empirically based ones (see Table 6.2). The theoretical resources refer to extant theory and can be divided between 'general theory' and what I term 'substantive theory'. General theory (or theoretician's theory) applies to generic features of social life and includes such questions as 'what is the nature of social activity and/or social

Table 6.2   *Sources of adaptive theory*

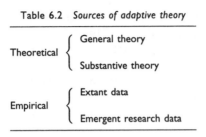

Theoretical	General theory
	Substantive theory
Empirical	Extant data
	Emergent research data

institutions?' or 'how do activities and institutions relate to each other in a general sense?' In this respect general theory is relevant and applies to many diverse empirical areas. Thus it differs from 'substantive theory' which is of relevance only to particular substantive areas (such as crime or deviance, medicine, education, work and industry, racialized relations, and so on).

My usage of the term 'substantive theory' is different from that of Glaser and Strauss (1967) who employ a distinction between substantive and formal theory. Their version of the distinction refers to the degree of generality and abstraction of the theory so that one might, for example, have a substantive theory of scientists' careers by taking a sample composed solely of scientists. However, one might want to go on to generate a formal theory of organizational careers by sampling any number of different kinds of career which fall within the formal area of organizational careers – scientists' careers being but one example. While I have no doubt that the notion of formal theory represents a more general and abstract type than that of substantive theory in Glaser and Strauss's terms, it certainly does not include general theory as I have defined it, since they dismiss the relevance of general theory for research. In this respect what I call substantive theory subsumes their notion of formal theory since it applies very much to specific empirical areas rather than to generic theoretical problems and issues in social life.

Both general and substantive theory provide ready-made resources which may be tapped into in the service of theory-generation in the context of applied primary research. In my view, they provide the sorts of resources that may aid the different forms of theory elaboration outlined in Chapters 3 and 4, both by thinking through the relations between extant concepts (fitting them into chains of theoretical reasoning) and by responding (accommodating and adapting) to the emergent data of research. Although either of these strategies is suitable and effective in its own right, I have stressed that the most powerful mode derives from the simultaneous and dialogical relation between both these forms of theory elaboration. While it is true that both·general theory and substantive theory may contribute in this fashion to ongoing theory-generation, it is worth pointing to some of the significant differences between general and substantive theory. This takes us back to some of the dimensions I mentioned in relation to clusterings of concepts in the previous section.

In particular, general and substantive theories tend to differ along the 'open' or 'closed' axis. Theoretical systems tend to be internally consistent and self-referential in order to be able to generalize across large slices of social life. The very scope of general theories (the extent of their relevance) requires that they are rigorously cross-referenced and that the concepts in which they are expressed are dense and inclusive. This inclusiveness often means that they also tend to set up boundaries and definite limits. This is coupled with the fact that theoretical systems are usually designed as original inter-ventions in ongoing debates and hence they are framed as explanatory rivals which are in competition with other theories. The inclusiveness, boundary maintenance and competitiveness have the effect of stressing their differences, incommensurability and incompatibility with other theories.

However, if general theories are to serve any serious organic role in theory-generation in social research, then they must not be viewed as repositories of certainty, truth, or even more or less adequate knowledge. Instead, they should be regarded as being able to expand or grow internally or produce new offshoots in the light of incoming evidence and/or theoretical elaboration. Both internal and external (those involving research) forms of theory-generation involve a sort of disciplined 'ransacking' of general theories and an examination of their constituent parts in order to search out aspects which may serve the creative purpose of further theory-generation. The collection and collation of concepts and ideas that results feeds into the emergence of new theory.

The same problem of 'relative closure' does not arise to the same extent with substantive theory. This is because substantive theories are usually more limited in scope, centring on the substantive area itself and limiting its references to wider areas. For example, theories concerning the operation of labour markets, such as segmentation theory, certainly make reference to contiguous areas such as class or work organization but do not make claims about the general nature of institutions or social interaction. In this respect they seem to be more immediately open to other influences (either theoretical or evidential) and the cross-fertilization of ideas. Of course there are generic problems of compatibility and commensurability concerning conceptual, epistemological and ontological matters and these are not all simply swept aside because of the relative openness of substantive theories. Nonetheless, their comparative lack of closure means that some of these problems are more easily overcome.

As far as the empirical raw materials are concerned, what I have termed 'extant data' represents the most wide-reaching and diffuse set of resources that can be drawn upon in the service of theory-generation. Extant data refers to all previous findings of social research and naturally includes both the large and small data sets and data bases that have accrued or have been developed in the recent and long-term past. However, extant data is not limited to the findings of social research as formally conceived. It ranges far and wide to include anything and everything that can be brought to bear in an evidential sense on the forms of knowledge and explanation that our social theories provide. Thus books and literature from disciplinary areas other than sociology, including popular literature, self-help and motivational material, novels, journals, diaries, magazines (popular, elite and esoteric), advertisements, photographs, films and theatre, and sporting events may be part of extant data – in short, any aspect of social life that is capable of representation in a form which allows it to be offered or referred to as evidence of social trends, customs, habits, types of work or recreation, and so forth. Anything which can be documented either visually or linguistically and which can therefore be pointed to as evidence of some aspect of social life or social reality may become a valuable resource which may stimulate theoretical thinking.

Of course, the fact that something may be used as evidence does not automatically mean that it will be accepted as valid, and in this respect conventional canons of proof and validity have to be achieved by evidence which has not been gathered in a systematic manner or for the purposes of social research. We have to distinguish here between extant data standing as evidence of some form of systematic (large-scale or far-reaching) explanation or theory, and extant data which stimulates a new line of conceptualization or theoretical thinking. In the latter case, evidential data which appears to be purely anecdotal, nebulous or of dubious provenance need not be simply dismissed on this basis if it can be used to redirect or reformulate theory, or if it acts as a spring board for creative theoretical thinking. The importance of extant data (as with extant theory) is that it encourages us to draw upon the widest possible range of resources when working within the confines of specific research projects. Just as an awareness of extant theory ensures that we do not simply attend to the emergent or grounded aspects of theory that flow from the current research, so too extant data allows us to be aware of other possible relevancies of information and evidence which may feed into theoretical thinking and theory-generation.

What I have called 'emergent research data' focus on the immediate findings and information that arise from the current research project. In this sense emergent data provide a continuous 'testing-out' of extant or prior theory and thus provide a direct feedback system which fashions the organic connection between theorizing and data collection and analysis. Also, emergent data is a potential resource for the suggestion of new concepts and theoretical ideas. In this sense some concepts are understood to be 'embedded' in data in so far as they are not simply given in, or apparent from, the theoretical materials at hand – as with the concept of typification. However, to say that some concepts are 'embedded' is not to suggest a form of empiricism whereby the data themselves directly 'suggest' or 'offer up' theoretical concepts. Embeddedness in this sense refers to the fact that newly uncovered empirical findings and data may reveal aspects of the world under consideration which prompt theoretical reflection in terms of extant and prior theory and which may then lead to conceptual formulation or reformulation.

This also underlines the point that 'facts' or information or data (whether newly emerged or extant) are never pristine and innocent. All data is already theoretically saturated either through 'contamination' by prior theorizing or through the preconceptions and common-sense presuppositions imported by the researcher (or generations of researchers). Thus, to speak of the manner in which adpative theory attempts to capture or fashion an 'organic' connection between theorizing and data collection and analysis is not to imply some essentialist link. Although adaptive theory allows for and indeed encourages a dialectical relation between the formulation of theoretical concepts, clusters and models and their reformulation or revisability in the light of emergent data collection and analysis, there is no implication that this presupposes some kind of a pre-theoretical (or epistemologically neutral) basis which is reflected in the term 'organic'. In this sense 'organicism' simply refers to the uncovering of research data and the simultaneous unfolding of conceptualization and theoretical reflection.

Modes of theory-generation

The fundamental basis of the adaptive approach rests on the twin employment of, and the subsequent interaction between, extant or 'prior' theoretical materials and emergent data from ongoing research. The dual approach ensures that extant or prior concepts and theory both shape and inform the analysis of data which emanates from ongoing research at the very same time that the emergent data itself shapes and moulds the existing theoretical materials. It is the dialectical interplay between these and the fusion that it entails which in turn produces the synthetic form of adaptive theory.

Figure 6.1   *The relations between extant theory, emergent data and adaptive theory*

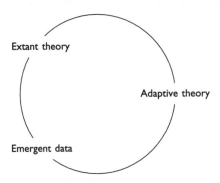

In Figure 6.1 the relations between extant theory, emergent data and the adaptive theory that results from their interaction is depicted as a continuous circuit of influences and effects. This reflects the fact that there is no unitary way of understanding the dynamics of the formation of adaptive theory. Since all the factors operate synchronically it is difficult to separate out the effects of the constitutent elements and this reflects its complex, ever-developing nature. In this sense the theory is continuously adaptive to the dictates of both theoretical reasoning and the 'factual' character of the empirical world. However, there are two distinct modes of adaptive theory which produce a tiered or contoured set of effects and influences. I shall deal with these under the headings of 'secondary effects' and 'adaptive theory proper'.

Secondary effects

The secondary effects of adaptive theory are an 'added extra' to the focal concern with emergent theory around the ongoing area of research. These refer to its relation with aspects of general theory *from the point of view of general theory*. In this sense it provides a direct link or bridge between general theorizing and empirical research. This tie-in ensures that the general theory in question (or aspects of it) receives the inputs (positive or negative) that flow from application in an empirical or substantive context. These 'concern' two related aspects of theorizing in terms of the development of extant theory. The first involves the 'testing-out' or 'validity' of various explanatory claims and other aspects of general theory (such as a concept, a model, a conceptual framework) in the context of an ongoing research project. The second concerns the revision, reformulation, addition or qualification of the explanatory scope and domain of the original theoretical materials, again as the result of direct engagement with empirical materials. The importance of this direct contact with empirical data is not to imply that general theory is completely lacking in empirical reference. Rather, the ongoing research provides a test-bed for the application of the theory in contexts that have not previously been considered, or been considered 'primary' or relevant to the concerns of the general theory in question.

For example, my use of a particular aspect of structuration theory – the 'dialectic of control' – in the context of research on actors' careers highlights the relation between these two aspects. In particular, I employed the dialectic of control to examine the relation between actors and agents (or 'personal managers'). By looking at their social relations from two points of view – the (reproduced) social relations between actors and agents as collectivities over time, and the way in which specific relationships between particular actors and their agents change over time – I was able to establish two things. First, that structuration theory had a useful general bearing on this substantive topic and that it therefore underscores the validity of particular features of the dialectic of control – and some aspects of the wider context of structuration theory. Secondly, the comparison between the collective and individual social relations between actors and agents suggested that the dialectic of control, as Giddens envisaged it, needed to be modified to take account of structural forms of power (Layder, 1997) as well as different properties of control at different levels of analysis (Layder, 1993).

Where there is a focal concern with the generation of theory from ongoing research, this sort of secondary effect occurs as an offshoot or by-product of the search for more specific kinds of theory-generation. As a consequence, this kind of 'addition' to general theory occurs in parallel with the organic emergence of a research-focused theory. However, in principle, this sort of relation with general theory can occur at any particular stage of any research process, including before the research has begun or after the data collection has been completed (Bloor and McIntosh, 1990; Layder et al., 1991). In this sense I am not claiming that this link with general theory is specific to adaptive theory, but rather I am suggesting that it is a routine and common feature of it. The principal difference between the use of general theory in conjunction with specific pieces of research in other contexts is that they usually involve a conscious, and sometimes exceptional, decision to 'import' a general theory, or elements of it, to help order the data and data analysis, whereas this approach automatically invokes extant theory as a routine means of stimulating theoretical ideas. In this sense these secondary effects work directly towards bridging the division between research and theory.

Another differentiating factor, as I mentioned previously, is that adaptive theory views general theories, in principle, as 'open' universes of meaning or discourse which are inherently revisable, reformulable, and so on, and not as unquestioned or total explanatory frameworks. This obviates the problems which arise when general theories are regarded as sacrosanct, all-encompassing perspectives into which any and all data can be squeezed or forced. With the latter, all the emergent data or evidence of the ongoing research is ordered via the master theory and thus tends to be interpreted as supporting or confirming the original theory. Such a posture leads to a stultification of theory development and has minimal consequences for the elaboration or amendment of general theory. Only where general theories are regarded as genuinely open discourses is it possible to make any real theoretical advances.

A further distinguishing feature has to do with the fact that secondary effects are off-shoots of the primary generation of research-focused theory. In the case of adaptive theory proper, there will always be some positive feedback from general theory into the research-focused theory – the real heart of adaptive theory – and this constitutes the primary effect. It is only in cases where there is no feedback into adaptive theory proper that secondary effects for general theory are produced. This contrasts with other usages of general theory in research in which it is employed as the principal means of ordering (or giving some pattern to) the research data. In this respect there is no room for the development of the kind of relatively autonomous (or even quasi-autonomous) pockets of theory which adaptive theory proper represents.

Adaptive theory proper

Unlike the secondary effects, adaptive theory proper is structured around, and in a certain sense emerges from, a research topic and problem. The 'emergence' of theory is a consequence of a simultaneous anchorage in theoretical materials (as well as empirical data) and in the shaping and moulding which derives from both these resources. The simultaneous privileging of theory and data in the emergence of new theory distinguishes this approach from that of grounded theory, which privileges data against prior theory. It is the importance of the dialogical relation between prior theory and data collection and analysis that gives the distinctive stamp to adaptive theory.

I shall give a concrete example shortly, but first let me say that there are two broad levels at which theory shapes the deliberations in a prior fashion. First, both general and substantive theory provide existing concepts (clusters) and models which may feed into the understanding of emergent data by 'suggesting' patterns or orderings of this data. However, by provisionally ordering data, the extant materials will be transformed to some degree as they are filtered and conditioned by the emergent data. Secondly, there is the possibility that new concepts and theoretical ideas will be revealed by, or emerge from, the data collection and analysis itself and this will also feed into theoretical deliberations. Therefore, the dual inputs of extant theoretical materials and emergent or embedded concepts will generate the composite form of the resultant (adaptive) theory.

Thus, during the research, a new entity – the adaptive theory itself – emerges as a third force in the proceedings and begins to act as a mediation between the extant theoretical materials and the data collection and analysis. As this third force begins to unfold, it starts to play a role as 'prior' theory at a different level or phase of the research process. The newly emergent adaptive theory will act as an ordering device, suggesting or imposing explanatory schemas and conceptual frames on incoming data in a manner similar to the extant theory (general and substantive). It too will connect and intermesh with data collection and analysis, and will eventually be modified and reshaped by these things. At the same time extant theory will lose its direct link with data collection and analysis since it will now be mediated by the emergent conceptual framework. In this sense the most important 'prior theory' will be that of the emergent adaptive theory which interposes itself between the original extant theoretical raw materials and the data uncovered by the social research.

Let me illustrate this. Say the original extant theoretical raw materials revolved around the issue of emotional labour and the topic of the research was how school teachers dealt with emotional issues in their work environment. The extant material may be both general theories of interaction (say Mead's or Goffman's) and substantive theories of emotional labour (Hochschild), while the data of research may be observations and/or surveys and/or interviews with teachers in the school setting. Although the extant theoretical materials may provide a well-founded provisional ordering and understanding of the incoming data, the researcher subsequently finds that the notion of emotional labour as it applies in the substantive area, say of flight attendants (Hochschild's main example), needs to be 'unpacked' and modified in order to draw out its implications for school teaching. This leads the researcher to develop a typology of different kinds of emotional labour in different kinds of social setting (from a secondary analysis of studies of different kinds of work and work environments).

The development of this typology subsequently becomes the centrepoint of the adaptive theory which then feeds into the data collection (say through extending the sampling to include pupils) and feeds back into the general theory (interactionism) and substantive theory (emotional labour). So that while the typology itself is shaped and modified by the extant theoretical materials and the incoming research data, the unfolding adaptive theory (the typology and related concepts) simultaneously shapes, modifies and orders the data and the extant materials. A complex set of mutual influences, feedback mechanisms and conduits, which has its own momentum and inner dynamic, is thereby formed. The typology that begins to shape up in this way becomes an additional and partly autonomous theoretical product (new theory) as well as providing new theoretical insights into the substantive area of school teaching as a form of work. While the main contours of the typology are being developed, the chances are that auxiliary concepts are 'being helped along'. These may act as satellites around the conceptual core, providing extended support for the overall theory. Together, these different strands of theorizing and conceptual development provide new theory generated by engagement in data collection and analysis around a specific research topic and by articulating with extant theoretical materials.

Conclusion

In this chapter I have tried to emphasize the philosophical, methodological and practical implications of a distinctive approach to understanding the relation between theory and social research. I have suggested that the approach I advocate is a judicious blend of inductive and deductive procedures – and the empiricist and rationalist theories of truth which underpin them. However, I have tried to go beyond the rather bland assertion that theorizing or research involve a soupçon of all the essential ingredients. I have specified the manner in which these different methodological procedures and theories of truth enter into research calculations and the practical possibilities for theory-generation.

These issues are pivotal to the way in which we conceive social science (or social analysis) in general and the core problem-focus of agency-structure or lifeworld–system interlocks. Only when we focus on how it is that social activities are intertwined with social institutions, culture and other reproduced aspects of the social world can we properly address the question of lifeworld–system inter-connections. Thus the 'subject matter' of adaptive theory concerns the multifarious ways in which aspects of the lifeworld (behaviour, activity, everyday life) intersect with systemic aspects of the social world (culture, institutions, power and control, reproduced positions, practices and social relations).

I have concentrated on the generation of theory from data collection and analysis, aspects of existing theory (both general and substantive) and a broad range of empirical materials, especially documentary resources from non-technical (sometimes 'popular') literature. Adaptive theory constantly fuses and accommodates aspects of prior theoretical ideas, concepts or conceptual clusters with theoretical elements that emerge from the ongoing collection of empirical data and its analysis. Theoretical models refine and readjust the direction of the research, lending shape to the constantly emerging research data. At the same time, the collection of empirical information and data helps reconfigure the theoretical model (or looser arrangements of concepts and ideas).

Such an approach allows for features which are essential for the construction of sound and robust theory and serves to draw general theory and social research closer together. First, where necessary, it permits a constant process of refinement, readjustment and reformu-lation of theory as it is developed. Secondly, it provides the con-ditions under which the validity and reliability of the theory may be routinely checked and monitored as the research proceeds. Finally, what I have termed secondary effects provide an additional means by which general theory may be developed (qualified, refined, recon-figured) through a link with the systematic collection of social research data and this helps to ensure that general theoretical per-pectives never congeal into dogma.

CHAPTER 7

SOME NEW RULES OF METHOD

I have been concerned not only to provide some 'rules of thumb' that facilitate theory-generation in the context of ongoing research, but also to outline some new rules of sociological method. I must reiterate that I do not mean that the approach I have sketched is solely designed to replace established or conventional approaches. In this respect I envision two general possibilities. First, that the strategies and methods that I advocate may be used in conjunction with more conventional ones with a view to further cross-fertilization of ideas about theory development. Secondly, the adaptive theory approach can be used in a more radical, 'alternative' sense as a set of new rules and strategies of sociological method which branch out on their own independent path. In the next section I shall approach these issues by making some comments about the general characteristics of adaptive theory. This discussion of some of the more practical rules-of-thumb of the approach serves to summarize some of its key features as I have described them in previous chapters. This will then be followed by a more general discussion of some of the theoretical and methodological implications for sociology and social research.

General characteristics of the adaptive theory approach

Pace and level of the development of theory

Although the substance of adaptive theory will begin to take shape sometime during the research, the exact point cannot be determined in advance. This is because factors like theoretical creativity, inspiration and the serendipitous or contingent nature of data collection do not conform to the logic of methodological rules or protocols and therefore cannot be guaranteed in advance. Similarly, the degree and rate of initial elaboration of the theory cannot be predicted since they depend upon variable circumstances which are specific to the research in question. Progress along both paths (point of initiation and rate of elaboration) may be slow or fast, smooth or disrupted depending on a whole host of factors – including the theoretical sensitivities of the researcher. The ability of the researcher to perceive conceptual connections and recognize empirical indicators is just as important as coming across the 'right' (appropriate, relevant) data and circumstances (access to data).

The continuous nature of adaptive theorizing

There are three main reasons that underwrite the continuous and processual nature of adaptive theorizing. First, as I have already indicated adaptive theory acknowledges the unpredictability of many factors involved in theory-generation, including the creative work and serendipitous incidents and circumstances surrounding the practicalities of research activity which lend weight to the idea that the process of theory-generation should be a continuous activity. Secondly, the adaptive approach regards every stage or phase of research as an opportunity for theory development. Thus theory-generation is never confined to a particular stage of research, such as the initial development of a theoretical framework or to a discussion of the 'conclusions' or 'findings'. The generation of adaptive theory operates at each and every moment of the research from the preparation and planning of data collection (including choice of methods and techniques, problems of access, and so on), through every phase of the actual collection and analysis of the data. As I have stressed theory-generation should proceed apace with data analysis and both should begin as soon as the initial data is gathered. The adaptive researcher-theorist should be alive to every moment of the research as a possible opportunity for the generation of concepts and theoretical ideas – even at late stages when the core concepts and categories have been established. As a consequence, the creative use of sampling and sampling techniques, the generation of codes and concept-indicator links, and the writing of theoretical memos are continuous features of the overall process. Such activities are never really 'completed' or discretely marked out as defined phases of research. Thirdly, the continuous nature of adaptive theorizing derives from the fact that it is most usefully regarded as a forever imperfect or incomplete product (see below, the open-ended nature of adaptive theory).

The range and types of adaptive theory

As I have suggested throughout, the range and forms that adaptive theory may take are quite diverse. The development of typologies (either behavioural or systemic, or both) and models which attempt to represent lifeworld–system interlocks are perhaps the most elaborate and complex forms – and vary in the extent of their 'elaborateness' and complexity. However, adaptive theory also refers to any element of the analytic process which may contribute to theory or theorizing in the long run. Thus, the development of codes, categories, and so on – even important extracts from theoretical memos – have to be regarded as integral components of the theoretical process.

Although such theoretical elements (or raw materials) must be regarded as important in their own right, they are also pivotal to the process of concept formation and the establishment of concept-indicator linkages. In this sense individual concepts represent a high-profile aspect of the process of adaptive theory regardless of whether they are understood to be part of a more encompassing cluster or network of concepts or even an integral aspect of a sophisticated model. Newly generated concepts, which 'stand apart' from the pack so to speak, may turn out to be as significant as others that are currently regarded as core or central. The open-ended and continuous characteristics of adaptive theory are complemented by its unfolding, cumulative and incremental nature.

The open-ended nature of adaptive theorizing

The overall shape of adaptive theory is not in the form of a vindicated hypothesis or a set of confirmed hypotheses. Neither is it a reformulated, revised or otherwise modified theory in the guise of an axiomatic set of statements suggesting the relationships between discretely measured variables (or even general law-like statements about human behaviour). Further, adaptive theory is not confined to describing the meaningful lifeworlds of particular people or groups. Rather, it attempts to map some of the lifeworld–system interlocks that form a synthesis of subjective and objective aspects of social life. As such, the form of the theory is both descriptive and explanatory and relies on concepts, networks and conceptual models of the social world which both shape and are shaped by that world.

As a result of these characteristics, adaptive theory should not be regarded as an end-point or definite conclusion to the theory-building process. Its adaptive nature points to its capacity to reformulate itself in response to new evidence and new ways of understanding this evidence. The cluster of concepts which repesent the latest stage of elaboration of the theory must always be regarded as potentially revisable both in the final stages of the research and with a view to future research. The adaptive theory that is an end-product of the research must only be viewed as an interim product which is forever incomplete because it is always potentially revisable and reformulable. I hasten to add here that all theories should be so regarded, although this would be denied by many and would thus require a radical shift of understanding of the nature of theory and its relation to evidence. By contrast, adaptive theory makes this an explicitly recognized part of its nature.

However, as I stressed at the end of Chapter 4, the lack of fixity or absoluteness of adaptive theory does not imply that the researcher (and/or theorist) should be tentative about the fruits of her or his labour. Nor does it imply that the research itself can never be terminated in a satisfactory fashion. By its very nature adaptive theory encourages, and as far as possible ensures, the continual checking and revising of emergent theory as the research progresses. In this sense the validity of theory so generated is not divorced from empirical evidence but is rather inherently bound up with it. By the conclusion of the research, the in-built checks, balances and controls should convince the researcher of the soundness of the core concepts, categories and clusters that form the basis of the adaptive theory. Thus research and theory-generation may be terminated in a satisfactory fashion – as a 'complete product' in terms of the immediate context of the research. However, the inherent openness of the adaptive approach requires that knowledge be viewed as always potentially revisable in the light of evidence which may be brought to bear and as a result of innovations in conceptualization and explanation.

New rules of method?

In so far as the advice and suggestions I have offered in this book can be regarded as radical departures from existing practices, then they imply new rules of method for social analysis and research which I shall now outline. They are all points that underpin the arguments in the book as a whole though I bring them together here in an explicit manner accompanied by brief comments.

1 Social analysis and research should operate on the assumption that social reality is variegated rather than uniform in nature. In formal terms this is to say that the social world is ontologically plural and implies the following:
(a) Analytic approaches which presuppose that social reality can be understood by reference to some single unifying principle or feature, such as discourses, reproduced practices, figurations, intersubjective meaning, actors' reasons and motives, the duality of structure, must

be abandoned since they embody and represent incomplete onto-
logies which lead to tendentious forms of analysis.

(b) The social world is constituted by multiple ontological domains,
possessing their own distinct properties and characteristics which
cannot be reduced to each other or some allegedly more encompassing principle or constitutive mechanism.

(c) It is essential to have methodological strategies which enable
researchers and analysts to tap into the subjective predispositions
and intersubjectively generated meanings that form the everyday
lifeworlds of social agents while at the same time also allowing
access to the objective social systemic aspects of society (reproduced
social relations, positions, practices, discourses and forms of power).
Such strategies allow the researcher to grasp the complex and multi-
faceted nature of social reality by simultaneously tracing the interconnections between different domains without neglecting the
differences between them.

(d) Although connected in various complex ways, the lifeworld–
system coupling rests upon a fundamental ontological distinction
between the historically emergent, socially reproduced conditions
transmitted from previous generations (system) and the contempora-
neous activities, meanings, reasons and motives of human beings in
everyday social interaction (the lifeworld). This coupling also
involves the conjunction and melding of different forms and frames
of temporality.

(e) On this basis we have to acknowledge that sociology and social
research *is* and *must be* concerned with a partly preconstituted
universe of objects *as well as* with aspects of social reality produced
by the active doings of subjects.

2 Social analysis and research should operate with a plural
knowledge base in order to maximize understanding and explanatory power. However, this must be accompanied by a recognition of
the difficulties that are created with regard to questions of the
compatibility and validity of different forms of knowledge. This
'plurality' implies the following:

(a) An openness and willingness to engage in dialogue with different forms, levels and types of theory and evidence, which may be
grounded in diverse (and to some extent antithetical) epistemological
positions.

(b) Due recognition must be given to underlying epistemological
assumptions which underwrite different theories and methodological principles (induction–deduction, empiricism–rationalism) and to
capitalize on their strengths while avoiding inherent weaknesses.

(c) All theories, methodological approaches, and so on must be
regarded as potentially open universes.

3   Social research should operate on the basis of a methodological pluralism and not in terms of a rigid adherence to a single or limited set of techniques and protocols. This subsumes many of the points raised in points 1 and 2 above but specifically refers to the following:

(a)   Social research should employ as many data collection techniques as possible in order to maximize its ability to tap into all social domains in depth.

(b)   Social research should not be about the application or assertion of one type of approach, especially where this approach limits itself to the analysis of one domain of social reality at the expense of other equally important domains.

4   The pluralism I have emphasized in points 1–3 above should not be confused with epistemological and methodological anarchism or relativism (Feyerabend, 1978).

(a)   It is important to be as open and flexible as possible in terms of applying 'rules' by drawing on a wide array of theoretical and empirical resources and methodological strategies and techniques. However, the point is to *accommodate* the useful aspects of diverse positions and approaches, not to abandon the notion of systematic method altogether. Clear and rigorous theoretical and methodological guidelines are absolutely necessary for the generation of robust theory with maximum explanatory range and power.

(b)   All theories should be regarded as 'interim products' which are revisable and reformulable in the light of empirical evidence and theoretical insights and arguments. Such a proviso ensures that the theory is a product of constant testing against empirical evidence and consequently increases soundness, validity and reliability.

(c)   Understanding theory and theorizing as an inherently 'unfinished or incomplete project' (in the light of further argument and evidence) helps to offset the tendency for established theories to be applied in a rigid and dogmatic manner irrespective of counterarguments and evidence which indicate the pressing need for amendments.

5   As specialist areas, general theory and social research will always possess their own relatively autonomous 'internal' concerns and problem foci. However, a pluralistic knowledge base, a commitment to methodological diversity and a recognition of the variegated nature of social ontology will help to offset the insularity of either theory or research. In turn this should help to promote the bridge-building efforts that are urgently required in order to create a genuinely cumulative body of social-scientific knowledge.

BIBLIOGRAPHY

Alexander, J. (1995) *Fin de siècle Social Theory*. London: Verso.

Archer, M. (1995) *Realist Social Theory: The Morphogenetic Approach*. Cambridge: Cambridge University Press.

Backett, K. (1990) 'Studying health in families', in S. Cunningham-Burley and N. McKeganey (eds), *Readings in Medical Sociology*. London: Routledge.

Bernstein, B. (1973) *Class Codes and Control* (vol. 1). London: Paladin.

Bhaskar, R. (1979) *The Possibility of Naturalism*. Brighton: Harvester.

Bloor, D. and McIntosh, J. (1990) 'Surveillance and concealment: a comparison of techniques of client resistance in therapeutic communities and health visiting', in S. Cunningham-Burley and N. McKeganey (eds), *Readings in Medical Sociology*. London: Routledge.

Blumer, H. (1954) 'What is wrong with social theory?', *American Sociological Review*, 19: 3–10.

Blumer, H. (1969) *Symbolic Interactionism*. Englewood Cliffs, NJ: Prentice-Hall.

Brewer, J. (1990) 'Talking about danger: the RUC and the paramilitary threat', *Sociology*, 24: 657–74.

Bruyn, S. (1966) *The Human Perspective in Sociology*. Englewood Cliffs, NJ: Prentice-Hall.

Bryant, C. (1995) *Practical Sociology*. Oxford: Polity Press.

Bryman, A. (1988) *Quantity and Quality in Social Research*. London: Unwin.

Bryman, A. and Burgess, R. (1994) *Analysing Qualitative Data*. London: Routledge.

Burns, T. and Stalker, G. (1961) *The Management of Innovation*. London: Tavistock.

Clegg, J., Standen, P. and Jones, G. (1996) 'Striking the balance: a grounded theory analysis of staff perspectives', *British Journal of Clinical Psychology*, 35: 249–64.

Denzin, N. (1990) 'Researching alcoholics and alcoholism in American society', *Studies in Symbolic Interaction*, 11: 81–101.

de Vaus, D. (1996) *Surveys in Social Research*. London: UCL Press.

Durkheim, E. (1952) *Suicide: A Study in Sociology*. London: Routledge.

Durkheim, E. (1964) *The Division of Labour in Society*. New York: Free Press.

Edwards, R. (1979) *Contested Terrain*. London: Heinemann.

Etzioni, A. (1961) *The Comparative Analysis of Complex Organisations*. New York: Free Press.

Feyerabend, P. (1978) *Against Method*. London: Verso.

Foucault, M. (1977) *Discipline and Punish: The Birth of the Prison*. Harmondsworth: Penguin.

Foucault, M. (1980) *Power and Knowledge*. Brighton: Harvester.

Giallombardo, R. (1966) 'Social roles in a prison for women', *Social Problems*, 13: 268–88.

Giddens, A. (1976) *New Rules of Sociological Method*. London: Hutchinson.

Giddens, A. (1979) *Central Problems in Social Theory*. London: Macmillan.

Giddens, A. (1984) *The Constitution of Society*. Oxford: Polity Press.

Giddens, A. (1987) *Social Theory and Modern Sociology*. Stanford, CA: Stanford University Press.

Glaser, B. (1994) *Emergence versus Forcing: Basics of Grounded Theory Analysis*. San Francisco: Sociology Press.

Glaser, B. and Strauss, A. (1965) *Awareness of Dying*. Chicago: Aldine.

Glaser, B. and Strauss, A. (1967) *The Discovery of Grounded Theory*. Chicago: Aldine.

Glaser, B. and Strauss, A. (1971) *Status Passage*. London: Routledge.

Glesne, C. and Peshkin, A. (1992) *Becoming Qualitative Researchers*. New York: Longman.

Goffman, E. (1967) *Interaction Ritual*. New York: Anchor.

Goffman, E. (1968) *Asylums*. Harmondsworth: Penguin.

Goffman, E. (1983) 'The interaction order sui generis', *American Sociological Review*, 48: 1–17.

Gouldner, A. (1954) *Patterns of Industrial Bureaucracy*. New York: Free Press.

Habermas, J. (1984) *The Theory of Communicative Action: Reason and Rationalization of Society* (vol. 1). Oxford: Polity Press.

Habermas, J. (1987) *The Theory of Communicative Action: The Critique of Functionalist Reason* (vol. 2). Oxford: Polity Press.

Hilbert, R. (1990) 'Ethnomethodology and the micro-macro order', *American Sociological Review*, 55: 794–808.

Hochschild, A. (1983) *The Managed Heart*. Berkeley, CA: University of California Press.

Hughes, E. (1937) 'Institutional office and the person', *American Journal of Sociology*, 43: 404–13.

Kanter, R. (1989) 'Careers and the wealth of nations: a macro perspective on the structure and implications of career forms', in A. Hall and B. Lawrence (eds), *Handbook of Career Theory*. Cambridge: Cambridge University Press.

Keat, R. and Urry, J. (1975) *Social Theory as Science*. London: Routledge.

Layder, D. (1984) 'Sources and levels of commitment in actors' careers', *Work and Occupations*, 11: 147–62.

Layder, D. (1985) 'Power, structure and agency', *Journal for the Theory of Social Behaviour*, 15: 131–49.

Layder, D. (1990) *The Realist Image in Social Science*. Basingstoke: Macmillan.

Layder, D. (1993) *New Strategies in Social Research*. Oxford: Polity Press.

Layder, D. (1994) *Understanding Social Theory*. London: Sage.

Layder, D. (1997) *Modern Social Theory: Key Debates and New Directions*. London: University College Press.

Layder, D., Ashton, D. and Sung, J. (1991) 'The empirical correlation of action and structure: the transition from school to work', *Sociology*, 25: 447–64.

Lemert, E. (1962) 'Paranoia and the dynamics of exclusion', *Sociometry*, 25: 2–20.

Lewins, F. (1992) *Social Science Methodology*. Melbourne: Macmillan.

Lofland, L. (1966) *In the Presence of Strangers*, Working paper 19. Michigan: Center for Research on Social Organization.

Marx, K. and Engels, F. (1968) *Selected Works*. London: Lawrence & Wishart.

McKeganey, N. (1990) 'Drug abuse in the community: needle sharing and the risks of HIV infection', in S. Cunningham-Burley and N. McKeganey (eds), *Readings in Medical Sociology*. London: Routledge.

McKeganey, N., Bernard, M. and Bloor, M. (1990) 'A comparison of HIV-related risk behaviour and reduction between female working prostitutes and male rent boys in Glasgow', *Sociology of Health and Illness*, 11: 274–92.

Mead, G. (1967) *Mind, Self and Society*. Chicago: Chicago University Press.

Merton, R. (1967) *On Theoretical Sociology*. New York: Free Press.

Mouzelis, N. (1995) *Sociological Theory: What Went Wrong?* London: Routledge.

Nijsmans, M. (1991) 'Professional culture and organisational morality: an ethnographic account of a therapeutic community', *British Journal of Sociology*, 42: 1–12.

O'Connell Davidson, J. (1995) 'British sex tourists in Thailand', in M. Maynard and J. Purvis (eds), *(Hetero) Sexual Politics*. London: Taylor & Francis.

O'Connell Davidson, J. (1998) *To Enter in These Bonds: Prostitution, Power and Freedom*. Oxford: Polity Press.

O'Connell Davidson, J. and Layder, D. (1994) *Methods, Sex and Madness*. London: Routledge.

Patton, M. (1990) *Qualitative Evaluation and Research Methods*. London: Sage.

Pawson, R. (1989) *A Measure for Measures*. London: Routledge.

Popper, K. (1972) *Objective Knowledge: An Evolutionary Approach*. Oxford: Oxford University Press.

Richie, J. and Spencer, L. (1994) 'Qualitative data analysis for applied policy research', in A. Bryman and R. Burgess (eds), *Qualitative Data Analysis*. London: Routledge.

Rock, P. (ed.) (1979) *The Making of Symbolic Interactionism*. London: Macmillan.

Rose, G. (1984) *Deciphering Sociological Research*. London: Macmillan.

Rosenau, P. (1992) *Post-modernism and the Social Sciences*. Princeton, NJ: Princeton University Press.

Scheff, T. (1966) *Being Mentally Ill*. Chicago: Aldine.

Schutz, A. (1972) *The Phenomenology of the Social World*. London: Heinemann.

Silverman, D. (1985) *Qualitative Methodology and Sociology*. Aldershot: Gower.

Silverman, D. (1993) *Analysing Qualitative Data*. London: Sage.

Stanley, L. and Wise, S. (1983) *Breaking Out*. London: Routledge.

Stebbins, R. (1970) 'Career: the subjective approach', *Sociological Quarterly*, 11: 32–49.

Strauss, A. (1987) *Qualitative Analysis for Social Scientists*. Cambridge: Cambridge University Press.

Strauss, A. and Corbin, T. (1990) *Basics of Qualitative Research*. London: Sage.

Turner, J. (1988) *A Theory of Social Interaction*. Oxford: Polity Press.

Vaughan, D. (1992) 'Theory elaboration and the heuristics of case analysis', in C. Ragin and H. Becker (eds), *What is a Case?* Cambridge: Cambridge University Press.

INDEX